W9-BXI-369

LIBERTY'S SECRETS

LIBERTY'S SECRETS

THE LOST WISDOM
of AMERICA'S FOUNDERS

JOSHUA CHARLES

 WND Books

LIBERTY'S SECRETS

Copyright © 2015 by Joshua Charles

All rights reserved. No part of this book may be reproduced in any form or by any means—electronic, mechanical, photocopying, scanning, or otherwise—without permission in writing from the publisher, except by a reviewer, who may quote brief passages in a review.

Scripture quotations are from the Holy Bible, King James Version (public domain).

Published by WND Books, Washington, D.C. WND Books is a registered trademark of WorldNetDaily.com, Inc. ("WND")

Book designed by Mark Karis

WND Books are distributed to the trade by:
Midpoint Trade Books
27 West 20th Street, Suite 1102
New York, New York 10011

WND Books are available at special discounts for bulk purchases. WND Books also publishes books in electronic formats. For more information call (541) 474-1776 or visit www.wndbooks.com.

Hardcover ISBN: 978-1-938067-59-4
eBook ISBN: 978-1-938067-60-0

Library of Congress Cataloging-in-Publication Data

Charles, Joshua.
Liberty's secret : the lost wisdom of America's founders / Joshua
Charles.
pages cm
ISBN 978-1-938067-59-4 (hardcover) -- ISBN 978-1-938067-60-0 (e-book)
1. United States--Politics and government--1775-1783. 2. United
States--Politics and government--1783-1789. 3. United States--Politics
and government--1789-1815. 4. United States--Politics and
government--Philosophy. 5. Liberty--Philosophy. 6. Statesmen--United
States--Quotations. 7. Legislators--United States--Quotations. 8.
Politicians--United States--Quotations. I. Title.
E302.1.C46 2015
973.3--dc23
                                                    2014038946

Printed in the United States of America
15 16 17 18 19 MPV 9 8 7 6 5 4 3 2 1

I dedicate this book to my Mom and Dad.

To my father, who always taught me there are no dreams worth giving only half your heart to.

And to my mother, who in teaching me to read put the entire universe, the great adventures, and the profound thoughts of the wise, the great, and the daring at my fingertips.

To these two indispensable and priceless gifts I owe every good thing in my life.

CONTENTS

Posterity! You will never know how much it cost the present generation to preserve your freedom! I hope you will make a good use of it. If you do not, I shall repent in heaven that I ever took half the pains to preserve it.

—JOHN ADAMS

ACKNOWLEDGMENTS

Primarily, I acknowledge my Messiah and Savior Yeshua (Jesus) for the extraordinary blessings he has granted me with such that I was able to complete this book. The relationships, resources, and skills with which he has blessed me, through no merit of my own, are the reason this book exists. He is faithful.

I am indebted to the Partners of the Rediscovery Project at the Public Policy Institute of William Jessup University which have made this research possible through their extraordinarily generous and faithful support: the Allyns, the Alongis, the Benzels, the Blues, the Brakenhoffs, the Burmans, the Carrolls, the Charless, the Clouses, the Crises, the Eberles, the Elders, the Garbers, the Giless, the Grahams, the Gravess, the Hellermans, the Hinmans, the Hixs, the Hsiaos, the Hunninghakes, the Jacobsens, the Kallingers, the Kirschs, the Larabees, the Lords, the Lorenzos, the Lynns, the Marcheks, the McClearys, the McDaniels, the McKinneys, the O'Connors, the Plumbs, the Rapinis, the Reas, the Selims, the Sledds, the Soliss, the Sommas, the Spencers, the Wilkinsons, and the Windheusers.

I'm grateful to my supervisors at the Public Policy Institute, Sosamma Samuel-Burnett and Phillip Escamilla, as well as our vice president for development, Eric Hogue, and last but not least, the president of William Jessup University, Dr. John Jackson. None of this would have been possible without your steadfast support and opening of doors for the Rediscovery Project.

I thank the mentors and friends who have inspired, sharpened, and challenged me, and who have dared to love me enough to be honest and genuine. First, my mentors: Shawn Spiess, Stephen Clouse, Dan Rudman, Alex Trochez, Vince Coakley, Doug Solis, Dave Perkins, and Mitch Wheeler. Without your guidance, your criticism, and your inspiration, I would not be who I am today. I'd be nothing and going nowhere. Words are insufficient thanks for what you are owed. The same goes for my "other mothers," Sue Boggs, Ellen Clouse, Amber Solis, and Susan Murff. With regard to this book in particular, a special thanks to Stephen and Ellen Clouse, who have at every point been extraordinarily generous in every way imaginable—you just give, give, give, and I have been so completely and utterly blessed by your presence in my life. You are family. A special thanks also goes to Wayne and Karladine Graves, who have been steadfast supporters in every way, and who have become dear friends and family throughout this whole process.

Second, to my "band of brothers": Ricardo Arguinzoni, Derek Evans, Ryan Black, Ben Allman, Jordan Crawford, Marcus Hollinger, Michael Stejskal, Derek Rempe, Connor Crist, Trent Sanders, Nate Simon, Jon Weiss, Will McCullough, too many other BYX brothers to mention, and (the two sisters) Gabrielle Jackson and Catherine Gunsalus. This life would be a lot more hellish, and a lot less livable without you all. I love you all immensely.

Special thanks to Justin Murff, Michael Onifer, and Ryan Dobbs, who, being too old to be peers but too young to be mentors, have been the best "big brothers" any guy could ask for. Whether it's been encouragement, wisdom, or the occasional roughing up when I've needed it, you guys do it all. Lots of love.

Additional special thanks to the Gunsalus and Channell families. I never thought I'd meet angels in person until I met you guys. Your love, encouragement, and grace are inspirational. You embody the life and mission of our servant Messiah.

Last but not least, I feel compelled to recognize our Founding Fathers. I feel like I have gotten to know them, and I have been utterly inspired by the words which they left for us.

INTRODUCTION

I wrote this book for one reason, and one reason only: to reintroduce my fellow countrymen to the Founders of our country and the vision of a free society they articulated, defended, and constructed, *in their own words*.

This project has been a long time coming, so it deserves a bit of background: I'm a twenty-seven-year-old Millennial. I was training to be a concert pianist from the time I was twelve, but Providence saw fit to direct me toward another path. I coauthored a book on the *Federalist Papers* in 2011, which turned out to be a bestseller. Now, four years later, and with nearly five years of full-time research under my belt on the writings of the Founders, I have arrived at the point where I am ready to share the results of my findings with those who may be willing to listen.

My reasons for doing this are multifaceted and numerous, but they all can be reduced to these two simple propositions: our country is in distress, and part of ameliorating this problem is to recover our heritage in an *honest* way. We no longer know where we come from, the grand story we fit into, and the great men and women who inspired the noble vision which birthed the United States of America, the first nation in history to be founded upon the reasoned consent of a people intent on governing themselves. Previous to this great experiment, all governments had been the result of happenstance, of conquest, of accident and force, but not of reason and virtue—not of *purpose*. That all changed with America, and it behooves us to reconstitute the vision bequeathed to us by our Founders if we are to maintain and pass down this noble endeavor to the next generation.

However, we live in a culture addicted to sound bites, to 24/7 news, to 140 character tweets, and to constant headlines from every corner of the globe, which by nature are almost always the implacable foes of deep thought, discourse, and expression. With this, we have seen a marked degradation in our ability to think and express not just profound thoughts but coherent ones. Our attention spans are simply no longer up to the task of such things.

Our public discourse has, as a result, too often been reduced to a meme, a graphic, a tweet, a Facebook post, and the result is that we are simply talking (more often yelling) past each other and not with each other. The art of conversation, honest and forthright, earnest and true, has largely been lost. We have gone from the days when whole towns of Americans would come out for multiple hours to view debates on the great issues of the day, as they did with Abraham Lincoln and Stephen Douglas, to having "debates" on television segments which are often no longer than a few minutes because their audiences cannot bear any more. As a result, we squeeze our side's talking points, our side's clichés, our side's stereotypes, into those few minutes we have allotted ourselves for "discussion" in order that we may gain one more convert.

Additionally, few of us are well-read enough (a problem our education system seems blithely unconcerned with) to discuss the lessons of the human experience (often simply called "history"), the vices and virtues of the great heroes of the past, and so instead of applying the accumulated wisdom available to us, we become bound up in a short-sighted and exaggerated prejudice in favor of the present, the contemporary, the now, and are satisfied with clichés about the old-fashioned past we have consigned to the dustbin of irrelevance. The "tyranny of the urgent," as I have heard it called, has overcome our willingness to sit still, to meditate, to immerse ourselves in the fruits of solitude, to pause and consider deeply. To do so is antithetical to the twenty-first century culture, which allows no time for pauses, no time for metaphorical

Sabbaths, and no time for those deeper things which we have become accustomed to discussing, and indeed now *enjoy* discussing in only superficial ways, if we discuss them at all. In such an environment, our history, heritage, heroes, and the wisdom of those who came before us have become irrelevant, for learning their lessons requires those things which the twenty-first century is least willing to encumber itself with: a book, and an attention span longer than a few minutes. Our own past has thereby become a "secret" to ourselves.

This scourge of superficiality has overcome our culture in successively more perilous forms of corrosion, infecting every area of our lives, even up to the august offices we have appointed to manage and direct our most pressing national concerns. Never before has the communication of political messages been more reliant on manipulation of the senses and the emotions as opposed to the convincing of the mind. We have gone from the days of the Nixon-Kennedy presidential debate, where the courtesy, substance, breadth and depth of knowledge we used to require of our leaders was on full display. Now, we evaluate the "debates" of those vying for the most powerful office on earth by the effectiveness of their poll-tested one-liners. Civility and substance be damned.

This has become the way to applause in the twenty-first century; this has become the path to obtaining a "following." If it's short and pithy enough; if it zings and stings; if it bites and has a comeback; if, in short, it is entertaining and amusing enough, we of the present are satisfied and count ourselves as having done our duty as citizens. We measure profundity in "likes," and substance with "retweets." If the ratings have gone up, we assume the merits of our views have done the same. Today, the issue is not so much that none of us has time to study the deeper things—the far more difficult reality we must confront is that few of us even want to do so.

In his seminal work *Amusing Ourselves to Death*, a book I consider perhaps the most important (after the Bible) for understanding the issues facing our century, Neil Postman brilliantly summarized the perils such a society is placed in as a result of its obsession with entertainment:

We were keeping our eye on 1984. When the year came and the prophecy didn't, thoughtful Americans sang softly in praise of themselves. The roots of liberal democracy had held. Wherever else the terror had happened, we, at least, had not been visited by Orwellian nightmares.

But we had forgotten that alongside Orwell's dark vision, there was another—slightly older, slightly less well known, equally chilling: Aldous Huxley's *Brave New World*. Contrary to common belief even among the educated, Huxley and Orwell did not prophesy the same thing. Orwell warns that we will be overcome by an externally imposed oppression. But in Huxley's vision, no Big Brother is required to deprive people of their autonomy, maturity and history. As he saw it, people will come to love their oppression, to adore the technologies that undo their capacities to think.

What Orwell feared were those who would ban books. What Huxley feared was that there would be no reason to ban a book, for there would be no one who wanted to read one. Orwell feared those who would deprive us of information. Huxley feared those who would give us so much that we would be reduced to passivity and egoism. Orwell feared that the truth would be concealed from us. Huxley feared the truth would be drowned in a sea of irrelevance. Orwell feared we would become a captive culture. Huxley feared we would become a trivial culture. . . . As Huxley remarked in *Brave New World Revisited*, the civil libertarians and rationalists who are ever on the alert to oppose tyranny "failed to take into account man's almost infinite appetite for distractions." In *1984*, Huxley added, people are controlled by inflicting pain. In *Brave New World*, they are controlled by inflicting pleasure. In short, Orwell feared that what we hate will ruin us. Huxley feared that what we love will ruin us.

This book is about the possibility that Huxley, not Orwell, was right.[1]

It is thus a great twist of irony that perhaps never before has mankind been so inundated with information and at the same time so bereft of wisdom. If this Republic is to continue, we must recognize this reality for what it is: an absurdity, and a farce unworthy of a people who mean to govern themselves.

This fundamental reality of the twenty-first century world has played a crucial role in determining how I have gone about doing my part to recover our heritage, for there are perhaps few around whom have developed so many myths and falsehoods, and about whom we so desperately need a reevaluation and a renaissance of awareness as the Founders of the United States of America. I determined after the success of my first book that I would not, for the time being, pursue a career as a commentator in the media, a blogger, or any other sort of ultravisible personality. It is one thing to be a fresh, young face repeating the same talking points to the delight of your respective niche. Such a thing was imminently possible after the publication of a bestselling book. But I wanted to actually have *something to say*, not just something to repeat. We are quite overstocked with those on each side of the great issues of our time who are willing to get in front of a camera, microphone, or computer, and essentially repeat what each side has determined to be its own "conventional wisdom," just with their own branding and "personal touch." But the desperate need of our time is to have those who are willing to do the laborious and rather nonglitzy task of earning the fruits of wisdom behind closed doors, out of sight and out of mind of the media machine, and then sharing what they have found with their fellow citizens. Anybody can learn how to repeat what everyone wants to hear repeated, and perhaps do it in a more convincing or charismatic way than the other guy. It is a far more difficult task to actually say something new, insightful, and thought-provoking, rather than offer that which only reinforces previously drawn conclusions.

Such has been the overarching goal of my work over the last few years. Whether I have attained to it will, in practical terms, largely be determined by you.

Which gets us to *Liberty's Secrets*, the goal of which, as I said earlier, was to allow the Founders, in their own words, unobscured (as much as possible) by bias, to articulate this grand system of human liberty of which they conceived in all its unknown and forgotten splendor. As important as the Declaration of Independence and the Constitution are (and even these we remain woefully ignorant of), the Founders left behind so much more—letters, diaries, newspaper editorials, speeches, memos, pamphlets, and even books which most Americans don't know exist and are not taught about in school. And yet, therein we would find the "secrets" of our liberty, the "secrets" of our history, and the "secrets" of what ultimately makes this free society of ours work. There alone, in the totality, do we discover the truth observed by Alexis de Tocqueville, one of America's most ardent admirers (and stridently friendly critics), that "Revolution in the United States was the result of a mature and thoughtful taste for freedom, and not a vague and ill-defined feeling for independence. It was not based upon the passions of disorder, but on the contrary love of order and the law directed its course."[2]

As will be shown, this "mature and thoughtful taste for freedom" was underpinned by two fundamental realities with which the Founders were both familiar and unwilling to ignore: human nature, and the lessons of history. Our Founders were, and likely remain, one of the most best-read groups of human beings in history. It is common to see many of them, with great fluidity and lucidness, intersperse their writings with lengthy quotations in Latin, Greek, or a number of other languages with which many of them were familiar, typically from some learned writer from the past. Even those who did not have formal educations, such as George Washington and Benjamin Franklin, filled their writings with allusions to historical figures, works of literature, Bible verses, and poetic metaphors based on the writings of Shakespeare and others. While today we measure literacy by the bare ability to read, literacy for our Founders was an entirely different proposition: it was familiarity with the great works of philosophy, history, poetry, and prose that formed the bedrock of Western civilization, and oftentimes other civilizations as well. It is no exaggeration to assert that our Founders were on an entirely different level of thought and historical and cultural awareness than most today.

It also bears mentioning that the Founders had much to say on numerous topics, not just politics. Perhaps one of the greatest "secrets" discovered in their writings is a seamless vision of liberty in which there are no neatly marked and hermetically sealed categories of "politics" and "nonpolitics," as if one could exist regardless of what was happening in the other. Rather, one is presented with a holistic and integrated vision of liberty in which politics no doubt plays an important rule, but where all efforts in the political realm make no difference if there is not at the same time education to create a knowledgeable citizenry; religion and morality to allow such a citizenry to govern themselves as much as possible on the individual and civil society levels before requiring the intervention of the coercive power of law; and economic freedom to reap the fruit of one's own labors, as well as provide for the general good of society. All of these things were integral parts of the Founders' vision of a free society and are severed from one another at our peril.

Thus, the Founders brought this deep well of knowledge into the systems of government which they designed for themselves and their posterity. While the results bore the marks of uniquely eighteenth-century phenomena, the vast majority integrate historical lessons which were exhibited over a period of thousands of years, lessons drawn from the Bible, from the Greeks and Romans, and from the annals of European and world history.

This all culminates in perhaps the greatest "secret" of all: the profound, eerie, and steadfast relevance of the Founders to today. Our culture so often exhibits a posture of what I call "chronological arrogance," the belief that being more contemporary is automatically more enlightened. We assume, in a stunning display of circular reasoning, that we are better than those in the past precisely because we are not in the past and they were. This is why we so often hear about being "on the right side of history" from those who are often completely ignorant of it. "History" for most people today is what has happened in the last decade. The age of "tolerance" cannot stomach the idea that old, dead white men (and women) might have some things to say that would pierce through the fog of unchallenged assumptions with which we have so often enveloped ourselves. Such are the heights of arrogance and the depths of ignorance which have dismembered the collective mind and memory of contemporary culture as America cuts itself off from the wisdom of the very Founders who instilled the values and developed the institutions which not only made its prosperity and pleasures possible, but whose corruption they predicted, and in terms which often precisely resemble that which we observe with our own eyes today.

It is a difficult thought for a modern person to stomach that someone who has been dead and six feet underground for centuries or longer has more insightful things to say about their world than their favorite commentator they see on the screen. But that is precisely what one finds when one reads the writings of the Founders in any sort of comprehensive way. There is an almost breathlessly timeless quality to their writings, a perennial relevance which can't help but be compelling. And it is because they never forgot the two pillars of human nature and the lessons of history (ironically, the two things modern culture deems the most malleable) that this is so. This phenomenon of relevance is so ubiquitous throughout the *corpus* of their works that I decided to coin a term for it: "one-niner," based on the famous Bible verse found in Ecclesiastes 1:9—"There is nothing new under the sun." My annotations of their writings are full of "1:9" in the margin, for much of what they said could have been written yesterday and would remain just as relevant. Reading writings such as these reveals a profound lesson: that history is rather aptly described as the cosmic hamster wheel of humanity. Have we progressed? Undoubtedly yes in some ways (primarily technologically, which oftentimes creates the illusion of more progress than has actually occurred). But in fundamental ways, we continue to struggle with the very same things our ancestors struggled with. The challenges mankind has dealt with may appear fundamentally different and only superficially the same over time, but a thorough knowledge of human nature and history shows that they are in fact superficially different and fundamentally the same. It was these fundamentals of the human experience upon which the Founders constructed our government and societal institutions. It therefore behooves us to learn, as our Founders did, from the collective wisdom and experience of *all* of humanity, not just those that happen to be alive. We have a vast treasure trove of human knowledge, wisdom, and experience at our fingertips. We ought not to limit ourselves to ourselves.

It is my hope that in your reading of this book, many of the myths on both "left" *and* "right" about the Founders will be revealed for the false caricatures and stereotypes they are. Unfortunately, various interests have tried to use or abuse them to fit their own agendas. As will be shown in this book *using their own words*, both narratives partake of some truth, but are at their core often profoundly wrong. Both are the result of not just a selective, "sound bite" reading of our Founders' writings (in line with the proclivities of our own time), but too often the use of completely false or misquoted "quotes," an unfortunate reality of the Internet Age. The genuine article has been lost, and thus the extremes have been legitimized and gained their own followings. I hope this book takes a decisive step toward reasserting the genuine article. Such a project runs the risk of angering many on different sides, to which I can only say, along with George Washington, that "Integrity and firmness is all I can promise—these, be the voyage long or short, never shall forsake me although I may be deserted by all men. For of the consolations which are to be derived from these (under any circumstances) the world cannot deprive me."[3]

This book represents my best presentation of the facts as I see them, after having gone through thousands upon thousands of pages of writings. My own views of the Founders have undergone a radical adjustment since the onset of this endeavor. Some former assumptions were reinforced. Others were destroyed. But in the deepest sense, my goal and my hope for both myself and my fellow countrymen were perhaps most aptly described by John Adams as follows:

It is very true, that a people who have declared themselves "a free state should know what freedom is, and have it represented in all its *lively and lovely features*, that they may grow zealous and jealous over it. They should also be made acquainted and thoroughly instructed in the means and rules of its preservation against the adulterous wiles and rapes of any projecting sophisters [sic] that may arise."[4]

We should, however, always bear in mind that the Founders were great, but not perfect human beings. They were, in fact, profoundly flawed, just like the rest of us. As historian David McCullough has often noted, it's not as if these fellow human beings walked around saying "My how fascinating it is to be in the past" or "How striking it is to be an historical figure." They were subject to the uncertainties and vicissitudes of life just as we are. In fact, life was oftentimes much more difficult for them than for us, for while sorrow has been visited upon every generation and the bitter cup of grief and suffering has spared none of us, life in the eighteenth century, yet alone in a country not yet fully settled, was difficult to an extent almost unfathomable to an American in the twenty-first, lacking as it did the technologies (particularly in the field of medicine) which have made life, by comparison, far easier, and far more convenient in our own day. They too had deep inner struggles as a result of their own egos, insecurities, and failures. George Washington, despite being a victorious general, could in no way be called a brilliant one. John Adams was a constantly beleaguered soul, often because of his own stubbornness and obstinacy. Thomas Jefferson was most certainly a racist by today's standards, and a philandering racist at that. Alexander Hamilton was an adulterer and egoist writ large. Benjamin Franklin could at times be cowardly under the cheap guise of "moderation." James Madison acknowledged the humanity of slaves, but could not bring himself to part with the material comforts they provided him. Abigail Adams was at times extraordinarily harsh and uncharitable toward her own children, despite the rectitude of her intentions. Similar sorts of things could be said of many other Founders. But acknowledging these flaws is to see but one part of them, and out of context. The full story is much more nuanced, full of fascination and pathos, triumph and defeat, and the all-too-human tales of endeavors unequal to the ideals upon which they were predicated. The story of the Founders is thus a profoundly *human* story of both triumph and tragedy, ideals and hypocrisy, hard-won progress and painfully recalcitrant regressions. Those who attempt to make it otherwise should be ignored.

At the same time, these men and women were indeed giants, not just of their own time but for all time. Some may ask what the point in being familiar with the Founders is. It is quite simply this: it is not every day that nations are founded, let alone nations which have been as consequential in world history as the United States. Some may hate them, others may love them. But no one can disagree that they were historical figures of immense and singular importance. They wrote the "user manuals" of America, they cast the vision, they took the first in a series of historically unprecedented steps toward the assertion of self-government and ordered liberty over a virtuous people under the rule of law. Without understanding the rationale and intent behind the design of our nation and its institutions, we are flying blind and likely to utilize them in ways which they were never designed to accommodate. For these reasons alone their words and actions are worthy of our closest attention and study.

One final aspect must be noted: while the Founders were immensely influential in charting America's course, they were, at the end of the day, still only individuals. They did not wield as much power in their own time as those of us in our own time may be tempted to think. Thus, it would be foolish to project onto the Founders the idea that they were out to fix all the wrongs in the world, or that even if such a goal were within their purview, that they would be capable of achieving it. The American Revolution was not about righting all wrongs, but about erecting a structure of self-government in which such wrongs could be, by the deliberate choice, reasoning, and effort of the people, corrected, and a "more perfect Union" could be constructed step by step. No such opportunity had yet presented itself in such a complete and all-encompassing manner prior to 1776. It is this fundamental failure to understand our Revolution in the grand context of world history which causes us to misapprehend its nature. Societies can bear only one revolution at a time. They may be social, political, or whatnot, but usually only one can be attained successfully at any given point under the guise of any given generation. This was a fundamental difference between the American and French Revolutions. The American Revolution was first a cultural revolution (prior to 1776), and only *then* a *geopolitical* revolution with victory over the British (1783), and only *then* a political revolution with the advent of the Constitution (1789). It was none of these things at the same time, but a progression over a number of *decades*. Indeed, the "Founders" of the Founders were the early Puritan pilgrims who had arrived on the shores of the New World in the seventeenth century, and whose example of self-government in the 150 years preceding the American Revolution proved to be a source of instruction and inspiration which they then applied to the newly born United States. The French Revolution, on the other hand, was an attempt by a people who had no previous experience of self-government to achieve all these revolutions at the same time, and hence its degeneration into anarchy and eventually a war-mongering dictatorship under the jackboot of Napoleon. Human nature can bear only so many revolutions at one time, a reality just as relevant today as it was then.

While this book is primarily focused on the words and vision of the Founders, a number of additional original sources dating from ancient times through the Enlightenment, as well as various figures who arrived on the scene immediately after the Founders, will be consulted as well. Of the former description will be included statesman such as the Roman Senator Cicero, the English philosopher John Locke, and the French political theorist Montesquieu, each of whom had a profound impact on the Founders. Of the latter description, I will primarily utilize the writings of Alexis de Tocqueville, who, as an adroit and discerning observer and admirer of both the Founders and American society during the generation immediately following the Founders, offers an incredibly penetrating and utterly relevant analysis and defense of the ideas which the Founders espoused. Commentary on current events will be minimal, as the words which will be used will typically be so obviously and universally relevant that further comment will not be necessary. I expect readers to ponder upon the subject themselves rather than feed them my own personal conclusions as far as contemporary events are concerned. At the same time, this book is neither a series of biographies, nor a narrative of events. Rather, it is a "biography of ideas," an analysis of the origin, significance, and justification for the ideas and vision espoused by our Founders. Nor should anyone think that whenever I refer to "the Founders," I am assuming they all had the exact same opinions on everything. They did not. In their own time, these disagreements were the source of frequent consternation. However, when compared with what our culture today believes, assumes, and values, they did share a substantial amount of agreement on various fundamental truths which are simply not as uniformly accepted today. In that sense, and only that sense, do I purport to assert what the Founders collectively believed.

Having described the goal of this book and the means by which that goal may be achieved, I conclude by asserting the spirit with which I have intended to write it, a spirit best captured in this passage from John Adams, then vice president, to his son John Quincy Adams:

> If you meddle with political subjects, let me advise you to never lose sight of decorum. Assume a dignity above all personal reflections: and avoid as much as possible a party spirit. The true interest and honor of your country should be your only object. And may you be a terror to those evil doers to whom truth and falsehood are equally but sport, honor but a phantom, and their own insignificant importance their only objects.[5]

I have at all times attempted to avoid the "party spirit" which is so endemic to the political gamesmanship that is frequently carried out in the name of our Founders. Thus, this book will, I believe, cast great doubt on a number of "left-wing" and "right-wing" myths, myths which have proven quite useful to the agendas of both, but which nonetheless remain false. But far more importantly, I hope that what is presented within these pages is an inspiration to my fellow citizens and countrymen. If your reaction is the same as mine over the years I have been digging through these documents, you will frequently feel a sense of amazement, surprise, and numerous "lightbulb moments." This is a heritage, and these are heroes that belong to all of us, regardless of our political persuasions. I hope this book helps equip my fellow citizens with the knowledge and wisdom which is their birthright as Americans, and which can explain to them not only why they are and ought to be free, but how they may remain free.

As I write this, I have recently finished watching the third season of Netflix's hit show, *House of Cards*. It is a fitting dramatic presentation of all the greatest fears our Founders had, and as such I hope as many people watch it as possible. It's only a "TV show," but it exemplifies so well the dangers inherent in the toxic buildup of concentrated power, and the corruption of power on the human soul. It sheds light on so many of the lessons of history which show us that we have every reason to be doubtful of, skeptical about, and disdainful toward the notion that Caesar can solve all our problems. Because in the final analysis, Caesar is not just a sinner like the rest of us: sin is the only reason he exists at all. This truth of human nature, exemplified throughout all of human history and well known to our Founders, ought to never be forgotten by anyone who cherishes their liberty.

John Adams once noted that "[To] know thyself is as useful a precept to nations as to men."[6] A nation can direct itself only if it knows itself—who it is, where it comes from, and where it is going.

It's time to get reacquainted.

LIBERTY'S SECRETS

1

FOUNDING PROPHETS:
HUMAN NATURE AND HISTORY

"**W**here, within the memory of man, would we find anything akin to what is happening before our very eyes in North America?"[1] So asked Alexis de Tocqueville, the Frenchman turned perhaps America's greatest admirer, in his famous book, *Democracy in America*. And his question was apt, for what was happening in America was unprecedented in history. A group of former British colonies founded by religious dissenters in the backwoods of a barely settled, sparsely populated "new world" had declared their independence from and won their freedom against the mightiest empire on earth. Not only that, but afterward, to the astonishment of the world, in what had been called "the greatest single effort of national deliberation that the world has ever seen,"[2] they devised for themselves a constitution with which to govern a union of thirteen unwieldy states. Never before had a people through reason, debate, and deliberation decided for themselves and their children upon a form of government most conducive to their happiness and prosperity. For the vast majority of human history, such matters had always been decided by force, accident, or birth—some were fit to rule, others fit to obey. Prior to 1776, brute force and power had decided most of mankind's fate, and here, in a still largely unsettled and unexplored portion of the globe, Tocqueville was witnessing the rise of a nation barely fifty years old that was already surpassing some of the greatest and most established countries in the world, countries that had represented the pinnacles of human civilization and achievement up to that point.

Such were the unlikely and inauspicious beginnings of what Thomas Jefferson would later call the "Empire of Liberty," the United States of America. It was in this context that a group of people known to us as the Founders laid the foundations of this new empire for the benefit of themselves and their posterity. They were men of vision, high ideals, and incredible learning. Despite being backwater colonists, they were among the most well-read people ever to have lived. They had studied the history of the past and present; they were familiar with the great heroes, both their virtues and their vices; many of them were learned in philosophy, religion, languages, and numerous other subjects. They were nothing short of Renaissance men, and it was their absorption of the lessons of history, along with the plain common sense derived from their own experience, that propelled them to dream new dreams, envision new realities, and forge a new world that they solemnly hoped would be an example to the rest of mankind. In other words, our Founders dreamed of what could be because they were steadfastly anchored in what had been.

And yet, despite their greatness, these men were far from perfect. Just as surely as they were men for all time, they were also men of their own time, subject in one degree or another to the faults, assumptions, and prejudices of their own age even while making lasting contributions to the ages. The Founders thereby straddled that most interesting of paradoxes in their being fully human in their frailties and errors while also achieving accomplishments that, if achieved in ancient times, may have been attributed to the mythological demigods of old. Reading their writings makes it clear that they knew they were building something for the ages, something that would make a singular mark on history. But they also knew that they were caught up in something they often felt unable to control, while at the same time they frequently felt a deep sense of inadequacy to the great task it seemed Providence had assigned to them to complete.

But it is this very paradox, the conundrum of superhuman achievements being accomplished by all-too-human men, that must be understood if we are to preserve that "Empire of Liberty" that they passed on to us. It is this anomaly that makes our Founders far more than just politicians and statesmen, but prophets. In the biblical sense, a prophet was not merely someone who foretold the future. In fact, this was often secondary to the primary task of speaking the truth to a world desperately in need of it. It is in this sense that the Founders were prophets in that they articulated eternal truths that frequently ended up being stunning (and eerily) accurate descriptions of times such as our own. And they had much to say on numerous topics (not just politics) much of which continues to strike a chord of core truth.

So what was the secret of the Founders' insights? In more modern terms, how did they "get it" so well? The answer is very simple: they understood human nature and history. That is it. They believed man was imperfect but nonetheless capable of great things. They believed he was driven by selfish motives far too often but was also capable of rising above his selfishness for the betterment of his fellows. And perhaps most crucially, they believed human nature included *both* aspects; it was not as if we could evolve or mold human nature into whatever pleasing image we sought to achieve. It is what it is, but even amid the sobering reality of its excesses and imperfections, it was capable of rising above them to achieve great things, though never on a permanent basis. The "dark side" always had to be kept in check through constant and unceasing vigilance.

George Washington once remarked, "We must take human nature as we find it. Perfection falls not to the share of mortals."[3] John Adams echoed his sentiments, remarking, "We mortals cannot work miracles; we struggle in vain against the constitution and course of nature."[4] Man was what he was, a flawed creature, and it was universally acknowledged by the Founders that perhaps the most dangerous aspect of his nature was his tendency to be prideful—"self-love," as Thomas Jefferson called it. Pride, the putting of oneself above and in exclusion of all others (or at least desiring to) was what made men murder, cheat, steal, and oppress, what made kings tyrants and rulers dictators. It was that by which men placed themselves higher than God and all of their fellow men, "an evil fruit," remarked John Adams, "[that] is sometimes ridiculous, and often pernicious."[5]

Adams referred to pride being in "the heart of man." It was thus intrinsic to his nature and could even be utilized in the pursuit of ostensibly good things, which made it all the more dangerous. Pride was, as Adams put it, a "passion for superiority" over one's fellow men, and he noted that it was the single most dominant feature of human nature.[6]

Benjamin Franklin seemed to concur in his *Autobiography*: "In reality there is perhaps no one of our natural passions so hard to subdue as *pride*. Disguise it, struggle with it, beat it down, stifle it, mortify it as much as one pleases, it is still alive, and will every now and then peep out and show itself."[7]

Thomas Jefferson once described the American concept of human nature to a French official: "The human character . . . requires in general constant and immediate control to prevent its being biased from right by the seduction of self-love."[8]

As we will discuss later, this is why the Founders were so skeptical of power. "Power naturally grows," Adams stated. "Why? Because human passions are insatiable. But that power alone can grow which already is too great; that which is unchecked, that which has no equal power to control it."[9] As Adams noted, "Power is intoxicating, encroaching, and dangerous, in nations as well as individuals."[10] He elucidated in his famous treatise defending the American forms of government: "There are few who love the public better than themselves, though all may have some affection for the public. . . . Self-interest, private avidity, ambition, and avarice will exist in every state of society and under every form of government."[11]

"All men would be tyrants if they could,"[12] Adams affirmed, and it was this truth that perhaps most profoundly shaped the Founders' views on government. Such were the unpleasant aspects of the human equation. It was for these reasons that Franklin, in his typically wry and whimsical manner, commented, "Mankind are very odd creatures: One half censure what they practice, the other half practice what they censure; the rest always say and do as they ought."[13]

It was because they accepted these truths as unalterable realities of human existence that they applied them in their conception of a free society and their construction of our forms of government. As we shall see, however, theirs was not an exercise in cynicism, but realism—they approached their pursuit of a better world from the premise that, in order to be made better, it must first be acknowledged for what it is. Too often, the Founders believed, our reason is overcome by our passions, and this was why they also believed virtue and knowledge were so incredibly important, not because they *changed* human nature, but because they helped *control* human nature. Adams brilliantly articulated this view in the lead-up to the Revolution:

> Human nature, depraved as it is, has interwoven in its very frame a love of truth, sincerity, and integrity, which must be overcome by art, education, and habit, before the man can become entirely ductile to the will of a dishonest master . . . Notwithstanding this, we see every day that our imaginations are so strong and our reason so weak, the charms of wealth and power are so enchanting, and the belief of future punishments [in hell] so faint, that men find ways to persuade themselves, to believe any absurdity, to submit to any prostitution, rather than forgo their wishes and desires. Their reason becomes at last an eloquent advocate on the side of their passions, and they bring themselves to believe that black is white, that vice is virtue, that folly is wisdom and eternity a moment.[14]

And despite their acknowledgment that men were capable of great things, they did not believe that man was thereby perfectible. Adams wrote to Jefferson, "I am a believer in the probable improvability and improvement, the ameliorability [*sic*] and amelioration in human affairs; though I never could understand the doctrine of the perfectibility of the human mind,"[15] a position on which Jefferson agreed.

As for history, they believed in the idea that there is a historical inertia that can and often does *include* progress, but because of the realities of human nature, also the seeds of regress, and it is only by sifting one from the other that the truth of any experience could be ascertained and applied to new situations and circumstances. From their perspective, history was often a tragic story of violence, oppression, and wrong. But it was also a tapestry on which could be seen great and mighty achievements. This gets to perhaps one of the greatest defining features of the "Founding Prophets": they tended to be exceedingly balanced in their views. It was no wonder James Madison referred to history as "an inexhaustible fund of entertainment and instruction,"[16] for while containing episodes of human greatness, it also held many instances of hypocritical absurdities, which had to be taken into account in determining the calculus of human nature. Adams synthesized both thoughts in this way: "All nations from the beginning have been agitated by the same passions. . . . Nations move by unalterable rules, and education, discipline, and laws make the greatest difference in their accomplishments, happiness, and perfection. It is the master artist alone [God] who finishes his building, his picture, or his clock."[17]

They also believed something quite counterintuitive: as unique as their accomplishments were, they knew history was full of repeats and variations on a set of fundamental themes. To simply say "history repeats itself" is too banal, for to "repeat" is to do again that which was done, and in exactly the same way. This never happens, and the Founders did not believe this was a characteristic of history. But history does tend to exhibit similar phenomena in every age, which seem to stem from certain fundamental realities. In this sense, it could be said that there are "strings" that run through history which, when plucked by each succeeding generation, produce similar tones. As on any stringed instrument, the tone may be flat here or sharp there, but it is fundamentally the same tone, and it was these basic truths that the Founders discerned throughout all of history, all of which stemmed from human nature. For this reason Jefferson told his friend Adams that, as far as their contributions to political philosophy were concerned, at the end of the day, "nothing new can be added by you or me to what has been said by others, and will be said in every age, in supporting of the conflicting opinions on government."[18]

Our Founding Prophets thus combined rigidity and flexibility in their appraisal of human affairs. Man was capable of great things but frequently fell far below that capability. History provided a long record of achievements but also tragic and ignominious failures. The Founders were virtuosos at handling the paradoxes of this reality and, instead of finding them incompatible, saw a proper understanding of their dynamics as the secret to achieving the greatest possible amount of human flourishing and happiness (which, as we shall see, they defined quite differently than our modern pop culture does). The Founders thus realized and embraced a most uncomfortable truth: we are all (themselves included), to one degree or another, hypocrites, simply by virtue of our own human nature. Abigail Adams wrote to her son, future president John Quincy Adams, how not only could a true understanding of human nature be attained, but its regressive features could also be tamed, while its peculiar excellences could be cultivated:

> It is from a wide and extensive view of mankind that a just and true estimate can be formed of the powers of human nature. She appears ennobled or deformed, as religion, government, laws, and custom guide or direct her. Fierce, rude, and savage in the uncultivated desert. Gloomy, bigoted, and superstitious where truth is veiled in obscurity and mystery. Ductile, pliant, elegant, and refined, you have seen her in that dress, as well as in the active, bold, hardy, and intrepid garb of your own country.
>
> Inquire of the historic page, and let your own observations second the inquiry. Whence arises the difference? And when compared, learn to cultivate those dispositions, and to practice those virtues, which tend most to the benefit and happiness of mankind.
>
> The great Author of our religion [Jesus] frequently inculcates

universal benevolence, and taught us both by precept and example when He promulgated peace and goodwill to man, a doctrine very different from that which actuates the hostile invaders and cruel ravagers of mighty kingdoms and nations.[19]

Not only did this outlook affect how they constructed the American system of government; it also affected their view of America's future. "There is no special providence for Americans, and their nature is the same with that of others,"[20] remarked Adams. And his fellow Founders shared the same sentiments, which is one of the reasons they put so much emphasis, as we will see, on virtue, knowledge, and a unique conception of liberty that would act as a preservative of the American experiment. They were under no delusions that Americans were any less subject to the imperfections of human nature, while at the same time they fully expected them to exhibit to the world the heights to which it could attain. But if there was any group of men who did not *idolize* America, it was her Founding Fathers, as evidenced by the way they attempted to frame her government and society. On the brink of Washington's final victory at Yorktown, Adams remarked to one of his fellow diplomatic colleagues in Europe, "I don't expect that America will turn the earth into a Heaven or a Hell. This world will continue to be earth and its inhabitants will continue to be men, and wars and follies will abound as much as ever."[21]

In fact, when it came to those who argued that America and Americans were somehow innately superior to any other nation, among the first to contend with them were the Founders, who believed such arrogance and pretense would have a degenerative effect on their countrymen. For example, Adams told a certain Mr. John Taylor, and in biblical terms, "We make ourselves popular, Mr. Taylor, by telling our fellow-citizens that we have made discoveries, conceived inventions, and made improvements. We may boast that we are the chosen people, we may even thank God that we are not like other men. But, after all, it will be but flattery, and the delusion, the self-deceit of the Pharisee [Luke 18:11]."[22]

It is crucial to understand this fact: the Founders were not in any sense striving to construct an *ideal* order. They did not believe such a thing existed. Rather, they were attempting to create a system that concurrently made the worst things less likely, and the attainment of the best things most likely. It was because they had ideals grounded in reality that they created such a magnificent reality based on such visionary ideals. They recognized that in order to come *closest* to those ideals (since consummating them was not possible), they had to acknowledge the deficiencies of human nature as observed in history. This most counterintuitive insight and wisdom made the Founders some of the greatest idealists who ever lived, precisely because they were able to put those ideals into practice to an extent most idealists could only imagine. The Founders thus avoided the downfall of most idealists: the inability to put their ideals into practice *at all* because of their own unwillingness to bow to the realities of history and human nature. They were pragmatic idealists, or idealistic pragmatists, for they knew the synergy of both is essential to human flourishing in an imperfect world. They knew, as Adams had written, "There is nothing in this world so excellent that it may not be abused."[23]

By incorporating the often-harsh lessons of human nature and history in our forms of government, they thereby included those ingredients which, while not the most glamorous, were the most essential to its success.

2

WHAT IS LIBERTY?

It was a brisk fall day. I was in Washington, DC, for the 2005 presidential inauguration, and I was visiting the National Archives building, the sacred depository of some of our nation's most treasured documents. My eyes were already watery as I approached the American Magna Carta, the Declaration of Independence. My watery eyes turned to teary eyes, and my throat tightened as I beheld the charter that brought America onto the world stage, the text that asserted not only the liberty of Americans, but of all people. Knowing that some of my greatest heroes' names had been signed on that hallowed parchment, and the sacrifices they endured to support and defend it, I could not contain my emotion.

But my tears of gratitude and joy would quickly become tears of frustration and despondency.

As I headed from the Declaration of Independence to the Constitution, I happened upon a group of teenagers who appeared to be at least juniors or seniors in high school. And then I heard the question that haunts me to this day, as a girl asked the security guard, "What's the difference between the Declaration of Independence and the Constitution?" The feelings that welled up within me had nothing to do with the fact that I loved history and maybe this girl didn't. Rather, I could not escape the fact that this young woman had likely spent more than a decade in the public education system, and she still could not distinguish the Declaration from the Constitution of the United States. She did not know even the bare facts about her liberty—where it came from and how it was asserted and defended.

In our own day, it has become crucial to once again not only ask but answer the question, what is liberty? Unfortunately, doing neither in a serious fashion has led to answers that are, at best, superficial and which perpetuate severe distortions of the liberty for which our Founding Fathers fought and upon which they based our system of government. For the average American citizen, perhaps most tragically among the young, *liberty* has become all but synonymous with "doing whatever I want to do." Many will add, "as long as I'm not hurting anybody else." *Liberty* in twenty-first-century America has been reduced to one simple catchphrase: *doing what I want.*

That may sound sufficient, and many will justify this definition of liberty as derived from the Founders. Unfortunately, it is inadequate (if not downright pernicious), and the connection made is only half true. The reasons for this will actually be unraveled *by* the Founders throughout this book. But at this juncture, it would be enlightening to discover how the Founders themselves articulated what they were fighting for, and the terms with which they described it. How did *they* conceive of liberty? How did *they* define their vision of a free society? What was the dream *they* were fighting for while sacrificing their homes, their time with their families, their fortunes, their security, some even their lives? What was it that would cause men such as John Adams to groan, "Posterity! You will never know how much it cost the present generation to preserve your freedom! I hope you will make a good use of it. If you do not, I shall repent in heaven that I ever took half the pains to preserve it."[1]

The tale is an inspiring one indeed, one whose cost we have no doubt forgotten, but which we must now remember. The problem has become even more vexing as more and more of our fellow citizens consult the words of our Founders less and less. What remains today in our civic memory is at best a clump of overused clichés, and at worst the most impossibly distorted and out-of-context quotes used by all sides of the political spectrum to advance their own agendas. We no longer know ourselves or our story.

THE AMERICAN STORY

It is impossible to understand the full American story, and the narrative our Founders believed themselves to be playing out, without going back to the very beginning of the New World: the Puritans (some of whom we know as "the Pilgrims" today).

The Puritans have largely been remembered as intrepid pioneers who fled Europe for the safe refuge of the New World so they could enjoy political and religious liberty. Fundamentally, this is all true, and this was largely how our Founders saw them. The majority of the first pilgrims to the New World were Puritans, highly religious and educated dissenters who were persecuted almost everywhere they went in Europe, particularly by established state churches, such as the Church of England and the Catholic Church. With the Reformation taking place at the beginning of the sixteenth century, the Bible became available in the languages of the common people for the first time since it was originally canonized in the fourth century. Previously it had largely been in Latin and could only be read by priests (and even some priests were not educated enough to read it). But when it became available in, among other languages, English, various religious sects around Europe began to form their own opinions of what the Bible said, often with interpretations that differed greatly from the established doctrine of the "official" churches. The Puritans were such a sect, and they were everywhere acknowledged as being peculiar in their incredible devotion to the notion of applying the teachings of the Bible itself, not the doctrines of "official" churches and Protestant churches, to every area of life—church, government, economics, and every other facet of society. While many today might dismiss them as religious fanatics, their ideas would have a monumental impact on world history that would improve the lives of millions. All the ideas that would become part of the American vision of a free society were in some way or another influenced by the Puritans. Tocqueville described the context in which this revolutionary intellectual and spiritual movement arose:

On the continent of Europe at the beginning of the seventeenth century, absolute monarchy everywhere stood triumphant on the ruins of the oligarchic and feudal liberty of the Middle Ages. At the heart of this splendor and literary excellence, the idea of rights had perhaps never been more entirely neglected. Never had nations enjoyed less political activity. Never had the ideas of true liberty less preoccupied people's minds. It was at that very time that these same principles, unknown or neglected by European nations, were being proclaimed in the deserts of the New World to become the future symbol of a great nation. The boldest theories of the human mind were distilled into practice in this apparently humble society which probably no statesman would have been bothered to consider.[2]

"The Puritans sought out a land so rough and so neglected that they might be allowed to live there as they wished and to worship God without restriction" he had noted earlier. "They tore themselves away from the comforts of their native land to obey a purely intellectual need. By suffering the inevitable deprivations of exile, their object was the triumph of an *idea*."[3] They saw themselves as replaying the famous story of the Exodus, the escape of the Jewish people from slavery in Egypt to the promised land of Israel. Europe, as the bastion of monarchical tyranny and feudal despotism, was the new Egypt. The Atlantic Ocean was the wilderness through which the children of Israel sojourned for forty years, and the New World, America, was the new promised land. As Thomas Paine observed, it seemed Providence had ordained these circumstances so that a land of liberty might be created in the New World: "The Reformation was preceded by the discovery of America, as if the Almighty graciously meant to open a sanctuary to the persecuted in future years, when home should afford neither friendship nor safety."[4]

Several months after the Battles of Lexington and Concord, the military engagements that effectively inaugurated the American Revolutionary War, the Second Continental Congress, in setting out its premises for taking up arms against the British, drew deeply from this well of heritage: "Our forefathers . . . left their native land to seek on these shores a residence for civil and religious freedom. At the expense of their blood, at the hazard of their fortunes, without the least charge to the country from which they removed, by unceasing labor and an unconquerable spirit, they effected settlements in the distant and inhospitable wilds of America."

For the Founders, to abandon the heritage of liberty and self-government bequeathed to them by their ancestors was totally unacceptable, as it was their duty to pass it on to the next generation as well. The congressional declaration continued:

> We have counted the cost of this contest [Luke 14:28], and find nothing so dreadful as voluntary slavery. Honor, justice, and humanity, forbid us tamely to surrender that freedom which we received from our gallant ancestors, and which our innocent posterity have a right to receive from us. We cannot endure the infamy and guilt of resigning succeeding generations to that wretchedness which inevitably awaits them if we basely entail hereditary bondage upon them.[5]

During the difficult days leading up to the Revolution, John Adams encouraged his countrymen by reminding them that it was their ancestors' hope of liberty that "conquered all discouragements, dangers, and trials!"[6]

It is no wonder that Tocqueville, in looking back on the arrival of the Puritans and the other Pilgrims in the New World, saw the same providential thread of history as Thomas Paine and the Founders: "I seem to see the whole destiny of America encapsulated in the first Puritan to land upon its shores, just as the first man led to the whole human race . . . Their fathers have given them the love of equality and freedom."[7]

Would men and women risk "the expenses of their blood," the "hazard of their fortunes," and by "unceasing labor" and an "unconquerable spirit," settle themselves in "the distant and inhospitable wilds of America," and suffer "all discouragements, dangers, and trials" for the mere sake of an idea of liberty as banal, uninspiring, and as vague as "doing whatever I want"?

No. They did it for something far more precious.

WHAT LIBERTY?

So what liberty were the Founders actually fighting for? This question will be answered throughout this entire book, but all the answers revolve around, and rise and fall upon, the power of a single idea: that human liberty, and the rights derived from it, are in no way whatsoever granted by other human beings or governments, but by God, the Creator Himself. Because of this, no man could be robbed of what was rightfully his—his life, his property, the fruits of his labor, his family, his religion, his thoughts, his intellectual powers, and more. "Human nature itself," John Adams wrote, "is evermore an advocate for liberty. There is also in human nature a resentment of injury, and indignation against wrong. A love of truth, and a veneration for virtue." These were divine endowments, and God required earthly governments to respect them as such. All the ideas the Founders inherited from the Puritans, and developed and put into practice themselves, are contingent upon this one. Without it, they all fall. But with it, they were able to devise perhaps the greatest form of government for a society that would in turn become the freest, the most prosperous, the most influential, and the most powerful ever seen in world history. And it all began with this: that rights come from God, not from man. From this original fountain flowed everything else.

When the Puritans were beginning to arrive in the New World, the idea then in vogue was the "divine right of kings," the notion that *the king*—no one else—was anointed by God to rule the common folk, and for that reason they owed him unquestioning obedience. Men needed the strong hand of a powerful government to guide them and prevent them from falling into anarchy, or so the idea went. What the Founders called "citizens" were in Europe called "subjects," as in subjects of, or subject to, the King. They had no rights, only privileges granted by the government. Most people in Europe were peasants, and because they had no inherent rights they typically died as peasants, as there were few opportunities for advancement if you were not connected with the rich and powerful, "the great" as Adams described them, who, he noted, "have accordingly laboured, in all Ages, to wrest from the Populace, both the Knowledge of their Rights and Wrongs, and the Power to assert the former, and redress the Latter."[8] Commenting on the bleak scene painted by history, particularly in Europe, Adams inquired, "Shall we conclude from these melancholy observations that human nature is incapable of liberty, that no honest equality can be preserved in society, and that such forcible causes are always at work as must reduce all men to a submission to despotism, monarchy, oligarchy, or aristocracy?"

His answer? "By no means."[9]

This all began to change with the opening of the Bible to the commoner for the first time after the Reformation. Upon reading it, the Puritans, and many other dissenters, didn't see the idea that some men were more equal than others, but that *all* men were equal before God, a contention they, and their progeny the Founders, would stake all their claims to liberty upon. Nowhere did they see God treating kings one way and treating everybody else another. Thomas Paine, in his famous pamphlet *Common Sense*, derided this idea, and not from humanistic or secular grounds, but from the Bible: "As the exalting one man [the king] so greatly above the rest cannot be justified on the equal rights of nature, so neither can it be defended on the authority of scripture."[10] Since all were equal before God, all shared the same inherent rights. "I say RIGHTS," Adams had written a decade earlier, "for such they have, undoubtedly, antecedent to all earthly government—*Rights* that cannot be repealed or restrained by human laws—*Rights* derived from the great legislator of the universe."[11]

This belief was the forward phalanx in the Revolutionary struggle. Other issues were involved, to be sure, but the foundation upon which they were all argued was this one. The Founders knew that their ancestors had fled Europe precisely because they sought to flee persecution and tyranny. They had arrived in the New World with grants from the king of England to set up their own independent legislatures, apart from Parliament, and with full powers, with the king's consent, to form their own laws for their own circumstances. For more than a century, the colonies in the New World experienced what has been termed the "benign neglect" of Great Britain, a time when they were independent in all but name, and Britain had very little to do with how they governed themselves. This all began to change in the 1760s, particularly after the French and Indian War. Parliament asserted its right to make laws that bound the Americans "IN ALL CASES WHATSOEVER." Such a claim was particularly egregious, not only because it violated what many of the colonists saw as their right to govern themselves through their own legislatures, independent of Parliament, granted to them by the king in their colonial charters, but also because they were not represented in Parliament, and were thus being ruled by a government in which they had no say whatsoever. "What is to defend us against so enormous, so unlimited a power?"[12] they asked. It was, at the end of the day, the same sort of claims to absolute and unbridled authority and power that their ancestors, the Puritans and others had fled to the New World to escape. John Jay, who would later be one of the authors of *The Federalist* and the first Chief Justice of the United States, aptly recounted the colonists' aggrieved sense of justice:

> What, among other things, can appear more unworthy of credit than that, in an enlightened age, in a civilized and Christian country, in a nation so celebrated for humanity as well as love of liberty and justice as the English once justly were, a prince should arise who, by the influence of corruption alone, should be able to reduce them into a combination to reduce three millions of his most loyal and affectionate subjects to absolute slavery, under a pretense of a right, appertaining to God alone, of binding them in all cases whatever, not even excepting cases of conscience and religion?[13]

Part of the untold story of the American Revolution is that the Founders were not initially attempting to completely overthrow the existing order. And contrary to popular belief, many of them were not opposed to monarchy in principle, particularly the British monarchy, which, since the Glorious Revolution of 1688, had been, at least in theory, subjected to the rule of law after a series of disastrous and bloody civil wars between Parliament and the king throughout the seventeenth century. They opposed monarchy that granted itself powers it did not have and status it had not earned or could not claim a right to, which is what they saw King George III doing. But in many cases, they defended their cause not by castigating the British Constitution, but by affirming what they saw as its bedrock principles. "Liberty is essential to the public good," wrote Adams, and it was liberty that distinguished the British constitution from any other. He continued:

> Liberty is its end, its use, its designation, drift and scope . . . It stands not on the supposition that kings are the favorites of heaven, that their power is more divine than the power of the people and unlimited but by their own will and discretion. It is not built on the doctrine that a few nobles or rich commons have a right to inherit the earth, and all the blessings and pleasures of it; and that the multitude, the million, the populace, the vulgar, the mob, the herd and the rabble, as the great always delight to call them, have no rights at all, and were made only for their use, to be robbed and butchered at their pleasure. No, it stands upon this principle, that the meanest and lowest of the people are, by the unalterable, indefeasible laws of God and nature as well entitled to the benefit of the air to breathe, light to see, food to eat, and clothes to wear as the nobles or the king. All men are born equal.[14]

Indeed, this idea did not arrive on the scene with the Founders, but had emerged among many seventeenth-century thinkers, like John Locke, and had accordingly developed for more than a century as the English gradually divested themselves more and more of the idea that monarchs could not be opposed because they were God's anointed. Locke, who greatly influenced the Founders, described the purpose of law under the British Constitution in much the same way Adams did, and both specifically denied the idea that liberty was simply doing "what I want":

The end of law is not to abolish or restrain, but *to preserve and enlarge freedom*: for in all the states of created beings capable of laws, *where there is no law, there is no freedom*. For *liberty* is to be free from restraint and violence from others which cannot be where there is no law. But freedom is not, as we are told, *a liberty for every man to do what he lists* [i.e., pleases] . . . But a *liberty* to dispose, and order, as he lists, his person, actions, possessions, and his whole property, within the allowance of those laws under which he is, and therein not to be subject to the arbitrary will of another, but freely follow his own.[15]

Montesquieu, a French political philosopher who also had a profound influence on the Founders, asserted the same idea: "In a state that is in a society where there are laws, liberty can consist only in having the power to do what one should want to do and in no way being constrained to do what one should not want to do."[16] For both, as we shall see in later chapters, liberty was more than one's individual sphere of action. Rather, it was an inherently *moral* idea, based on its endowment to man by God, and therefore was not subject to the arbitrary whims of man.

It was precisely because the British king and Parliament had asserted an *arbitrary* power over their American colonies, subject to no other control except their own, that the Founders determined that, while the British Constitution was intended to foster liberty, the British government had abandoned this original purpose. By doing so, it had in effect abandoned and cheapened the rights and privileges of its American subjects. These included freedom of the press, the right to a trial by a jury of one's peers, the right of self-government under colonial legislatures founded upon the authority of royal charters, and many others that would later become integrated into the US Constitution and the Bill of Rights. All were intrinsic to the British Constitution, yet, the British government was violating them all, in one way or another. In doing so, contended the Founders, it was the British, not the Americans, who were acting contrary to the will of God.

It was for this reason they had such confidence in the American cause.

As the conflict between the colonies and the mother country became more intense, Adams staked the justice of the American cause on fundamentally religious and moral principles: "But the gallant struggle . . . on the Continent of NORTH AMERICA is founded in principles so indisputable in the moral law, in the revealed Law of God [the Bible], in the true Constitution of Britain, and in the most apparent welfare of the British nation, as well as of the whole body of the people in America that it rejoices my very soul."[17]

"Let it be known," he thundered the year before, "that British liberties are not the grants of princes of Parliaments, but original rights, conditions of original contracts, coequal with prerogative and coeval with government; that many of our rights are inherent and essential, agreed on as maxims and established as preliminaries even before a Parliament existed." In his view, then, the colonists had "an indisputable right to demand them against all the power and authority on earth."[18]

Other Founders had written similarly: "The sacred rights of mankind are not to be rummaged for among old parchments or musty records," wrote Alexander Hamilton, in his 1765 work, *A Farmer Refuted*. "They are written, as with a sunbeam, in the whole volume of human nature by the hand of the Divinity itself, and can never be erased or obscured by mortal power."

Samuel Adams had asserted the same idea: "Just and true liberty, equal and impartial liberty, in matters spiritual and temporal, is a thing that all men are clearly entitled to by the eternal and immutable laws of God and nature, as well as by the law of nations, and all well-grounded municipal laws, which must have their foundation in the former."[19]

"Be it remembered," John Adams enjoined, "that liberty must at all hazards be supported. We have a right to it derived from our Maker. But if we have not, our fathers have earned and bought it for us at the expense of their ease, their estates, their pleasure, and their blood."[20]

Upon reaching the point of no return, the crescendo and drum roll of the Revolution had climaxed on this simple, profound, and history-molding idea, preserved for all time in our Declaration of Independence:

"We hold these truths to be self-evident, that all men are created equal; that they are endowed by their Creator with certain unalienable rights, that among these are life, Liberty, and the pursuit of happiness."

And it all started with a few Puritan dissenters who had dared to take the Bible, which they were finally able to read for the very first time, seriously.

THE CAUSE OF LIBERTY

Just as the idea that rights come from God was the great conviction of the American Revolution, it was in fact only the first and primary answer to a broader question: Can man govern himself? Was he capable of exercising his reason and virtue to establish a government of his own volition? In opening the *Federalist Papers*, Alexander Hamilton noted that it was America's task to find out: "It seems to have been reserved to the people of this country to decide, by their conduct and example, the important question, whether societies of men are really capable or not of establishing good government from reflection and choice, or whether they are forever destined to depend for their political constitutions on accident and force."[21]

Tyrants through the ages had given this question a firm no, for only kings had divinely endowed rights. The Founders, however, said yes, for they believed, as did their Puritan ancestors, that all men are divinely endowed with rights. But they also believed that liberty was possible only if the assertion of such rights were accompanied by a like assertion of the moral and rational faculties with which to exercise those rights for the benefit of themselves and others. Liberty, for them, did not make sense, and was not even possible, if the assertion of rights were not accompanied by the corollary assertion of duties. People had a right to worship God as they desired because they had a duty to worship God as well as they knew how. They had the right to speak their minds because they had a duty to use their minds in pursuit of productive ends. And they had the right to their property because they had the duty to acquire it honestly and steward it wisely. Citizens who utilize their liberty in such ways as to govern themselves do not require an impersonal, removed, and ponderous government to tell them, let alone compel them, to do what they already know and compel themselves to do. This was, in a nutshell, the liberty our Founders believed was worth dying for.

For now, it remains for us to step back and catch a glimpse of the big picture our Founders envisioned, for theirs was a vision not ultimately for themselves, but for millions yet unborn in a future yet unseen. By securing the gift of liberty for future generations of Americans, they believed they were better securing it for everyone, everywhere.

"Our cause is noble, it is the cause of mankind! And the danger to it is to be apprehended from ourselves,"[22] George Washington had written at a critical time during the war. He was echoing the sentiments of Thomas Paine, who had himself written in *Common Sense*, "The cause of America is in a great measure the cause of all mankind." He explained why: "Every spot of the old world is overrun with oppression. Freedom hath been hunted round the globe. Asia, and Africa, have long expelled her. Europe regards her like a stranger, and England hath given her warning to depart. O! Receive the fugitive, and prepare in time an asylum for mankind."[23]

"This new world," he noted, "hath been the asylum for the persecuted lovers of civil and religious liberty from *every part* of Europe."[24] Samuel Adams noted with similar enthusiasm the singular position in which America had been placed: "Courage, then, my countrymen, our contest is not only whether we ourselves shall be free, but whether there shall be left to mankind an asylum on earth for civil and religious liberty." Nowhere else would "freedom of thought and the right of private judgment, in matters of conscience," which had been "driven from every other corner of the earth," be secure except in America, "their last asylum."[25]

Paine penned perhaps the most famous words regarding the golden opportunity the American Revolution presented to the world: "We have it in our power to begin the world over again. A situation similar to the present hath not happened since the days of Noah until now.

The birthday of a new world is at hand, and a race of men, perhaps as numerous as all Europe contains, are to receive their portion of freedom from the event of a few months."[26]

John Adams expressed similar sentiments in his *Thoughts on Government*, penned in 1776:

> You and I, my dear friend, have been sent into life at a time when the greatest law-givers of antiquity would have wished to have lived. How few of the human race have ever enjoyed an opportunity of making an election of government more than of air, soil, or climate, for themselves or their children? When? Before the present epocha [*sic*], had three millions of people full power and a fair opportunity to form and establish the wisest and happiest government that human wisdom can contrive?

George Washington described the American Revolution in terms reminiscent of a capstone being providentially placed upon an edifice whose construction had been centuries, if not millennia, in the making. Very much in line with the thinking of many of his Puritan and Pilgrim ancestors, he specifically cited the Bible, and its ever-increasing diffusion around the world, as the primary cause behind the establishment of liberty in America:

> The foundation of our Empire was not laid in the gloomy age of ignorance and superstition, but at an epocha [*sic*] when the rights of mankind were better understood and more clearly defined than at any former period, the researches of the human mind, after social happiness, have been carried to a great extent, the treasures of knowledge acquired by the labors of philosophers, sages, and legislatures through a long succession of years are laid open for our use, and their collected wisdom may be happily applied in the establishment of our forms of government. The free cultivation of letters, the unbounded extension of commerce, the progressive refinement of manners [i.e., morals], the growing liberality of sentiment, and above all, the pure and benign light of Revelation [the Bible] have had a meliorating

influence on mankind and increased the blessings of society. At this auspicious period, the United States came into existence as a nation, and if their citizens should not be completely free and happy, the fault will be entirely their own.[27]

John Adams called this vision of America "our virtuous vision of a Kingdom of the just,"[28] and it was this noble vision that provided the Founders and the generation of which they were a part the strength and fortitude to bear all discouragements and trials in order to attain it. Adams described to his wife, Abigail, his conviction that it was their duty to at all times be cognizant of the fact that the task in which they were engaged was not merely for themselves, but for future generations:

> You and I, my dear, have reason, if ever mortals had, to be thoughtful, to look forward beyond the transitory scene. Whatever is preparing for us, let us be prepared to receive. It is time for us to subdue our passions of every kind. The prospect before us is an ocean of uncertainties in which no pleasing objects appear. We have few hopes, excepting that of preserving our honor and our conscience untainted, and a free Constitution to our country. Let me be sure of these, and, amidst all my weaknesses, I cannot be overcome. With these, I can be happy in extreme poverty, in humble insignificance, nay I hope and believe, in death. Without them, I should be miserable with a crown upon my head, millions in my coffers, and a gaping, idolizing multitude at my feet.[29]

His cousin Samuel Adams obviously felt the same way: "If ye love wealth better than liberty, the tranquility of servitude than the animated contest of freedom—go home from us in peace," he said. "We ask not your counsels or arms. Crouch down and lick the hands which feed you. May your chains sit lightly upon you, and may posterity forget that you were our countrymen!"[30]

George Washington wrote that he had "sacrificed every private consideration and personal enjoyment to the earnest and pressing solicitation of those who saw and knew the alarming situation of our public concerns, and had no other end in view but to promote the interests of their country."[31] Indeed, his estate, Mount Vernon, was in utter disrepair by the end of the war. In the span of eight years, he had been able to visit it once, and then only very briefly. The majority of the time, the war was often more akin to an organized retreat from the often stronger British forces than Washington would have preferred. Disaster was always just around the corner, and the continental army was always on the brink of defeat. But despite such tribulations, Washington and many other Founders expressed a constant confidence in Providence, the "Supreme Judge of the world" referred to in the Declaration of Independence, whose beneficent dispensations they had so often witnessed. "It is impossible for the man of pious reflection not to perceive in it a finger of that Almighty Hand which has been so frequently and signally extended to our relief in the critical stages of the revolution" James Madison had written in Federalist No. 37. They recognized that what was happening was far bigger than they, their country, and their time. As John Adams observed, "In such great changes and commotions, individuals are but atoms. It is scarcely worthwhile to consider what the consequences will be to us. What will be the effects upon present and future millions, and millions of millions, is a question very interesting to benevolence, natural, and Christian. God grant they may, I firmly believe they will, be happy."[32]

Thomas Paine wrote in *Common Sense*, "The sun never shined on a cause of greater worth. Tis not the affair of a city, a country, a province, or a kingdom, but of a continent—of at least one eighth part of the habitable globe. Tis not the concern of a day, a year, or an age. Posterity are virtually involved in the contest, and will be more or less affected, even to the end of time, by the proceedings now."

For many of the Founders, time away from family was an all-too-heart-wrenching if not necessary sacrifice given the exigencies of the times in order to gain freedom, the prize they believed their children were even more entitled to than they themselves. Adams wrote movingly to his son John Quincy back home:

I hope you and your sister and brothers will take proper notice of these great events and remember under whose wise and kind Providence they are all conducted. Not a sparrow falls, nor a hair is lost, but by the direction of infinite wisdom [allusion to Matthew 10:29]. Much less are cities conquered and evacuated. I hope that you will all remember how many losses, dangers, and inconveniences have been borne by your parents, and the inhabitants of Boston in general, for the sake of preserving freedom for you and yours, and I hope you will all follow the virtuous example, if, in any future time, your country's liberties shall be in danger, and suffer every human evil rather than give them up.[33]

A year after the signing of the Declaration of Independence, Adams again encouraged his children to take note of the times in which they lived:

If it should be the design of Providence that you should live to grow up, you will naturally feel a curiosity to learn the history of the causes which have produced the late Revolution of our government. No study in which you can engage will be more worthy of you. It will become you to make yourself master of all the considerable characters which have figured upon the stage of civil, political, or military life. This you ought to do with utmost candor, benevolence, and impartiality . . . You will wonder, my dear son, at my writing to you at your tender age such dry things as these. But if you keep this letter, you will in some future period thank your father for writing it.[34]

After the war had already been won and the country was struggling to secure its hard-fought liberty with a new Constitution, Adams continued to enjoin both the current and younger generations of Americans to not lose sight of the possibilities within their grasp. Indeed, he had harsh words, particularly for the young, who so flippantly took for granted the liberty secured for them by their elders:

Objects stupendous in their magnitudes and motions strike us from quarters and fill us with amazement! When we recollect that the wisdom or the folly, the virtue or the vice, the liberty or servitude, of those millions now beheld by us, only as Columbus saw these times in vision, are certainly to be influenced, perhaps decided, by the manners, examples, principles, and political institutions of the present generation, that mind must be hardened into stone that is not melted into reverence and awe. With such affecting scenes before his eyes, is there, can there be a young American indolent and incurious, surrendered up to dissipation and frivolity, vain of imitating the loosest manners of countries which can never be made much better or much worse? A profligate American youth must be profligate indeed and richly merits the scorn of all mankind.[35]

So committed was he to the cause of liberty, and so determined to pass it on to his children, that he informed his wife that, should they ever complain or curse him in their later years for his long spans of absence during the Revolution (as he was a member of Congress), then they were not worthy of the cause for which he had fought for them:

But I will not bear the reproaches of my children. I will tell them that I studied and labored to procure a free Constitution of government for them to solace themselves under, and if they do not prefer this to ample fortune, to easy and elegance, they are not my children, and I care not what becomes of them. They shall live upon thin diet, wear mean clothes, and work hard, with cheerful hearts and free spirits, or they may be the children of the earth or of no one for me.[36]

Many of the Founders could certainly have echoed, along with Adams, that "When these things shall be once well finished, or in a way of being so, I shall think that I have answered the end of my creation, and sing with pleasure my *nunc dimmittes* [Song of Simeon, Luke 2:29–32]."[37]

As the Fourth of July, 1776, inexorably approached and the conflict with Britain continued to intensify, Congress, after expressing the great pains the American people had taken to remedy the situation, combatively declared the righteousness of the liberty for which they had slowly, but now with the greatest conviction, taken up arms to defend:

> Our cause is just. Our union is perfect. . . . we most solemnly, before God and the world, declare that, exerting the utmost energy of those powers which our beneficent Creator hath graciously bestowed upon us, the arms we have been compelled by our enemies to assume we will, in defiance of every hazard, with unabating firmness and perseverance, employ for the preservation of our liberties, being with our [one] mind resolved to die free men rather than live slaves.[38]

Responding to British threats to subjugate what they were now describing as the American rebellion, Benjamin Franklin wrote one of his former colleagues in London (from his time as an unofficial representative of several of the colonies), "[America] will not be destroyed: God will protect and prosper it . . . We know you may do us a great deal of mischief, but we are determined to bear it patiently as long as we can. But if you flatter yourselves with beating us into submission, you know neither the people nor the *country*."[39]

At long last, with all alternatives exhausted, with their olive branches rejected, with British troops occupying Boston and thousands more, including foreign mercenaries, on the way, Congress decided that the time had come to declare independence from Great Britain. John Adams described the occasion to his wife:

> Yesterday, the greatest question was decided which ever was debated in America, and a greater perhaps never was or will be decided among men . . . It is the will of Heaven that the two countries should be sundered forever. It may be the will of Heaven that America shall suffer calamities still more wasting and distresses yet more dreadful . . . I am not without apprehensions from this quarter. But I must submit all my hopes and fears to an overruling Providence in which . . . I firmly believe.[40]

In a fit of enthusiasm, he wrote her yet another letter the very same day. Somewhat comically in retrospect, he labeled the second of July (instead of the fourth) as the great day of remembrance. What Adams was referring to was the day on which the Declaration was officially approved, while the document itself was dated on the fourth. His sentiments, nonetheless, were crystal clear:

> The second day of July 1776 will be the most memorable epocha [*sic*] in the history of America. I am apt to believe that it will be celebrated by succeeding generations as the great anniversary festival. It ought to be commemorated as the day of deliverance by solemn acts of devotion to God Almighty. It ought to be solemnized with pomp and parade, with shows, games, sports, guns, bells, bonfires and illuminations from one end of this continent to the other from this time forward forever more. You will think me transported with enthusiasm, but I am not. I am well aware of the toil and blood and treasure that it will cost us to maintain this Declaration and support and defend these States. Yet through all the gloom I can see the rays of ravishing light and glory. I can see that the end is more than worth all the means, and that posterity will triumph in that day's transaction, even although we should rue it, which I trust in God we shall not.[41]

"Objects of the most stupendous magnitude, measures in which the lives and liberties of millions, born and unborn, are most essentially interested, are now before us," he wrote elsewhere. "We are in the very midst of a Revolution, the most complete, unexpected, and remarkable of any in the history of nations."[42]

The fight would be long, and it would be extremely difficult. But it was worth it. It was more than worth it. The gift of liberty would at all costs be passed down to posterity. As a diplomat during the war, Adams described the attitude of Americans to his European colleagues: "They think the cause of their country a sacred trust deposited in their hands by Providence for the happiness of millions yet unborn. They now think their liberty can never be safe under the government of any European nation, the idea of coming again under which strikes them with horror."[43]

Upon signing of the peace treaty with Great Britain, Washington, in bidding farewell to the men he had so gallantly led for nearly a decade of war, reflected in astonishment that "it is universally acknowledged that the enlarged prospects of happiness, opened by the confirmation of our independence and sovereignty almost exceeds the power of description."[44] At the end of his presidency, and thus at the conclusion of his entire public life, Washington commended his countrymen to always remember that their first and primary identity was not as citizens of their own states, but as Americans, for that was the capacity in which they had sacrificed, bled, and won their liberty together: "The name of AMERICAN . . . must always exalt the just pride of patriotism . . . With slight shades of difference, you have the same religion, manners, habits and political principles. You have in common cause fought and triumphed together. The independence and liberty you possess are the work of joint councils, and joint efforts, of common dangers, sufferings, and successes."[45]

But none of it would have happened without a radical change in culture among the American people themselves in the ten to fifteen years preceding the fateful 1776. This was the true American Revolution. A culture of liberty had ultimately made liberty possible. Perhaps the greatest summary of this transformation comes from John Adams:

> The American Revolution was not a common event . . . But what do we mean by the American Revolution? Do we mean the American war? The Revolution was effected before the war commenced. The Revolution was in the minds and hearts of the people; a change in their religious sentiments of their duties and obligations . . . but when they saw those [governmental] powers renouncing all the principles of authority, and bent upon the destruction of all the securities of their lives, liberties, and properties, they thought it their duty to pray for the continental congress and all the thirteen State congresses . . . believing allegiance and protection to be reciprocal, when protection was withdrawn, they thought allegiance was dissolved . . . *This radical change in the principles, opinions, sentiments, and affections of the people, was the real American Revolution.*[46]

This was the liberty our Founders fought for, and the liberty we need to regain ourselves. But to do that, we must uncover what our Founders actually had to say about it. What did they say about government in general, the Constitution in particular, and the other foundation stones of the liberty they intended to be ours? These shall be the objects of our continuing quest for liberty's secrets.

3

GOVERNMENT OF THE PEOPLE: LIBERTY'S PROTECTOR

The Founders believed that government was necessary to the success of liberty, a proposition John Adams said "is proved, as has been often already said, by the constitution of human nature, by the experience of the world, and the concurrent testimony of all history."

Unfortunately, man was capable of governing himself virtuously only *part* of the time—his own nature prevented him from doing so perfectly at *all* times. His passions were apt to gain the upper hand over his reason. Such a view was based on a Judeo-Christian view of human nature as having inherent dignity and worth, but also being flawed, or to use a more theological term, "fallen." "Government, like dress, is the badge of lost innocence," Thomas Paine noted, in a clear reference to the story of the Fall of Adam and Eve in the book of Genesis. "Here then is the origin and rise of government, namely a mode rendered necessary by the inability of moral virtue to govern the world," Paine concluded.[1] Adams brilliantly summarized both the implications and necessities imposed by the realities of human nature:

> The moral government of God and his vicegerent [manager] Conscience, ought to be sufficient to restrain men to obedience, to justice, and benevolence at all times and in all places. We must therefore descend from the dignity of our nature when we think of civil government at all. But the nature of mankind is one thing, and the reason of mankind another, and the first has the same relation to

the last as the whole to a part. The passions and appetites are parts of human nature as well as reason and the moral sense. In the institution of government it must be remembered that, although reason ought always to govern individuals, it certainly never did since the Fall [Genesis 3], and never will till the Millennium [the reign of perfect peace and righteousness prophesied in the Bible]; and human nature must be taken as it is, as it has been, and will be.[2]

But what exactly was it that human nature fell short of? The requirements of natural law, or the "Law of Nature and Nature's God" as Jefferson phrased it in the Declaration of Independence. This law was the objective, divinely defined standard by which all human rights were endowed and actions judged. The Founders did not contend that the natural law could be known *perfectly*, but it was nonetheless known to all human beings in one way or another through the "vice-regent, conscience" as Adams called it. George Washington called it the "celestial fire."[3] All men, they believed, knew deep down that they were morally obligated to treat their fellow man as they would like to be treated. In other words, the Golden Rule was not just some innocuous moral precept, but the basis of all rights and morality. The sum of the natural law was therefore that all men had inalienable rights and were required to respect the inalienable rights of their fellow men, rights such as life, liberty, and property. The natural law was thus a way of conceiving of an objective morality that, although not known perfectly by all men, applied equally to all.

But this idea was not original to the Founders. Rather, they inherited it from a long line of thinkers largely associated with the Judeo-Christian tradition, but also several of the great figures of Greece and Rome. The Roman statesman, Cicero, was particularly influential when it came to the formation of the Founders' views on natural law, as his writings were standard texts for many schoolchildren in the eighteenth century. Here is how he described the "true law":

> True law is in keeping with the dictates both of reason and of nature. It applies universally to everyone. It is unchanging and eternal. Its commands are summons to duty, and its prohibitions declare that nothing

wrongful must be done. As far as good men are concerned, both its commands and its prohibitions are effective, though neither have any effect on men who are bad. To attempt to invalidate this law is sinful. Nor is it possible to repeal any part of it, much less to abolish it altogether. From its obligations neither Senate nor people can release us. And to explain or interpret it we need no one outside ourselves . . . The maker, and umpire, and proposer of this law will be God, the single master and ruler of us all. If a man fails to obey God, then he will be in flight from his own self, repudiating his own human nature. As a consequence, even if he escapes the normal punishment for wrongdoing, he will suffer the penalties of the gravest possible sort.[4]

John Locke made a similar observation, "For though the law of nature be plain and intelligible to all rational creatures, yet men being biased by their interest, as well as ignorant for want of study of it, are not apt to allow of it as a law binding to them in the application of it to their particular cases."[5]

James Madison seemed to agree: "We all know that conscience is not a sufficient safeguard, and besides, that conscience itself may be deluded, may be misled, by an unconscious bias into acts which an enlightened conscience would forbid."[6]

Adams justified the existence of government by using the same principle: "It would be as reasonable to say that all government is altogether unnecessary because it is the duty of all men to deny themselves and obey the laws of nature and the laws of God. However clear the duty, we know it will not be performed, and, therefore, it is our duty to enter into associations and compel one another to do some of it."[7]

Although people could exhibit many good attributes, and even though "these favorable attributes of the human character are all valuable, as auxiliaries," Madison asserted that "they will not serve as a substitute for the coercive provision belonging to government and law."[8] His coauthor on the *Federalist Papers*, Alexander Hamilton, made a similar comment when he observed that "it is not safe to trust to the virtue of any people."[9] If men perfectly observed the natural law, then "man would need no other lawgiver" Paine opined. But because he did not observe it, "he finds it necessary to surrender up a part of his property to furnish means for the protection of the rest."[10] History had exhibited the sobering reality that men rarely observed the natural law voluntarily, and thus a coercive power was necessary. This, in essence, was the basis of government's existence according to the Founders. Madison put it succinctly: "But what is government itself but the greatest of all reflections on human nature? If men were angels, no government would be necessary. If angels were to govern men, neither external nor internal controls on government would be necessary."[11]

Thus, government arose out of the need for imperfect men to protect their rights from being violated by other imperfect men. By doing so they would preserve liberty and thereby fulfill the requirements of the natural law. For the Founders, all the various duties and functions of government could be deduced from this single point.

At the same time, since government's existence was based on the natural law, it could not claim to be above it. To assert that it could would be to conclude that the power tasked with enforcing a law was superior to the law itself, a manifestly absurd notion. Montesquieu, a French political philosopher who greatly influenced the Founders, wrote of such a notion: "To say that there is nothing just or unjust but what positive laws [i.e., laws made by government] ordain or prohibit is to say that before a circle was drawn, all its radii were not equal."[12] To apply his analogy to government would be akin to saying, "Since we need some sort of government to enforce the natural law, we need to make sure government defines the natural law first." It is a contradiction in terms. Unlike the problem of the chicken and the egg, the natural law came first, the Founders believed, and government existed only because men did not keep it.

From this philosophy of the origins of government arose two categories into which the various purposes of government were divided: the overall goals of government and the structural needs required to attain those goals. In other words, ends and means. It is the first category to which we turn now.

THE PURPOSES OF GOVERNMENT

The Founders put forward several fundamental principles by which they defined the overall purposes of government. First, government exists for man, not man for government. Second, government exists to protect the rights of citizens, not violate or bestow them. Third, government is accountable to the people and rules by their consent.

The Founders believed that the key to the greatest amount of human happiness was for individuals to live, and by extension governments to govern, in accordance with the natural law. This is why they believed that government was meant for the benefit of the governed, not the governors. All men were created equal and endowed with equal rights by the Creator before government existed. It was therefore incumbent upon the government to protect those rights in a manner that encouraged the greatest welfare of all. John Adams opined, "We ought to consider what is the end of government before we determine which is the best form . . . The happiness of society is the end of government . . . From this principle it will follow that the form of government which communicates ease, comfort, security, or, in one word, happiness, to the greatest number of persons, and in the greatest degree, is the best."[13]

Congress used similar wording to justify taking up arms against the British: "But a reverence for our great Creator, principles of humanity, and the dictates of common sense must convince all those who reflect upon the subject that government was instituted to promote the welfare of mankind, and ought to be administered for that attainment of that end."[14]

It was precisely for this reason that governments were subject to the very same natural law as the citizens they ruled, as Locke contended:

> Thus, the law of nature stands as an eternal rule to all men, *legislators* as well as others. The *rules* that they make for other men's actions must, as well as their own and other men's actions, be conformable to the law of nature, i.e. to the will of God, of which that is a declaration, and the *fundamental law of nature* being *the perseveration of mankind*, no human sanction can be good or valid against it. . . . For the law of nature being unwritten, and so nowhere to be found but in the

37

minds of men, they who through passion or interest shall mis-cite or misapply it cannot so easily be convinced of their mistake where there is no established judge.[15]

Since it was subject to the natural law, the only just objects of government's attention were the "happiness of society" and the "welfare of mankind" per the protection of his divinely endowed rights. This was often phrased by the Founders as the protection of each man's property. But "property" was not simply the *things* one possessed, but also included one's life, beliefs, skills, and so forth. James Madison referred to "the property which individuals have in their opinions, their religion, their person, and their faculties."[16] All of these were to be the objects of government's protection. This idea went all the way back, once again, to the great Cicero, who stridently defended the right to property and described government's role in its protection in terms remarkably similar to those of John Locke and the Founders:

> It is also incumbent on everyone who holds a high governable office to make absolutely sure that the private property of all citizens is safeguarded, and that the State does not encroach on these rights in any way whatever . . . Indeed, the principal reason why, in the first place, states and cities were ever organized at all was to defend private property. It is true that people had come together into communities spontaneously by a natural instinct. But the reason why they sought the shelter of cities was because they wanted to safeguard their own personal possessions . . . It is, I repeat, the special function of every state and every city to guarantee that each of its citizens shall be allowed the free and unassailed enjoyment of his own property.[17]

This gets to a subject of particular importance today, when more people are claiming that our rights are bestowed and defined by government, not the "law of Nature and Nature's God," as our Founders contended. Those who make this argument typically do so by conjecturing that, since we live in a "democracy" (according to our Founders, we don't; more on that later), "the government *is* us." Thomas Paine quite directly addressed this very argument in the very first lines of his famous *Common Sense*:

> Some writers have so confounded society with government as to leave little or no distinction between them, whereas they are not only different but have different origins. Society is produced by our wants, and government by our wickedness. The former promotes our happiness *positively* by uniting our affections, the latter *negatively* by restraining our vices. The one encourages intercourse, the other creates distinctions. The first is a patron, the last a punisher. Society in every state is a blessing, but government, even in its best state, is but a necessary evil, in its worst state an intolerable one.

For Paine, "society" was what we would today call the "civil society," the realm of human interaction in which we engage with each other voluntarily and conduct ourselves as we should in accordance with the natural law (covered in more detail in chapter 7). This again reflects the Founders' belief that man *could* act in accordance with the natural law, but that because he often didn't, government was necessary. Government, then, exists to protect the rights, including the right to property, that by our own nature we tend to violate.

Since government had been tasked with protecting the rights to property of everyone under its jurisdiction, it could not then turn around and violate those property rights itself. After all, the power of government was *bestowed* by the people's consent in order to protect their rights. "Hence," observed Locke, "it is a mistake to think that the supreme *legislative power* of any commonwealth can do what it will, and dispose of the estates of the subject *arbitrarily*, or take any part of them at pleasure." Referring to the natural rights of the citizen before the existence of government, Locke observed that "this is all he doth, or can give up to the common-wealth, and by it to the *legislative power*, so that the legislative can have no more than this . . . It is a power that hath no other end but preservation, and therefore can never have a right to destroy, enslave, or designedly to impoverish the subjects."[18] This naturally limited the extent and manner in which government could exercise power, "for," as Locke observed, "wherever the power that is put in any hands for the government of the people, and the preservation of their properties is applied to other ends, and made use of to impoverish, harass, or subdue them to the arbitrary and irregular commands of those that have it, there it presently becomes *tyranny*, whether those that thus use it are one or many."[19] And since government did not endow rights, but was instead tasked with protecting them, it could by definition not *bestow* additional rights, except the right of equal justice under law (i.e., civil rights), which gets to the third principle, that government is accountable to the people.

Since government is delegated certain powers by the people, it is, as a trustee, accountable to the people for the manner in which it exercises those powers. Responding to the then-common charge from Europeans that America would never succeed because it did not have a monarch and allowed the people too much liberty, President Jefferson wrote, "Sometimes it is said that man cannot be trusted with the government of himself. Can he, then, be trusted with the government of others? Or have we found angels in the forms of kings to govern them? Let history answer this question."[20]

For Jefferson, and the Founders as a whole, history had proven the exact opposite: the presumption that there was a semidivine group of people, such as monarchs or dictators, who alone were fit to rule the people without being directly accountable to them had led to the greatest miseries in human history.

For the Founders, all human governments had been based on some "principle or passion in the minds of the people," as Adams said: fear, honor, or virtue. Within these three categories could be many forms, but every form was derived from this primary passion of the people. Fear had been "the foundation of most governments," and was so "sordid and brutal" by nature that "Americans will not be likely to approve of any political institution which is founded on it." The Founders considered all despotic and tyrannical governments as rooted in fear. As an example of a fear-based government, they frequently referred to the Ottoman Empire, "the Turks," or even to the absolute monarchy in France, in which the king was not controlled by any parliament or other political body. Honor, on the other hand, while "truly sacred," was not as high a principle as virtue. Honor was what compelled a constitutional monarch, such as a king or queen, to maintain peace, order, and justice in his or her kingdom, not only because they were personally invested in the kingdom's success (after all, it was "theirs"), but there were some mechanisms by which his or her power could be checked, such as by Parliament in Great Britain (which held the power of the purse and many other important legislative functions). But the highest principle of them all was virtue, which was the foundation of republics. "Will not every sober man acknowledge it better calculated to promote the general happiness than any other form?" Adams asked. A republic is a form of government in which the people "depute [delegate] power from the many to a few of the most wise and good" for the purpose of making laws for the common good. And because ultimate sovereignty was in the people, not an institution, a king, or a dictator, those laws necessarily applied to everyone. "The very definition of a Republic" Adams commented, "is 'an Empire of Laws, and not men.'"[21]

Thomas Paine, in *Common Sense*, expressed it this way: "Let a day be solemnly set apart for proclaiming the charter [a constitution]. Let it be brought forth placed on the divine law, the word of God [the Bible]. Let a crown be placed thereon, by which the world may know that so far as we approve of monarchy, that in America THE LAW IS KING."

For the Founders, a republic founded upon such principles was their answer to the age-old question of "whether societies of men are really capable or not of establishing good government from reflection and choice, or whether they are forever destined to depend for their political constitutions on accident and force," as Alexander Hamilton phrased it in the *Federalist Papers*.[22] As Adams had asked, "Can authority be more amiable and respectable when it descends from accidents or institutions established in remote antiquity than when it springs fresh from the hearts and judgments of an honest and enlightened people?"[23] For the Founders, the answer was a firm no.

Thus, a *republic* is defined as a form of government founded on the virtue of the people[24] in which the people delegate their power to elected representatives who legislate and enforce laws for the common good. These laws must apply equally to all citizens, including those in government. Because a republic is based on the virtue of the people, it is by nature the offspring of the people and has only those powers that the people have sovereignly delegated to it. It is dependent upon the idea that the people can govern themselves, and are thus capable, and have the right to construct and deconstruct their government in whatever way they deem the most conducive to the common good. John Locke phrased it this way: "But if a long train of abuses, prevarications, and artifices, all tending the same way, make the design visible to the people, and they cannot but feel what they lie under, and see wither they are going, tis not to be wondered that they should then rouse themselves and endeavor to put the rule into such hands which may secure to them the ends for which government was at first erected."[25]

The Declaration of Independence contains a phrase that is striking in its resemblance: "But when a long train of abuses and usurpations, pursuing invariably the same Object evinces a design to reduce them under absolute Despotism, it is their right, it is their duty, to throw off such Government, and to provide new Guards for their future security."

During the tumultuous final days of the Roman Republic and the rise of the Empire under the virtual rule of a single man (at that time, Julius Caesar), Cicero emphasized the same principle of the accountability of rulers, writing that "political leaders must be left in no doubt how far the limits of their authority extend. And the citizens, too, must be made fully aware of the extent of their obligations to obey the functionaries in question."[26]

This was particularly true in the American conception of government, in which those who governed the people were supposed to be not only limited in their authority, but directly accountable to the people for their conduct and actions. Adams explained: "They [the people] have a right, an indisputable, unalienable, indefeasible, divine right to that most dreaded and envied kind of knowledge, I mean of the characters and conduct of their rulers. Rulers are no more than attorneys, agents, and trustees for the people . . . the people have a right to revoke the authority that they themselves have deputed and to constitute abler and better agents, attorneys, and trustees."[27]

George Washington expressed a similar sentiment as commander in chief. Even when he had been delegated broad, nearly unlimited powers by Congress to win the war, he still conducted himself as one ultimately accountable to the public. This fiduciary responsibility to the people made even a man of his high stature humble before those who had delegated such powers to him: "As I have no other view than to promote the public good . . . I would not desire in the least degree to suppress a free spirit of enquiry into any part of my conduct," he once wrote, later adding, "My heart tells me it has been my unremitted aim to do the best circumstances would permit. Yet I may have been very often mistaken in my judgment of the means, and may, in many instances, deserve the imputation of error."

Thomas Jefferson, likewise, expressed his conviction that "while in public service especially, I thought the public entitled to frankness, and intimately to know whom they employed."[28]

And yet, there is a glaring problem: how could a government made up of fallen men govern fallen men in such a way as to maintain their liberty? After all, Madison observed that "the essence of government is power, and power, lodged as it must be in human hands, will ever be liable to abuse."[29] History had shown very few examples of men exercising self-denial when in possession of power. Adams commented:

> To expect self-denial from men when they have a majority in their favor and consequently power to gratify themselves is to disbelieve all history and universal experience; it is to disbelieve Revelation and the Word of God [the Bible], which informs us the heart is deceitful above all things and desperately wicked [Jeremiah 17:9]. There have been examples of self-denial and will be again, but such exalted virtue never yet existed in any large body of men and lasted long . . . There

is no man so blind as not to see that to talk of founding a government upon a supposition that nations and great bodies of men, left to themselves, will practice a course of self-denial is either to babble like a new-born infant or to deceive like an unprincipled imposter.[30]

This is why Adams wrote to his friend and fellow signer of the Declaration of Independence, Benjamin Rush, "Philosophy, morality, religion, reason, all concur in your conclusion that 'Man can be governed only by accommodating laws to his nature.'"[31] Upon giving men power, how could you prevent them from abusing it and usurping more? This is why Madison famously noted in Federalist No. 51 that "in framing a government which is to be administered by men over men, the great difficulty lies in this: you must first enable the government to control the governed, and in the next place oblige it to control itself." This gets to the structural aspect of the purpose of government—how does one group of fallen men (the government) maintain the liberty of other fallen men (citizens) without becoming tyrannical? While this question will be answered in more detail in the next chapter on the Constitution, the Founders articulated several fundamental principles that must be understood before we approach the Constitution itself.

THE STRUCTURE OF GOVERNMENT

In 1787 James Madison ably summarized the structural challenge of government in a letter written to his friend Thomas Jefferson: "The great desideratum [desired goal] in government is so to modify the sovereignty as that it may be sufficiently neutral between different parts of the society to control one part from invading the rights of another, and at the same time sufficiently controlled itself from setting up an interest adverse to that of the entire society."

Based on their knowledge of human nature and history, the Founders knew that at the end of the day, whenever power had been delegated, given, or simply taken by anybody, it was *eventually* abused. Why was this? Beyond the correct, but vague answer of "human nature," the Founders attributed it to, among other things, the existence of parties. By "parties," they did not necessarily mean political parties as we think of them today, but rather, the existence of different interests, typically dictated by the amount or type of property one had. "In every political society, parties are unavoidable," Madison noted. "A difference of interests, real or supposed, is the most natural and fruitful source of them."[32]

Jefferson explained the origin of parties in a similar fashion: "The same political parties which now agitate the US have existed thro' all time. Whether the power of the people, or that of the ἄριςτοι [aristocrats] should prevail, were questions which kept the states of Greece and Rome in eternal convulsions; as they now schismatize [sic] every people whose minds and mouths are not shut up by the gag of a despot."[33] He wrote elsewhere:

> Men by their constitutions are naturally divided into two parties. 1. Those who fear and distrust the people, and wish to draw all powers from them into the hands of the higher classes. 2ndly those who identify themselves with the people, have confidence in them, cherish and consider them as the most honest safe, although not the most wise depository of the public interests. In every country these two parties exist, and in every one where they are free to think, speak, and write, they will declare themselves. Call them therefore liberals and serviles [sic], Jacobins and Ultras, whigs and tories, republicans and federalists, aristocrats and democrats or by whatever name you please, they are the same parties still and pursue the same object.[34]

Thus, according to the Founders, embedded within human nature itself was the predilection to have different interests and thus form "parties." As Tocqueville noted, "human institutions may be altered, but not man himself. Whatever the general efforts of society to keep citizens equal and similar, the personal pride of individuals will always strive to rise above the common level and will hope to achieve some inequality to their own advantage."[35] Such was the history of all ages, and the Founders were under no delusions that they could change this fundamental aspect of the human character.

While Jefferson's definition of parties was rather binary on occasion, many of the Founders saw interests, or "parties," as typically divided between the *one*, the *few*, and the *many*. The "one" would be the absolute ruler—a king or a dictator. The "few" were those close to the absolute ruler—nobles, aristocrats, or in more modern terms, those we would call the "connected." The "many" comprised the majority of citizens, both the poor and what we might call the "middle class." The form of government each of these parties wanted to obtain was, respectively: a dictatorship or monarchy (rule by one), an aristocracy (rule by the few), and a democracy (rule by the many). Notice that a republic is not on this list.

Given the unavoidable existence of such parties, the question for the Founders then became how best to manage them. They could not simply be eliminated by legislation. Since liberty and the protection of God-given rights was the end they sought, tyranny naturally became that which they sought to avoid. And how did they define tyranny? Tyranny was the accumulation of *all* legal power (a monopoly on force) in the hands of a single individual or party, which would inevitably lead it to dominate and subjugate the others. So strong was his belief in this truth that Adams referred to it as the "fundamental article of my political creed," describing it this way: "Despotism, or unlimited sovereignty, or absolute power, is the same in a majority of a popular assembly, an aristocratical [*sic*] council, an oligarchical junto, and a single emperor. Equally arbitrary, cruel, bloody, and in every respect diabolical."[36]

Additionally, the Founders understood law itself as falling into three categories of power: the power of *making* laws, the power of *enforcing* laws, and the power of *applying* or *interpreting* laws when there is a conflict. This forms the basis of the three branches of government we are all familiar with today: a legislative, executive, and judicial branch. In the same way, whether all power is gathered into the hands of the one, the few, or the many, the Founders knew that if the power to make, enforce, and interpret laws were all consolidated into one branch of government, or completely consolidated in the federal government at the expense of the state governments, it would likewise be far more subject to abuse. It was for these reasons that Madison wrote in Federalist No. 47 that "the accumulation of all powers of legislation, executive, and judiciary in the same hands, whether of one, a few, or many, and whether hereditary, self-appointed, or elective, may justly be pronounced the very definition of tyranny."

The Founders' solution was simple, yet revolutionary: divide power—do not let any single party or branch of government have a monopoly on power; otherwise, as history had exhibited without fail, liberty would die. From this reality the Founders derived the need for what is commonly called "separation of powers" into three distinct branches, so power could be properly divided and distributed between the one, the few, and the many. This was not because they saw one as more naturally righteous than the other. On the contrary, because of their thorough knowledge of human nature and history, they were equally skeptical of them all: if any of these had absolute power, or even preponderant power, they would abuse it; they already had. And since the difference between parties was often a question of wealth, they also believed there was no inherent virtue which resulted from either riches or poverty or being right in the middle. All were equally prone to the ravages of human nature. All were equally entitled to the protection of their rights by the laws, and all were equally prone to award themselves to the detriment of the others if possessed of too much power.

This is the foundation of the system of "checks and balances," the idea that each party needed to be monitored by every other party—each must have powers by which to affirm its own rights, as well as powers by which to maintain the equilibrium of the others. Adams articulated it this way:

> The essence of a free government consists in an effectual control of rivalries. The executive and the legislative powers are natural rivals; and if each has not an effectual control over the other, the weaker will ever be the lamb in the paws of the wolf. The nation which will not adopt an equilibrium of power must adopt a despotism. There is

no other alternative. Rivalries must be controlled or they will throw all things into confusion, and there is nothing but despotism or a balance of power which can control them.[37]

For the Founders, the only alternative to such a balance of powers was not the rule of law and liberty, but force and power. In his magisterial *Defense*, written just before the Constitution was ratified, Adams had written:

> But it is of great importance [for the United States] to begin well. Misarrangements [*sic*] now made will have great, extensive, and distant consequences, and we are now employed, how little soever we may think of it, in making establishments which will affect the happiness of a hundred millions of inhabitants at a time in a period not very distant. All nations, under all governments, must have parties. The great secret is to control them. There are but two ways, either by a monarchy and standing army or by a balance in the constitution. Where the people have a voice and there is no balance, there will be everlasting fluctuations, revolutions, and horrors, until a standing army with a general at its head commands the peace, or the necessity of an equilibrium is made apparent to all and is adopted by all.[38]

Notice here that Adams does not seem particularly deferential to the idea of the people having unlimited power. Indeed, this attitude was shared by many of the Founders, who were horrified by "democracy," which for them was the rule of the many. "The power of the people has been confused with the liberty of the people,"[39] Montesquieu had noted, an assumption which is all too often made today as well. On the contrary, the Founders asserted that "the people," or the majority of a society, with no checks and balances, had been just as tyrannical as their aristocratic and monarchical counterparts. Adams explained:

> An excellent writer has said, somewhat incautiously, that a people will never oppress themselves or invade their own rights. This compliment, if applied to human nature, or to mankind, or to any nation or people

in being or in memory, is more than has been merited. . . . All kinds of experience show that great numbers of individuals do oppress great numbers of other individuals, that parties often, if not always, oppress other parties, and majorities almost universally minorities. . . . But if one party agrees to oppress another, or the majority the minority, the people still oppress themselves, for one part of them oppress another. . . . But if the people never, jointly nor severally, think of usurping the rights of others, what occasion can there be for any government at all?[40]

While the Founders asserted that "the people" were the source of all legitimate authority, they said this with the understanding that the people (the one, the few, and the many) were virtuous, for as noted earlier, virtue was for them the foundation of a republic, and the single best guarantee that the rights of all would be defended under law, not just the rights of the wealthy and the powerful (see chapters 5 and 6). But, as is common today as well, many in their own day were prone to flattering the "democratic" portion of society (i.e., regular people) at the expense of the one or the many, which many of the Founders eschewed. This is precisely why they never intended for the United States to be a "democracy," for a democracy by definition was rule by majority at all times, which they saw as essentially the rule of the mob. A "democracy," for the Founders, had no need of a constitution, for its one and only rule was that the majority always rule, which is incompatible with a constitution that limits and specifies governmental powers. Cicero best articulated the Founders' objection to "democracy": "There is no form of government to which I should more readily deny the definition of a state than one which is entirely under the control of the masses. . . . [M]ass government . . . is just as tyrannical as if a single person were the ruler, and indeed an even nastier despot, because there is nothing more disgusting than the sort of monstrosity which fictitiously assumes the name and guise of the people."[41]

It was precisely this usurpation over the rights of one party by another that the Founders sought to avoid. This included the many oppressing the one and the few, for they were citizens as equally entitled to the protection of their rights as the "regular guy," for whom the Founders tended to have no particular affection simply because he was "regular."

However, Adams quite forcefully indicted *all* three parties, and made a case that none should be completely or even mostly trusted compared to the others: "Despotical, monarchical, aristocratical, and democratical fury, have all been employed in this work of destruction of everything that could give us true light, and a clear insight of antiquity. For every one of these parties, when possessed of power, or when they have been undermost [*sic*], and struggling to get uppermost, has been equally prone to every species of fraud and violence and usurpation."[42]

He made the very same case in his famous *Defence*:

> It is very easy to flatter the democratical portion of society by making such distinctions between them and the monarchical and aristocratical. But flattery is as base an artifice and as pernicious a vice when offered to the people as when given to the others. There is no reason to believe the one much honester [*sic*] or wiser than the other. They are all of the same clay, their minds and bodies are alike. The two latter have more knowledge and sagacity, derived from education, and more advantages for acquiring wisdom and virtue. As to usurping others' rights, they are all three equally guilty when unlimited in power. No wise man will trust either with an opportunity, and every judicious legislator will set all three to watch and control each other. We may appeal to every page of history we have hitherto turned over, for proofs irrefragable, that the people, when they have been unchecked, have been as unjust, tyrannical, brutal, barbarous, and cruel as any king or senate possessed of uncontrollable power. The majority has eternally and without one exception usurped over the rights of the minority.[43]

Whenever a majority engaged in such oppression, it was acting according to might, not right. Jefferson believed that "the majority, oppressing an individual, is guilty of a crime, abuses its strength, and by acting on the law of the strongest breaks up the foundations of society."

He explained in his 1801 inaugural address: "Though the will of the majority is in all cases to prevail, that will to be rightful must be reasonable; that the minority possess their equal rights, which equal law must protect, and to violate would be oppression."

Thus, such majorities needed to be checked and balanced in some way, for the Founders were attempting to construct a government that, wrote Madison, would "protect all parties, the weaker as well as the more powerful,"[44] with laws that were "not to be varied in particular cases, but to have one rule for rich and poor, for the favorite at court, and the country man at plough,"[45] as Locke said. If the many had all power, what would prevent them from oppressing the few? If the few had all power, what would prevent them from doing the same to the many? And likewise with the one? The unanimous and unequivocal answer of history was that nothing would stop them. Hence Adams's observation: "Longitude, and the philosopher's stone, have not been sought with more earnestness by philosophers than a guardian of the laws has been studied by legislators from Plato to Montesquieu. But every project has been found to be no better than committing the lamb to the custody of the wolf, except that one which is called a *balance of power*."[46]

The Founders also recognized that differences in wealth naturally created different interests, and this was inherent to the nature of man and could not be legislated away. Thus, both should be made to check and balance the other, as Adams explained:

> It is agreed that the end of all government is the good and ease of the people in a secure enjoyment of their rights without oppression. But it must be remembered that the rich are *people* as well as the poor, that they have rights as well as others, that they have as clear and as *sacred* a right to their large property as others have to theirs which is smaller; that oppression to them is as possible and as wicked as to others; that stealing, robbing, cheating are the same crimes and sins, whether committed against them or others. The rich, therefore, ought to have an effectual barrier in the constitution against being robbed, plundered, and murdered, as well as the poor . . . The poor

should have a bulwark against the same dangers and oppressions . . . In every society where property exists, there will ever be a struggle between rich and poor. . . . They will either be made by numbers to plunder the few who are rich, or by influence to fleece the many who are poor. Both rich and poor, then, must be made independent, that equal justice may be done and equal liberty enjoyed by all.[47]

The "insight of antiquity" revealed that the same struggle took place thousands of years before as in their own day, as Madison noted: "In Greece and Rome, the rich and poor, the creditors and debtors, as well as the patricians and plebeians, alternately oppressed each other with equal unmercifulness."

The same lessons, Adams contended, had been exhibited in the realm of religion as well, not because the pursuit of spiritual power was any more pernicious than the pursuit of financial, political, or military power, but because it, likewise, was based on a flawed human nature that was prone to seek power at the expense of others: "Checks and balances . . . are our only security for the progress of mind, as well as the security of body. Every species of Christians would persecute desists as soon as either sect would persecute each other if it had unchecked and unbalanced power. Nay, the deists would persecute Christians, and atheists would persecute desists with as unrelenting cruelty as any Christians would persecute them or one another. Know thyself, human nature!"[48]

And the Founders were just as skeptical of the few as the many, the rich and powerful as much as the masses of common folk. Adams, concurring with Jefferson, wrote:

Your ἄριστοι [aristocrats] are the most difficult animals to manage of anything in the whole theory and practice of government. They will not suffer themselves to be governed. They not only exert all their own subtlety, industry, and courage, but they employ the commonalty to knock to pieces every plan and model that the most honest architects in legislation can invent to keep them within bounds . . . Yet birth and wealth together have prevailed over virtue and talents in all ages.[49]

Ultimately, all such questions of parties, interests, who would check and balance whom, human nature, history, and the like, all revolved around one primary concern of the Founders: What was the best way to incorporate these realities into a structure of government that would most effectively protect and preserve liberty? How could you prevent the few from robbing the many, the many from robbing the few, the strong from oppressing the weak, or the weak from plundering the strong? In short, how could you compel all members of all parties to respect the rights of everyone else? Adams phrased both these questions, and the Founders' answers, this way:

> The great question will forever remain *who shall work*? Our species cannot all be idle. Leisure for study must ever be the portion of a few. The number employed in government must forever be very small. Food, raiment, and habitations, the indispensable wants of all, are not to be obtained without the continual toil of ninety-nine in a hundred of mankind. . . . The controversy between the rich and the poor, the laborious and the idle, the learned and the ignorant, distinctions as old as the creation and as extensive as the globe, distinctions which no art or policy, no degree of virtue or philosophy can ever wholly destroy, will continue, and rivalries will spring out of them. These parties will be represented in the legislature, and must be balanced, or one will oppress the other. . . . Property must be secured, or liberty cannot exist. But if unlimited or unbalanced power of disposing property be put into the hands of those who have no property, France will find, as we have found, the lamb committed to the custody of the wolf. . . . The great art of lawgiving consists in balancing the poor against the rich in the legislature and in constituting the legislative a perfect balance against the executive power at the same time.[50]

How was this balance to be achieved? As previously mentioned, this is where "separation of powers" comes in, an idea covered more fully in the next chapter. More than a decade before the Constitution was even being drafted, Adams opined: "In a large society, inhabiting an extensive country, it is impossible that the whole should assemble to make laws. The first necessary step then is to depute [delegate] power from the many to a few of the most wise and good." This was the first step to forming the legislature. However, in accordance with the belief of many of the Founders that a single assembly with all power was as prone to vice, folly, and "hasty results and absurd judgments" as a single individual, the legislature should be divided into two houses to provide "some controlling power."[51] The lower house could be more "democratic" (representative of the people as a whole), and an upper house, with fewer members, could represent the more "aristocratic" portion of society and, by their presumably greater wisdom and experience, help control and direct the often misdirected and ebulliently rambunctious energy for which lower houses were famous. All of these ideas were to be incorporated in the Constitution more than a decade later.

What of the power of enforcing laws? If the ability to make and enforce laws were made *completely* independent of each other, Adams argued they would "oppose and encroach upon each other until the contest shall end in war, and the whole power, legislative and executive, be usurped by the strongest." To avoid this problem, Adams suggested "giving the executive power a negative upon the legislative, otherwise this will be continually encroaching upon that."[52] This would later become known as the *veto power* under the Constitution, the ability of the president to reject an act of Congress if he felt it unwise or unconstitutional. The Framers at the Constitutional Convention would go one step further and arm Congress with a similar power to override such a veto, although it would require a supermajority to do so. And what of the application or interpretation of the law? Adams suggested a separate and independent judicial branch be constituted for that very purpose, and for the same reasons as the other two branches: checks and balances.

But how did the Founders actually put these theories of government into practice? How did they codify them in the Constitution? This is the subject to which we now turn.

4

THE CONSTITUTION: LIBERTY'S CHARTER

The creation of the United States Constitution was a singularly unique event in man's quest for self-government. Never before had an entire society created a form of government through reason, debate, and the application of ideas rather than the application of force. The signing of the Magna Carta (Latin for "Great Charter") in 1215, though incredibly important, was in no way comparable. The Magna Carta was signed by an English king who was being forced by feudal lords and vassals to sign a document primarily concerned with recognizing *their* ancient rights, and codifying that recognition in law. In retrospect, it was an enormous step forward, but it fell far short of peacefully forming a new government from the ground up. Indeed, as significant as it was, the Magna Carta was the result of the use of force, or at the very least, the threat of it. Perhaps the only other *possible* contender was the English Bill of Rights, passed by Parliament in 1689 after the "Glorious Revolution" of 1688. While this parliamentary statute enshrined many of the rights that would also find their way into the American Bill of Rights, it was but one law passed by an ancient assembly that had evolved very slowly over centuries, not the formation of an entirely new government. James Madison aptly summarized the phenomenon of the Constitution when he wrote that "in Europe, charters of liberty have been granted by power. America has set the example . . . of charters of power granted by liberty."[1] In other words, the American people were telling the government of their own creation what *its* powers were, not being told by that government what their liberties were.

The way this constitution was formed thus proved to be unique in the annals of history. Before 1776, the colonies had largely governed themselves with little British interference for nearly 150 years. Consequently, local governments were highly developed at the time of the Constitutional Convention, and each state was essentially its own country. This quirk of history would turn out to be yet another twist of Providence, as the Constitution that organically emerged from such a context was, in sharp contrast to Europe, constructed from the ground up. Tocqueville observed: "In European nations, the initial movements of power resided with the upper echelons of society and passed gradually and always in a partial manner to the other sections of society. By contrast, in America, we can state that the organization of the township preceded that of the county, the county that of the state, the state that of the Union."[2]

But for a time, it did not appear that a constitution would even be formed. Earlier, the newly independent American States had lived under an extremely weak confederation, and Congress had little power to do much of anything. In a practical sense, the individual states under the Articles of Confederation were almost countries unto themselves and they often conducted their own foreign affairs, concluded their own commercial treaties, coined their own money, and so forth. The newly independent nation was barely a nation, and many in Europe predicted that because of its abandonment of monarchy, it would fall into chaos and anarchy, which brought great dread to many of the Founders, perhaps foremost among them George Washington: "What a triumph for the advocates of despotism to find that we are incapable of governing ourselves, and that systems founded on the basis of equal liberty are merely ideal and fallacious! Would to God that wise measures may be taken in time to avert the consequences we have but too much reason to apprehend."[3]

If America was unable to govern itself, the Founders feared it would prove the naysayers to be right: that man needed the strong arm of force in order to be governed rather than being capable of self-government. A few months before the opening of the Constitutional Convention,

Washington again expressed his profound apprehension concerning the very real possibility of the failure of the American experiment: "Among men of reflection, few will be found I believe who are not *beginning* to think that our system is better in theory than practice—and that, notwithstanding the boasted virtue of America, it is more than probable we shall exhibit the last melancholy proof that mankind are not competent to their own government without the means of coercion in the Sovereign."[4]

Other Founders expressed very similar and equally distressed concerns for this great experiment. This caused them to view with awe and reverence the product of the Constitutional Convention after a summer's worth of work in 1787. Madison, traditionally labeled the "Father of the Constitution," asserted that "the Union of so many states is, in the eyes of the world, a wonder; the harmonious establishment of a common government over them all, a miracle."[5] The fact that an assembly of men representing such divergent interests and concerns had come together and formed a constitution they intended to operate upon all of them was utterly remarkable. Washington called the fruit of their labors "the best fabric of human government and happiness that has ever been presented for the acceptance of mankind."[6] James Wilson, a fellow Convention delegate who also played an important role in bringing together the final product, declared to his constituents in Pennsylvania that he was "bold to assert that it [the Constitution] is the best form of government which has ever been offered to the world."[7] John Adams, the primary author of the Massachusetts Constitution and a longtime advocate of many of the principles incorporated into the new Constitution, recalled in his 1797 inaugural address that he read the Constitution "with great satisfaction, as the result of good heads prompted by good hearts, as an experiment better adapted to the genius, character, situation, and relations of this nation and country than any which had ever been proposed or suggested."

Thomas Jefferson expressed a similar view in a letter to Adams: "A constitution has been acquired, which, though neither of us thinks perfect, yet both consider as competent to render our fellow citizens the happiest and the securest on whom the sun has ever shone."[8]

In another, he articulated how he saw the Constitution within the context of history:

> Never was a finer canvass presented to work on than our countrymen. All of them engaged in agriculture or the pursuits of honest industry independent in their circumstances, enlightened as to their rights and firm in their habits of order and obedience to the laws. This I hope will be the age of experiments in government, and that their basis will be founded in principles of honesty, not of mere force. We have seen no instance of this since the days of the Roman republic, nor do we read of any before that. Either force or corruption has been the principle of every modern government.[9]

None of them believed the Constitution was perfect but that it nonetheless represented a singularly revolutionary step forward in the affairs of mankind. "The conception of such an idea," Adams wrote, "and the deliberate union of so great and various a people in such a plan is, without all partiality or prejudice, if not the greatest exertion of human understanding, the greatest single effort of national deliberation that the world has ever seen."[10] Similarly, while he did not agree with everything it contained, Washington wrote that he was "convinced it approached nearer to perfection than any government hitherto instituted among men." He continued:

> You will permit me to say that a greater drama is now acting on this theater than has heretofore been brought on the American stage, or any other in the world. We exhibit at present the novel and astonishing spectacle of a whole people deliberating calmly on what form of government will be most conducive to their happiness, and deciding with an unexpected degree of unanimity in favor of a system which they conceive calculated to answer the purpose.

Washington reflected on the magnitude as well as the providential nature of the opportunities that lay before the American people should they adopt the Constitution:

> I begin to look forward with a kind of political faith to scenes of national happiness which have not heretofore been offered for the fruition of the most favored nations. The natural political and moral circumstances of our nascent empire justify the anticipation. We have an almost unbounded territory whose natural advantages for agriculture and commerce equal those of any on the globe. In a civil point of view we have unequalled privilege of choosing our own political institutions and of improving upon the experience of mankind in the formation of a Confederated government where due energy will not be incompatible with unalienable rights of freemen. To complete the picture, I may observe that the information and morals of our citizens appear to be peculiarly favorable for the introduction of such a plan of government as I have now just described. [11]

So how did they do it?

PRINCIPLES FIRST

Clearly the Founders were very aware of the magnitude of what they had accomplished. But the question we must again ask is *why* and *how* they were able to do so. We have already outlined the large, more general concepts, but how did these actually make their way into the Constitution itself?

These were questions hotly debated at the Constitution Convention. One thing was for sure: the longevity of the Constitution depended on the implementation of sound principles, for as Adams had noted, "If they set out wrong, they will never be able to return, unless it be by accident, to the right path."[12] While the great goal was to secure liberty upon a sound foundation, it was, as Madison observed, "a melancholy reflection that liberty should be equally exposed to danger whether the government have too much or too little power, and that the line which divides these extremes should be so inaccurately defined by experience."[13]

This sense of balance was necessary given the realities of human nature. Madison summed up the primary challenge in Federalist No. 51: "In framing a government which is to be administered by men over men, the great difficulty lies in this: you must first enable the government to control the governed, and in the next place oblige it to control itself."

Thomas Paine famously noted that "when we are planning for posterity, we ought to remember that virtue is not hereditary." As Alexander Hamilton queried, "What government ever uniformly consulted its true interest in opposition to the temptations of momentary exigencies? What nation was ever blessed with a constant succession of upright and wise administrators?"[14] Accordingly, the Founders knew that the structure of the new federal government itself, as well as how it related to the state governments, must be designed in such a way so as to prevent the rise of tyranny if just such a set of virtueless leaders were to arrive on the scene. To do this, it was necessary to divide power, as shown in chapter 3.

But contrary to what we are often taught, that the Founders were simply interested in dividing power between three branches, they were also concerned that no single group of citizens would ever have any such concentrated power either. As alluded to in chapter 3, the Founders saw society in terms of the one, the few, and the many: the would-be dictator; the wealthy, powerful, and connected; and the mass of regular people. They trusted none of these, and therefore incorporated the power of each of them into the Constitution so as to arm all of them with the ability to counter the oppression of the others. It is this lesser-known aspect of the Constitution that will be the focus of this chapter.

Jefferson spoke of the purpose of the Constitution as a means by which to "fortify us against the degeneracy of one government, and the concentration of all its powers in the hands of the one, the few, the well-born, or the many."[15] By "one" government, Jefferson meant a government in which power was not divided, but concentrated in one body, one group, or one person. Other Founders often referred to this as a "simple" government. This was unacceptable to the Founders, as in every age the temptations of power had proved simply too alluring to resist. Adams expounded the problem:

> No simple form of government can possibly secure men against the violence of power . . . Monarchy [turns into] despotism, aristocracy [into] oligarchy, and democracy will soon degenerate into an anarchy, such an anarchy that every man will do what is right in his own eyes [an allusion to Judges 21:25], and no man's life or property or reputation or liberty will be secure and every one of these will soon mold itself into a system of subordination of all the moral virtues and intellectual abilities, all the powers of wealth, beauty, wit, and science, to the wanton pleasures, the capricious will, and the execrable cruelty of one or a very few.[16]

Notice that for the Founders, "democracy" was among the forms of government they most despised, for it put *all* power into the masses, "the many," who had proven just as likely to abuse the rights of others as the one or the few. Madison noted in Federalist No. 10 that it was precisely such unbounded power held by the masses that made it no surprise "that such democracies have proven to be as short in their lives as they were violent in their deaths, having been examples of turbulence and conflict, and thus incompatible with personal security or property rights." In this sense, our Founders did not worship the common man or think he was somehow less susceptible to the temptations of human nature than a rich or powerful man. Therefore, rather than a "simple" government, they sought to construct a "compound" government that mixed and matched various powers and sovereignties so that no one group, either in government or in society, ever became powerful enough to oppress the others. Thus, the structure of the Constitution itself presupposes certain fundamental principles of liberty and human nature that are not subject to the whims of a majority. This would not be a Constitution in which a majority of society ("democracy"), or a majority of money ("aristocracy"), or a majority of power ("monarchy") could always, and without opposition, dictate the course of government. It would be a finely tuned mechanism by which each would be prevented from attaining absolute supremacy, and thus the liberty of all would be secured.

This was exactly why the new Constitution divided legal power into three branches, legislative, executive, and judicial, which would become Congress, the president, and the judiciary, "For what was the government divided into three branches, but that each should watch over the others, and oppose their usurpations?"[17] Jefferson asked. Madison agreed, and asserted the notion (particularly in the *Federalist Papers*) that tyranny existed wherever all executive, legislative, and judicial power existed in one place, whether in the one, the few, or the many, and thus needed to be separated so that each power would check and balance the other. Adams explained that "three branches of power have an unalterable foundation in nature; that they exist in every society natural and artificial, and that, if all of them are not acknowledged in any constitution of government, it will be found to be imperfect, unstable, and soon enslaved."[18]

But again, the Founders had not arrived at this conclusion on their own simply as a matter of theory. On the contrary, great thinkers from many ages, going back to ancient times, had advocated a "mixed" constitution of government, in which the interests of the one, the few, and the many were divided against each other so as to keep any of them from attaining absolute rule. Montesquieu, for example, wrote that such an arrangement of power was necessary because political liberty "is present only when power is not abused, but it has eternally been observed that any man who has power is led to abuse it: he continues until he finds his limits. . . So that one cannot abuse power, power must check power by the arrangement of things."[19] He had written elsewhere in his famous *Spirit of the Laws* that "one must give one power a ballast, so to speak, to put it in a position to resist another. This is a masterpiece of legislation that chance rarely produces and prudence is rarely allowed to produce."[20]

As a practical example, when responding to the idea that the judiciary had the power to dictate what the Constitution meant to the other branches, Jefferson articulated what he believed to be the essence of both the separation of powers and checks and balances that applied to all the branches:

> But nothing in the Constitution has given them a right to decide for the executive more than to the executive to decide for them. Both magistracies are equally independent in the sphere of action assigned to them. The judges, believing the law constitutional, had a right to pass a sentence of fine and imprisonment, because that power was placed in their hands by the Constitution. But the executive, believing the law to be unconstitutional, was bound to remit the execution of it, because that power has been confided to him by the Constitution. That instrument [the Constitution] meant that its co-ordinate branches should be checks on each other. But the opinion which gives to the judges the right to decide what laws are constitutional, and what are not, not only for themselves in their own sphere of action, but for the legislature and executive also in their spheres, would make the judiciary a despotic branch.[21]

It was the desire of the Founders, at all costs, to prevent the rise of any such "despotic branch" within the federal government, first by separating powers, and then by arming each sovereignty, or branch, with the power to check and balance the others, thus maintaining equilibrium. How they achieved this is relatively well-known by most, so it is to those aspects of their ingenious structure that have been most forgotten, and which are arguably most essential, to which we turn.

SEPARATION OF POWERS, ENUMERATED POWERS, AND FEDERALISM

Perhaps the greatest constitutional innovations of the Founders are those that, to the average citizen, would be the greatest "secrets," by which I mean enumerated powers and federalism. The three branches provided an internal federal mechanism by which power was divided, and the subdivided powers could keep each other in check. However, the Constitution divided the power of the federal government not only within itself but also between it and the state governments. The portion of power delegated to the federal government is encompassed within its enumerated powers. The powers that were not delegated, on the other hand, remain with the states. These two things together constitute the idea of "federalism."

The United States has a "federal" government, but Britain does not, nor does France, China, Israel, or many other nations. These other countries have what, in modern political science terms, is called a "unitary" government, but which the Founders would have called a "national" government. So what is the difference? Very simple: in a national government, the central government has all of the power, and any subdivisions within its jurisdiction (e.g., provinces) are simply the way central government has decided to organize itself most effectively. Therefore, when a national government issues laws, they apply directly to the citizens of that nation, and the provinces have no say in the matter. In a federal government, on the other hand, the central government has only "limited" powers, and any subdivisions have their own set of powers that even the central government cannot violate.

The idea of "enumerated powers" simply refers to those powers that the Constitution delegated to the federal government (leaving the rest to the states), the primary list of which is found in Article I, Section 8, which enumerates the subjects on which Congress can legislate. The result was that "its jurisdiction extends to certain enumerated objects only," Madison commented in Federalist No. 39, "and leaves to the several states a residuary and inviolable sovereignty over all other objects."

This is an absolutely essential "secret" that we must rediscover if we are to properly understand the Constitution. Many today presume that as long as the mechanical features of separation of powers and checks and balances are maintained, the federal government can write laws on any subject it wants (provided it doesn't violate the Bill of Rights). But that is how a "national" government operates, and ours is not a "national" government, but a federal one, founded primarily for "the common defense of the members, the preservation of the public peace as well against internal convulsions as external attacks, the regulation of commerce with other nations and between the States, the superintendence of our intercourse, political and commercial, with foreign countries."[22]

Madison often commented upon "the peculiar manner in which the federal government is limited. It is not a general grant, out of which particular powers are excepted—it is a grant of particular powers only, leaving the general mass in other hands."[23] He explained further:

> The powers delegated by the proposed Constitution to the federal government are few and defined. Those which are to remain in the state governments are numerous and indefinite. The former will be exercised principally on external objects as war, peace, negotiation, and foreign commerce; with which last the power of taxation will, for the most part, be connected. The powers reserved to the several states will extend to all the objects which, in the ordinary course of affairs, concern the lives, liberties, and properties of the people, and the internal order, improvement, and prosperity of the state. The operations of the federal government will be most extensive and important in times of war and danger; those of the state governments in times of peace and security.[24]

Tocqueville succinctly summarized the type of political society created by the Constitution as one "in which several peoples are fused into one nation with regard to certain shared interests, while remaining as separate confederates for all else."[25] Jefferson expounded this principle of the Constitution:

> The true theory of our Constitution is surely the wisest and best, that the states are independent as to everything within themselves, and united as to everything respecting foreign nations. Let the general government be reduced to foreign concerns only, and let our affairs be disentangled from those of all other nations, except as to commerce, which the merchants will manage the better the more they are left free to manage themselves, and our general government may be reduced

to a very simple organization, and a very inexpensive one: a few plain duties to be performed by a few servants.[26]

For Jefferson, the maintenance of these limited powers was essential to maintaining liberty: "I consider the foundation of the Constitution as laid on this ground: That [all] powers not delegated to the United States by the Constitution, nor prohibited by it to the States, are reserved to the States respectively, or to the people. To take a single step beyond the boundaries thus specially drawn around the powers of Congress is to take possession of a boundless field of power, no longer susceptible of any definition."[27]

Thus, the federal government would have not only internal mechanisms by which it would be checked and balanced against tyranny, but, through federalism, external mechanisms as well, making federalism perhaps the least known, but arguably most important "check and balance" the Founders incorporated in the Constitution. Madison described its rationale this way:

> Power being found by universal experience liable to abuses, a distribution of it into separate departments has become a first principle of free governments . . . there is less opportunity to usurp what is not granted . . . The power delegated by the people is first divided between the general government and the state governments . . . so, it is to be hoped, do the two governments possess each the means of preventing or correcting unconstitutional encroachments of the other . . . The people who are the authors of this blessing must also be its guardians.[28]

The fact that the state governments would themselves retain a large portion of sovereignty would make them potent engines by which to prevent tyrannical moves on the part of the federal government, as Jefferson noted:

> But the true barriers of our liberty in this country are our State governments; and the wisest conservative power ever contrived by man, is that of which our Revolution and present government found us

possessed. Seventeen distinct States, amalgamated into one as to their foreign concerns but single and independent as to their internal administration, regularly organized with legislature and governor resting on the choice of the people, and enlightened by a free press, can never be so fascinated by the arts of one man as to submit voluntarily to his usurpation.[29]

This principle, however, also applied to the people themselves, he said, not just the government constructed by the Constitution: "We [Americans] think experience has proved it safer for the mass of individuals composing the society to reserve to themselves personally the exercise of all rightful powers to which they are competent, and to delegate those to which they are not competent to deputies named, and removable for unfaithful conduct by themselves immediately."[30]

But federalism had another justification beyond simply acting as a barrier to tyranny: it would simply make things work better. By delegating power to those most capable of wielding it effectively, it could be exercised in a more efficient way. Thus, power should stay as close as possible to those who are the most capable of managing it. This, for Jefferson, was the essence of "good government": "It is not by the consolidation or concentration of powers, but by their distribution, that good government is effected . . . Were we directed from Washington when to sow, and when to reap, we should soon want bread," he wrote. "It is by this partition of cares, descending in graduation from general to particular, that the mass of human affairs may be best managed for the good and prosperity of all."[31]

He described his scheme in further detail to a colleague:

The way to have good and safe government is not to trust it all to one, but to divide it among the many, distributing to every one exactly the functions he is competent to. Let the national government be entrusted with the defense of the nation, and its foreign and federal relations; the State governments with the civil rights, laws, police, and administration of what concerns the State generally; the counties with the local concerns of the counties, and each ward direct the interests within itself. It is by dividing and subdividing these republics from the great national one down through all its subordinations until it ends in the administration of every man's farm by himself; by placing under everyone what his own eye may superintend, that all will be done for the best. What has destroyed liberty and the rights of man in every government which has ever existed under the sun? The generalizing and concentrating all cares and powers into one body.[32]

"My proposition had, for a further object," he wrote elsewhere, "to impart to these wards those portions of self-government for which they are best qualified, by confiding to them the care of their poor, their roads, police, elections, the nomination of jurors, administration of justice in small cases, elementary exercises of militia; in short, to have made them little republics, with a warden at the head of each, for all those concerns which, being under their eye, they would better manage than the larger republics of the county or State."[33] Notice how many basic functions Jefferson saw as part of the function of local governments, *not* the federal government, which, by virtue of its remoteness, as well as the fact that it presided over the nation as a whole, would be wholly incompetent to carry them out. Instead, the federal government was tasked with focusing on those things that applied to the nation as a whole. Jefferson went further:

> The secret will be found to be in making himself [man] the depository of the powers respecting himself, so far as he is competent to them, and delegating only what is beyond his competence by a synthetical process to higher and higher orders of functionaries, so as to trust fewer and fewer powers in proportion as the trustees become more and more oligarchical. The elementary republics of the wards, the county republics, the States republics, and the republic of the Union, would form a gradation of authorities, standing each on the basis of law, holding every one its delegated share of powers, and constituting truly a system of fundamental balances and checks for the government.[34]

Madison, likewise, believed such an arrangement would allow the States to become, to use a more modern term, "laboratories of democracy," in which various solutions to public policy problems could be experimented with: "Among the advantages distinguishing our compound government it is not the least that it affords so many opportunities and chances in the local legislatures for salutary innovations by some, which may be adopted by others, or for more important experiments which, if unsuccessful, will be of limited injury, and may even prove salutary as beacons to others."[35]

This is why the Constitution not only divided power within the federal government, but between the federal government and the states. The federal government was delegated a limited set of powers and the state governments retained the general powers which were not so delegated. Such a system was meant not only to maintain the maximum liberty of all, but to assign to that government, whether federal or state, only those powers which it was capable of wielding in a competent manner.

CONCLUSION

The Constitution is the integration of ideals with reality, the ideal being human liberty, the reality being human nature. If you wanted to design a federal government that could accomplish whatever goals it had in mind as efficiently as possible, the Constitution our Founders bequeathed to us is woefully inadequate. Except perhaps the preamble, it is entirely bereft of soaring rhetoric, because it is not an expression of ideals. Rather, it is the application of a set of realities in such a way as to best maintain a set of ideals. The Constitution delegated the federal government a specific set of powers, precisely arranged to allow it the due strength to govern both the people and itself so that liberty could both thrive and flourish, and the peace and security of society could be maintained. Its purpose was to establish an institutional framework whose goal was to *secure* and *safeguard* liberty. The Constitution, therefore, is not that which defines liberty. The Founders believed that liberty, as a gift from God, existed before government. Rather, the Constitution is defined by liberty. If liberty is our gold, the Constitution is our safe.

But here is the caveat: our Constitution was designed to allow future generations to change their political system to better suit their own times and circumstances. In other words, government can be expanded lawfully, and our Founders set up a constitutional mechanism (Article V) for this to happen. Washington candidly admitted, "I do not conceive that we are more inspired—have more wisdom—or possess more virtue than those who will come after us."[36] Elsewhere, he explained:

> Is there not a Constitutional door open for alterations and amendments, and is it not probable that real defects will be as readily discovered after, as before, trial? And will not posterity be as ready to apply the remedy as ourselves, if there is occasion for it, when the mode is provided? To think otherwise will, in my judgment, be ascribing more of the *amor patria* [Latin for "love of country"]—more wisdom—and more foresight to ourselves than I conceive we are entitled to.[37]

Likewise, Jefferson discounted the notion that the Constitution was perfect and beyond reproach: "Some men look at constitutions with sanctimonious reverence, and deem them like the Ark of the Covenant, too sacred to be touched. They ascribe to the men of the preceding age a wisdom more than human, and suppose that what they did to be beyond amendment. I knew that age well. I belonged to it, and labored with it. It deserved well of its country."[38]

But that is exactly why the Founders left to us a method by which to amend it, something that has been done twenty-seven times. As we shall see, however, in chapter 9, for this very reason, the Founders were absolutely opposed to changing the meaning of the words in the Constitution or "updating" it through a subjective reinterpretation of its terms to "fit the times"—that is, to make it a "living Constitution," in which the Constitution is "amended" not through the amendment process, but through changing the definition of words based on individual interpretation. If words could mean anything, then the Constitution would essentially become meaningless.

But herein lies the heart of the matter, and it strikes at the very purpose of the Constitution: it was intended to establish a government of limited powers. However, "limited" does not necessarily mean "small." Rather, for the Founders, a limited government was one whose powers had been specifically defined by the people themselves through a written constitution in which the words mean what they say. If those powers need to be changed, reduced, or expanded, then they can be amended through an objective process involving the people as a whole, not a subjective one in which a judge's or politician's "interpretation" of the Constitution is able to fundamentally change its meaning for the whole society. This is the inverse of what our Founders intended and it completely undermines the form of government that the Constitution designed. While many of the Founders were no doubt keen on what today would be called a "small" government, the essence of "limited," for them, was that the limits of power would be defined, not that those powers would necessarily be few in number. In this sense, they would far prefer a "big" government whose powers had been specifically defined and expanded by the whole society through amending the Constitution, over a "small" government which, despite being small, had nonetheless perhaps gone beyond those powers delegated to it by the Constitution simply by changing the meaning of its words. A "big" government of the former description would, according to the Founders, be the "limited" government; whereas the "small" government of the latter description would be the unlimited and thus a tyrannical one. And yet, as Washington observed, tyranny was exactly what the Constitution was meant to prevent: "It will at least be a recommendation to the proposed Constitution that it is provided with more checks and barriers against the introduction of tyranny, and those of a nature less liable to be surmounted, than any government hitherto instituted among mortals hath possessed."[39]

This indeed goes to the heart of it all: Is the Constitution, and thus our republic, ultimately defined by "We the People," or by the government it established? Were the Constitution and those who exercised power in its name the ultimate touchstone of American liberty, or was it the spirit and culture of the people themselves? For the Founders, there was only one answer to this, brilliantly summarized by Jefferson: "Where then is our republicanism to be found? Not in our Constitution certainly, but merely in the spirit of our people. That would oblige even a despot to govern us republicanly [*sic*]. Owing to this spirit, and to nothing in the form of our Constitution, all things have gone well."[40]

5

RELIGION, VIRTUE, AND MORALITY:
LIBERTY'S SENTINELS, PART I

The prophetic nature of the Founders was based on their understanding of two fundamental principles: their deep knowledge of and submission to the realities of human nature, and the lessons of history. The first they were not particularly optimistic about, and the second they knew exhibited more examples of human misery than of flourishing. At the same time, they thundered with confidence about the inherent dignity of human nature and the rights to which all citizens were equal heirs by the "laws of nature and nature's God," as declared in the Declaration of Independence. The purpose of government, they asserted, was to protect those God-given rights that not only precede but are the basis of its existence. Such was the political foundation of our free society.

So why had such a fine proposition not been observed in history? The Founders' answer to this question was complicated and multifaceted, but it came down to one fundamental proposition: the inability or unwillingness of a *society*, and the individuals of which it was composed, to exercise self-government. James Madison perhaps phrased it most succinctly when he said that the basis of "all our political experiments" was "the capacity of mankind for self-government."[1] But "self-government" was not primarily a political concept. As we shall see, "self-government" for the Founders was not only a societal concept but an individual concept as well. Bear in mind that the "political experiments" of the Founders culminated in the creation of a government based not only on the *authority* of the people but also on the *reason* of the people, applied to the *moral* end of human liberty. They therefore tied the concept of self-government to the unique properties of their own "political experiments" and *not* to the idea of government itself in all forms. Only a people capable of self-government were capable of a free society and conversely, self-government is immaterial in a dictatorship or other tyranny.

So what was it then? For the Founders, self-government meant the presence of two things: virtue (i.e., morality) and knowledge. As Samuel Adams put it, "If virtue and knowledge are diffused among the people, they will never be enslaved. This will be their great security." But how could they believe that citizens were capable of such a thing given what they observed in human nature and history? Because the Founders, whether they were individual adherents or not, adopted the profoundly Judeo-Christian concept of man's dual nature: his dignity and his depravity, his greatness and his wickedness. Man's greatness, endowed by God, required his rights to be respected. At the same time, his depravity meant that this often did not happen and necessitated the existence of government in the first place. But government itself was made of men and needed to control itself as well. Thus, the Founders asserted that the self-government necessary for a free society to exist was both collective and individual: it required the submission of both citizen and state to the dictates of morality and reason. Because of this Judeo-Christian view of human nature, the Founders believed man was a morally accountable agent, not a materialistic automaton, and was thus capable of choosing self-government, despite the fact that history had often exhibited the dispiriting spectacle of men giving in to their passions for wealth, power, glory, or pleasure.

Thus, the American vision of a free society articulated by our Founders requires much more than simply a particular type of government, but a particular type of people whose moral and intellectual constitution enables them to exercise self-government, first as individuals, then collectively through their governors. Alexis de Tocqueville succinctly summarized this notion as follows: "It is, indeed, difficult to imagine how men who have completely given up the habit of self-government could successfully choose those who should do it for them."[2]

This is why the Founders, as much as they spoke about government, more often spoke about the idea of self-government founded on virtue and knowledge as the palladium of a free society. As John Adams noted during the Revolution, he was convinced that it was the "wisdom, integrity, and humanity" of the people that would make it possible for them to devise new constitutions of government for their states.[3] As president, he applied the same observation to the federal constitution: "The existence of such a government as ours for any length of time is a full proof of a general dissemination of knowledge and virtue throughout the whole body of the people."[4]

George Washington asserted the exact same thing during his own presidency: "'Tis substantially true, that virtue or morality is a necessary spring of popular government. The rule indeed extends with more or less force to every species of free government. Who that is a sincere friend to it, can look with indifference upon attempts to shake the foundation of the fabric?"[5]

Self-government is the great sentinel and protector of liberty, its very life source. Without it, liberty cannot exist, and in its absence, tyranny commences. Self-government is that which qualifies individuals and peoples for liberty. Our Founders knew that in any civilized society, there had to be a force that could act to control the ravages of human nature, namely, government. But if the people over whom that government operated meant to be free, then they themselves must work to control their own human nature through moral behavior and intellectual enlightenment, or else they would need to be compelled to do so through the force of government. As Irish statesman Edmund Burke noted of the almost mathematical quality of self-government in a society that intended to be free, "The less there is within, the more there must be without."[6] The Founders understood that the key to maintaining a free society was for the individuals of that society to conduct themselves, as much as possible, as if they needed no government. This could be accomplished only by virtue applied by knowledge. It was because men had evinced an inability to govern themselves without coercion that government was required in the first place. It followed that the more individuals surrendered their powers of self-government through immorality, apathy, and ignorance, the more the convincing power of individual conscience would be replaced by the coercive power of government control upon those who had tired of self-control. This is why Jefferson asserted that the great preservative of American freedom would, in the final analysis, not be the Constitution, but the people over whom it operated. The Constitution was meant to enable the United States to be the stage on which the human flourishing made possible by morally ordered liberty could be displayed to the world. But the people themselves needed to act their part.

This is why, as we shall see in the next two chapters, the Founders championed both virtue and knowledge. Let's look at virtue first.

WHAT IS VIRTUE?

First, we have to know exactly what the Founders meant by "virtue" if we are to understand what they had to say about it. Perhaps the best summary of all (or most) of the virtues to which the Founders referred is provided by Benjamin Franklin in his *Autobiography*. The names of the virtues with Franklin's own description of their precepts were:

1. **Temperance**: Eat not to dullness, drink not to elevation.

2. **Silence**: Speak not but what may benefit others or yourself. Avoid trifling conversation.

3. **Order**: Let all your things have their places. Let each part of your business have its time.

4. **Resolution**: Resolve to perform what you ought. Perform without fail what you resolve.

5. **Frugality**: Make no expense but to do good to others or yourself, i.e. waste nothing.

6.   **Industry**: Lose no time—be always employed in something useful—cut off all unnecessary actions.

7.   **Sincerity**: Use no hurtful deceit. Think innocently and justly, and, if you speak, speak accordingly.

8.   **Justice**: Wrong none by doing injuries or omitting the benefits that are your duty.

9.   **Moderation**: Avoid extremes. Forbear resenting injuries so much as you think they deserve.

10.   **Cleanliness**: Tolerate no uncleanness in body, clothes, or habitation.

11.   **Tranquility**: Be not disturbed at trifles, or at accidents common or unavoidable.

12.   **Chastity**: Rarely use venery [sexual intercourse] but for health or offspring. Never to dullness, weakness, or the injury of your own or another's peace or reputation.

13.   **Humility**: Imitate Jesus and Socrates.[7]

According to the Founders, virtue is moral action based on duty to oneself and one's fellow man, and as such enables the greatest degree of human flourishing possible. It is what enables and inspires citizens to order not only their own affairs but also the affairs of society without being compelled to do so by force (i.e., government), which is why they saw it as essential to liberty. They understood virtue to be intimately connected with the idea of stewardship, or the responsible management of those things under one's own control. Going through Franklin's list, we will see that the virtues he named ultimately come down to self-control, the stewarding of one's appetites and passions:

1.   *Temperance* is stewardship of one's appetites and body.

2.   *Silence* is stewardship of one's tongue.

3. *Order* is stewardship of one's belongings and property.

4. *Resolution* is stewardship of one's commitments.

5. *Frugality* is stewardship of one's money.

6. *Industry* is stewardship of one's time and energy.

7. *Sincerity* is stewardship of one's relationships.

8. *Justice* is stewardship of one's fellow man.

9. *Moderation* is stewardship of the extremes to which one is prone.

10. *Cleanliness* is stewardship of one's surroundings.

11. *Tranquility* is stewardship of one's mind.

12. *Chastity* is stewardship of one's sexuality and body.

13. *Humility* is stewardship of one's soul.

Stewardship, then, at the end of the day, is also self-government, as it requires the control of one's desires and appetites in the short term to better secure the benefits of the long term. Jefferson echoed Franklin's enthusiasm for the practice of virtue when he wrote to his nephew, "The moral sense, or conscience, is as much a part of man as his leg or arm . . . It may be strengthened by exercise, as may any particular limb of the body."[8]

Virtue was also the basis of the Founders' idea of happiness, which is absolutely crucial to understand if we are to properly interpret what they meant when they wrote "Life, Liberty, and the Pursuit of Happiness." While our modern notion of "happiness" tends to revolve around the idea of personal "success," actualization, and pleasure, for the Founders, success and pleasure in and of themselves had very little to do with happiness. Rather, happiness was the result of having fulfilled one's moral obligations to oneself and others, living the good life. This was an idea they inherited from their Puritan ancestors as well as from the "historians, orators, poets, and philosophers of Greece and Rome," with whom the Puritans were "quite familiar"[9] according to Adams.

Cicero, the great Roman senator and opponent of Julius Caesar, summed up the classical view of happiness when he stated that "moral excellence is what guarantees happiness," further noting that "everything that is morally good and fine and distinguished is infinitely productive of joy." Thus, happiness was the satisfaction that resulted from carrying out one's moral obligations and duties in the world. "Anyone who has attained it [moral goodness]," he noted, "has found not only happiness, but happiness that is complete and supreme."[10] It thus becomes apparent why John Adams asserted that "happiness, whether in despotism or democracy, whether in slavery or liberty, can never be found without virtue."[11] Franklin agreed, writing as "Poor Richard" that "virtue and happiness are mother and daughter."[12]

Virtue for the Founders was thus neither a human invention nor one that could be compelled by the force of law. Rather, it resulted from the willful submission of every aspect of one's life to the universal and unchanging requirements of reason and morality. But as history had shown, men were not prone to behave virtuously, because they more often behaved according to their own passions and desires rather than reason. Adams described the problem this way:

> Nature and truth, or rather truth and right, are invariably the same in all times and in all places. And reason, pure unbiased reason, perceives them alike in all times and in all places. But passion, prejudice, interest, custom, and fancy are infinitely precarious. If therefore we suffer our understandings to be blinded or perverted by any of these, the chance is that of millions to one that we shall embrace error. And hence arises that endless variety of opinions entertained by mankind.[13]

For the Founders, virtue was thus based on the "law of nature and nature's God" spoken of in the Declaration of Independence—a transcendent and universal set of moral duties required of man whether he liked it or not, because they were best for him and society, and thus the basis of true happiness. Cicero described "virtues" as follows: "The virtues blossom forth in their various forms and manifestations, and it is revealed to us what nature has ordained as the ultimate good and evil, the principles on which human obligations ought to be based, and the rules we must adopt for the conduct of our lives. And it is the exploration of these and similar questions which brings us to the conclusion . . . that moral goodness is enough by itself to create a happy life."[14]

In 1789 George Washington reaffirmed the transcendent, divine basis of morality in his first inaugural address: "The propitious smiles of Heaven can never be expected on a nation that disregards the eternal rules of order and right, which Heaven itself has ordained." He also asserted the same classical definition of happiness and the general good it produces: "The foundations of our national policy will be laid in the pure and immutable principles of private morality . . . there is no truth more thoroughly established than that there exists in the economy and course of nature an insoluble union between virtue and happiness, between duty and advantage, between the genuine maxims of an honest and magnanimous policy, and the solid rewards of public prosperity and felicity."

Quite contrary to the modern notion of feeling "inhibited" or "oppressed" by moral duties and restraints based upon religious obligations, the Founders believed such things were the foundation of both personal and national happiness. Franklin wrote, "Sin is not hurtful because it is forbidden, but it is forbidden because it's hurtful. Nor is a duty beneficial because it is commanded, but it is commanded because it's beneficial."[15]

We thus arrive at a complete definition of virtue according to the Founders: virtue is the elevation of reason over passion, which results from the voluntary submission of one's behavior to divinely transcendent and universally binding moral obligations to oneself and others, resulting in the greatest possible degree of human liberty, happiness, and flourishing for both individuals and societies.

RELIGION AND VIRTUE

The Founders' notions of virtue were, as we shall see, profoundly religious in nature and intimately connected with the Judeo-Christian system of moral values. But what did the Founders mean when they said "religion"? Often they meant Christianity, for that was without question the dominant religion of the colonies, with no other religion even coming close in strength. However, "religion" was also a more general term by which the Founders referred to a system of morality based on Judeo-Christian principles, but which did not necessarily always include every doctrine of orthodox Christianity. Franklin provided a succinct summary of the "American religion" (his own personal beliefs) that, while very dependent on Judeo-Christian assumptions and values, lists a minimum set of religious "essentials" subscribed to by all of the Founders whether or not they were orthodox Christians:

> Here is my creed: I believe in one God, Creator of the Universe. That he governs it by his Providence. That he ought to be worshipped. That the most acceptable service we ought render to him is doing good to his other children. That the soul of man is immortal, and will be treated with justice in another life respecting its conduct in this. These I take to be the fundamental principles of all sound religion, and I regard them as you do in whatever sect I meet with them.[16]

Within that context, the Founders' writings make it clear that they saw religion as essential to the preservation of virtue, and thus liberty itself, for it made man accountable to God, whether in this life or the next. What one believed to be true, or whatever one might justify according to one's own selfish desires, would one day be judged against the standard of divine truth and justice. Injustice in this life, therefore, could never escape the judgment of ultimate justice in the next. Thus, the Founders believed that if there were no God and no ultimate justice, "morality" would be identified not with what is right and true, but by whatever best served the interests of power.

While the Founders saw religion as serving the aforementioned purposes, their belief in it was based not only on its practical efficacy but also on what they saw as the self-evident truth—that a Creator had brought the universe into existence and the unavoidable moral implications of such a reality. In other words, every single one of them at a minimum believed that religion was not just generally beneficial, but *true*, per the "creed" outlined by Franklin, as it provided the only rational foundation for both the physical and moral constitution of the universe.

GOD AND THE HUMAN SOUL: THE EXISTENCE OF THE UNIVERSE AND MORALITY

Belief in God and the immortality of the human soul was universal among the Founders, which is incontrovertibly evident from the most cursory review of their writings. While not all of them were orthodox Christians, their thoughts on atheism ranged from extreme caution to outright disdain. For them, belief in God was natural to man because it was in accordance with his nature, and they agreed with Tocqueville when he noted (while describing the virtual absence of atheism in America) that "men cannot detach themselves from religious beliefs except by some wrong-headed thinking, and by a sort of moral violence inflicted upon their true nature . . . Unbelief is an accident; faith is the only permanent state of mankind."[17]

They saw the fingerprints of God everywhere they looked, and their conclusion that He existed was not even necessarily dependent on the Bible or any specific set of religious dogma but on the very nature of the cosmos. Writing to his friend John Adams toward the end of his life, Jefferson explained his views:

> I hold (without appeal to revelation) that when we take a view of the Universe, in its parts general or particular, it is impossible for the human mind not to perceive and feel a conviction of design, consummate skill, and the indefinite power in every atom of its composition . . . We see, too, evident proofs of the necessity of a superintending power to maintain the Universe in its course and order . . . So irresistible are these evidences of an intelligent and powerful Agent that, of the infinite numbers of men who have existed through all time, they have believed, in the proportion of a million at least to unit, in the hypothesis of an eternal pre-existence of a creator, rather than in that of a self-existent Universe. Surely this unanimous sentiment renders this more probable than that of a few in the other hypothesis.[18]

Even Thomas Paine, who in the second half of his life was an ardent opponent of orthodox Christianity (mostly Catholicism) and the clergy and did not believe the Bible was divinely inspired, wrote at the same time, "All the principles of science are of divine origin. Man cannot make or invent or contrive principles. He can only discover them, and he ought to look through the discovery to the Author."[19]

Paine criticized any teaching of "natural philosophy" (i.e., science) that asserted that the universe was simply "an accomplishment" (i.e., self-existent). He also criticized those teachers who "labor with studied ingenuity to ascribe everything they behold to innate properties of matter and jump over all the rest by saying that matter is eternal" and thereby encouraged the "evil" of atheism. "Instead of looking through the works of creation to the Creator Himself, they stop short and employ the knowledge they acquire to create doubts of His existence," he lamented. "When we examine an extraordinary piece of machinery, an astonishing pile of architecture, a well-executed statue, or a highly-finished painting . . . our ideas are naturally led to think of the extensive genius and talent of the artist. When we study the elements of geometry, we think of Euclid. When we speak of gravitation, we think of Newton. How, then, is it that when we study the works of God in creation, we stop short and do not think of God?"[20]

For these reasons, among others, Jefferson rejected being an atheist, "which," as he put it, "I can never be."[21] His friend John Adams noted, "I never heard of an irreligious character in Greek or Roman history, nor in any other history, nor have I known one in life who was not a rascal. Name one if you can, living or dead."[22] Nor did the Founders see science and religion as opposed to one another, as is all too common today. Rather, as President Adams asserted in a letter to university students, they were not only mutually compatible, but mutually necessary for one another: "When you look up to me with confidence as the patron of science, liberty, and religion, you melt my heart. These are the choicest blessings of humanity; they have an inseparable union. Without their joint influence no society can be great, flourishing, or happy."[23]

Just as much as the existence of God was essential to their understanding of the physical constitution of the universe, its combination with their belief in the immortality of the soul was crucial to their understanding of the moral constitution of the world, as it was the means by which God judged the good and evil acts committed in this life, whether noticed by man or not. Tocqueville ascribed a great deal of the accomplishments of the Puritans/Pilgrims and their progeny (the Founders) to this belief, which he described as so "indispensable to man's greatness that its effects are striking,"[24] for it kept him morally anchored, never able to escape ultimate justice. It was for this reason that the Founders considered belief in God as the cornerstone of all morality, but not because man could do no good apart from God commanding him to do so. Quite the contrary: part of their conception of the "law of nature and nature's God" was the idea that all men had at least portions of this law inscribed into their very being, and that most men knew the basics of right and wrong because God had given them a conscience. The problem was that, because of their fallen nature, they did not obey their consciences as they should. Adams elaborated:

> The law of nature would be sufficient for the government of men if they would consult their reason and obey their consciences. It is not the fault of the law of nature, but of themselves, that it is not obeyed; it is not the fault of the law of nature that men are obliged to have recourse to civil government at all, but of themselves; it is not the fault of the ten commandments, but of themselves, that Jews or Christians are ever known to steal, murder, covet, or blaspheme. But the legislator who should say the law of nature is enough, if you do not obey it, it will be your own fault, therefore no other government is necessary, would be thought to trifle.[25]

This brings us to a very important fact that we must remember when it comes to the Founders: they did not believe that religion *made* men good, but rather that it provided the best encouragement and incentive to be good, for it taught them that their choices had consequences in eternity, not just in the moment. Even if consequences could be avoided in the now, God would exact justice in the hereafter.

This had been a Judeo-Christian teaching from time immemorial and was well known to the Founders. The problem was not that man had no knowledge of good and evil and therefore needed a religious commandment to tell him, but rather that human nature commonly bowed to the dictates of the passions, rather than reason, and thereby abandoned conscience and committed evil anyway. The Founders realized that our human nature could, and often did, pervert the plain dictates of conscience, allowing us to convince ourselves that right is wrong and wrong is right if it suits our own desires. As Adams noted, "Human reason and human conscience, though I believe there are such things, are not a match for human passions, human imaginations, and human enthusiasm." Our passions would corrupt our minds, our minds would justify our passions, and in turn our passions would become even more corrupt, a deadly cycle with horrific consequences for individuals and society. "Our passions, ambition, avarice, love, resentment, etc. possess so much metaphysical subtlety and so much overpowering eloquence that they insinuate themselves into the understanding and the conscience and convert both to their party," Adams wrote. "And I may be deceived as much as any of them when I say that power must never be trusted without a check."[26]

That "check," at least as far as voluntary self-restraint was concerned, was religion. The Founders understood that mankind's capacity for self-delusion was boundless; therefore, moral obligations must be placed on a divine rather than a humanistic footing if anyone could assert any truth or notion of right and wrong at all. It was for this reason that religious commandments such as "do not murder," "do not steal," and "do not commit adultery" were necessary, not because man was completely incapable of avoiding these sins without God commanding him to, but because, since He *had* commanded them, man had no intellectual excuse for ever allowing his passions or personal desires to blind his judgment and excuse him of his moral obligations. Religion thus anchored the definition of morality on God and asserted its obligations on man by acting as a powerful regulator of the inherently negative aspects of human nature. James Madison explained the importance of this truth: "The belief in a God All Powerful wise and good, is so essential to the moral order of the world and to the happiness of man, that arguments which enforce it cannot be drawn from too many sources nor adapted with too much solicitude to the different characters and capacities to be impressed with it."[27]

Adams asserted the same thing and specifically acknowledged that Judaism, through the Bible, had bequeathed to the world what he considered the most essential ingredient of human civilization:

> I will insist that the Hebrews have done more to civilize men than any other nation. If I were an atheist, and believed in blind eternal fate, I should still believe that fate had ordained the Jews to be the most essential instrument for civilizing the nations. If I were an atheist of the other sect, who believe or pretend to believe that all is ordered by chance, I should believe that chance had ordered the Jews to preserve and propagate to all mankind the doctrine of a supreme, intelligent, wise, almighty sovereign of the universe, which I believe to be the great essential principle of all morality, and consequently of all civilization.[28]

For the Founders, the most effective catalyst of virtue was religion, for it reminded man that he is not God and he therefore cannot shape morality according to his own selfish desires. It was the subversion of this principle that they identified as the cause behind the American and French Revolutions taking such radically different courses: it was ultimately a difference of theology.

GOD AND THE AMERICAN AND FRENCH REVOLUTIONS

The Founders believed in the existence of a God, which they deemed the most rational basis for the existence of the universe, morality, and reason itself. The French Revolution was predicated on almost the exact opposite idea.

While many today assume that the notion of blind chance being the operative force in the universe's creation and development arrived on the scene with Charles Darwin, this is not the case. In fact, it was a notion quite popular among many of the continental European intellectuals of the time, most of whom were French, and most of whom tended to be atheists and/or materialists (which were practically the same). They contended that the universe had not been created but had either existed eternally or was the result of inherent properties in matter itself. But among the French intelligentsia, the one who had the most profound effect on the Founders, Montesquieu, directly contradicted this position in his famous work, *The Spirit of the Laws*: "Those who have said that *a blind fate has produced all the effects that we see in the world* have said a great absurdity," he wrote, "for what greater absurdity is there than a blind fate that could have produced intelligent beings?"[29]

For Montesquieu and the Founders, the universe was simply too full of information, order, and harmony to ascribe it to blind chance. "What is chance?" asked Adams. "It is motion; it is action; it is event; it is phenomenon without cause. Chance is no cause at all; it is nothing."[30]

In addition to their denial, or at least extreme doubt of the existence of a Creator, many of the French intellectuals in like manner either doubted or denied the existence and immortality of the human soul. They therefore denied the two theological pillars upon which the Founders based their ideas of virtue, and as such, it was no surprise that the French Revolution, which claimed to be the heir of the American Revolution, devolved into a bloodbath of violence and oppression unrestrained by any religious principle.

While both revolutions were similar in their assertion of human rights, they offered fundamentally different explanations of the origin of such rights. The American Revolution was premised on men being "endowed by their Creator with certain unalienable rights," while the French Revolution asserted man's rights were based purely on reason, apart from any notions of divinity or religion. A statue of a deified "Reason" was erected in the Notre Dame cathedral in Paris, and the revolution was predicated upon principles that were explicitly and directly opposed to religion, Christianity in particular. Adams noted the differences between the two revolutions when he wrote to his friend Richard Price that "Diderot and D'Alembert, Voltaire and Rousseau," all French atheists and materialists, "have contributed to this great event more than Sidney, Locke, or Hoadly," English political philosophers who explicitly asserted that the "laws of nature and nature's God" were the foundation of man's rights and moral obligations, and who had a profound impact on the American Revolution. The French, on the other hand, based man's rights on the consensus of "the nation." The rights of man were what man, through the nation, had decided they would be. For this reason, Adams admitted to Price as early as 1790, "I own to you, I know not what to make of a republic of thirty million atheists,"[31] and he predicted there would be rampant violence and bloodshed.

But that was not all. Several of the Founders, Adams in particular, believed that the principles of the French Revolution not only directly undermined the basis of human rights and obligations but also destroyed the very idea of human liberty. If man was simply matter in motion, then his entire destiny had already been determined by physical laws and constants (today known as "determinism"), making liberty a meaningless idea. And yet, this was the view of many of the leading French intellectuals. "And what was their philosophy?" Adams inquired:

> Atheism—pure, unadulterated atheism.[32] . . . The universe was matter only, and eternal. Spirit was a word without a meaning. Liberty was a word without a meaning. There was no liberty in the universe; liberty was a word void of sense. Every thought, word, passion, sentiment, feeling, all motion and action was necessary [determinism]. All beings and attributes were of eternal necessity; conscience, morality, were all nothing but fate. This was their creed, and this was to perfect human nature, and convert the earth into a paradise of pleasure . . . Why, then, should we abhor the word "God," and fall in love with the word "fate"? We know there exists energy and intellect enough to produce such a world as this, which is a sublime and beautiful one, and a very

benevolent one, notwithstanding all our snarling; and a happy one, if it is not made otherwise by our own fault.[33]

Alexander Hamilton, who described the French Revolution as "the most cruel, sanguinary, and violent that ever stained the annals of mankind," also predicted its failure due to the fact that it was explicitly opposed to Christianity, "a state of things which annihilates the foundations of social order and true liberty, confounds all moral distinctions and *substitutes to* the mild and beneficent religion of the Gospel a gloomy, persecuting, and desolating atheism."[34]

It was precisely because the French Revolution rejected the Judeo-Christian notion of the fallen nature of man in exchange for the idea that he could be perfected by reason that they engaged in the wanton violence and cruelty of the guillotine: it was all worth it because they were creating a new, ideal world that had to be purged of its impure elements.

The French Revolution was thereby founded on principles that fundamentally contradicted the divine basis of the existence of the universe, man's rights, his moral obligations, and his very liberty, upon which the Founders, partaking of both the classical and Judeo-Christian tradition, asserted them. With God removed, several of the Founders, Adams in particular, predicted the French Revolution would operate according to the bloody principles of "might makes right." "A nation of atheists," he had warned, would likely lead to "the destruction of a million of human beings."[35] Adams explained his prophecy of a forthcoming deluge of blood in biblical terms and ascribed it to the utter rejection of religion by the leaders of the French Revolution:

> The temper and principles prevailing at present in that quarter of the world have a tendency to as general and total a destruction as ever befell Tyre and Sidon[,] Sodom and Gomorrah. If all religion and governments, all arts and sciences are destroyed, the trees will grow up, cities will molder into common earth, and a few human beings may be left naked to chase the wild beasts with bows and arrows. . . . I hope in all events that religion and learning will find an asylum in America.[36]

In this, he disagreed (at the time) with Jefferson. But even Jefferson was forced to admit decades later, after the Reign of Terror, the Napoleonic Wars, and the other violent outbursts that came out of the French Revolution, that Adams had been completely right in his assessment, acknowledging, "Your prophecies . . . proved truer than mine."[37] When Jefferson asked Adams why he had predicted what he did, Adams explained that the power of God had been replaced by the arrogant, usurping power of man, and conscience was thereby disconnected from its transcendent anchors. Thus, those in power believed whatever they did was moral: "Power always sincerely, conscientiously, *de tres bon foi* ["in very good faith"], believes itself right. Power always thinks it has a great soul, and vast views, beyond the comprehension of the weak, and that it is doing God's service, when it is violating all his laws."[38] It was for this reason that, as much as religion had been abused for centuries in European history, Adams argued it could not compare with the atrocities committed in the name of *"Liberté, Égalité, Fraternité"* during the French Revolution: "It is a serious problem to resolve whether all the abuses of Christianity, even in the darkest ages when the Pope deposed princes and laid nations under his interdict, were ever so bloody and cruel, ever bore down the independence of the human mind with such terror and intolerance, or taught doctrines which required such implicit credulity to believe, as the present reign of pretended philosophy in France."[39]

As president, Adams had to deal directly with the revolutionary French government and easily noted the difference between an American society that assented to general religious principles and a French society that rejected them:

> You may find the moral principles, sanctified and sanctioned by religion, are the only bond of union, the only ground of confidence of the people in one another, of the people in the government, and the government in the people. Avarice, ambition, and pleasure, can never be the foundations of reformations or revolutions for the better. These passions have dictated the aim at universal domination, trampled on

the rights of neutrality, despised the faith of solemn contracts, insulted ambassadors, and rejected offers of friendship.[40]

For the Founders, the purpose of reason—which Adams referred to as "a revelation from its maker"[41] and Jefferson as an "oracle given you by heaven"[42]—was to better align human actions with the "law of nature and nature's God" by the taming of human passions and the application of knowledge. The leaders of the French Revolution believed precisely the opposite, that God didn't really exist (and if He did, He was largely irrelevant), and that reason was man's alone, and thus his to utilize toward whatever ends he himself determined. Though the Founders knew perfection "falls not to the share of mortals,"[43] the French believed that man could be perfected through reason, and therefore any barriers to creating the world of their dreams needed to be destroyed, for this was tantamount to obstructing man's perfection. The differences between the two revolutions thus turned out to be theological at root, and for this reason, while on the surface they were superficially similar, they were in fact fundamentally different, as Adams prophesied, other Founders criticized, and the facts of history verified.

RELIGION AND VIRTUE: THE ANCHORS OF THE SOUL

As a young man, Adams asked the same question most human beings have asked in one form or another: what is the meaning of life? His answer placed the divine at the center of it:

What is the proper business of mankind in this life? We come into the world naked and destitute of all the conveniences and necessaries of life. And if we were not provided for and nourished by our parents or others should inevitably perish as soon as born. We increase in strength of body and mind by slow and insensible degrees. One-third of our time is consumed in sleep, and three-fourths of the remainder is spent in procuring a mere animal sustenance. And if we live to the age of three score and ten and then set down to make an estimate in our minds of the happiness we have enjoyed and the misery we have suffered, we shall find, I am apt to think, that the overbalance of happiness is quite inconsiderable. We shall find that we have been through the greatest part of our lives pursuing shadows, and empty but glittering phantoms rather than substances. We shall find that we have applied our whole vigor, all our faculties, in the pursuit of honor or wealth or learning or some other such delusive trifle instead of the real and everlasting excellences of piety and virtue. Habits of contemplating the Deity and his transcendent excellences, and correspondent habits of complacency in and dependence upon him, habits of reverence and gratitude to God, and habits of love and compassion to our fellow men, and habits of temperance, recollection and self-government will afford us a real and substantial pleasure. We may then exult in a consciousness of the favor of God, and the prospect of everlasting felicity.[44]

It is no surprise that Adams accorded religion a prime role as the great regulator of human actions. Man is a reasonable creature, to be sure, but his passions were apt to get the best of him, and the contemplation of the divine, the raising of his sights beyond himself and his surroundings, was the most effective way to curtail his selfish tendencies and restore the reason necessary to live a virtuous life. Franklin described his beliefs in a remarkably similar fashion:

> I conclude that believing a Providence we have the foundation of all true religion; for we should love and revere that Deity for his goodness and thank him for his benefits; we should adore him for his Wisdom, fear him for his Power, and pray to him for his Favor and Protection; and this religion will be a powerful regulator of our actions, give us peace and tranquility within our own minds, and render us benevolent, useful, and beneficial to others.[45]

Religion thus tended to order the soul of man in such a way as to maintain both his mind and his heart. True religion thus served to ameliorate the effects of man's most dangerous vice, the one which had led to his most destructive actions and the greatest suffering of his fellow human beings: pride. The widespread belief among the Founders in divine providence, or the divine ordaining of history, was yet another extension of this principle so fatal to human conceit and arrogance. As Adams noted during the Revolutionary War:

> I am of your mind that Providence is working the general happiness, and whether we cooperate in it, with a good will, or without, cooperate we must. We mortals feel very big sometimes, and think ourselves acting a grand role when in truth it is the irresistible course of events that hurries us on, and we have in fact very little influence in them. The utmost that is permitted to us is to assist, and it is our duty to be very cautious that what we do is directed to a right end.[46]

This is why Tocqueville, in commenting on the effect religion had on the American soul, described with penetrating insight how it not only tended to anchor the souls of individuals, but contributed to the well-being of society by anchoring morality to a divine foundation rather than the latest whims and fads of men:

> There is almost no human action, however individual one supposes it to be, which does not originate in a very general idea men have about God, his connections with the human race, the nature of their souls, and their duties toward their fellows. We have to accept that these ideas are the shared source from which all others flow. Men have therefore, a huge interest in creating fixed ideas about God, their soul, their general duties toward their creator and fellow men, for any doubt about these first concerns would put all their actions at risk and would condemn them in some way to confusion and impotence. This is therefore the most important matter upon which each of us should have settled ideas . . . Fixed ideas about God and human nature are vital to the daily practice of their [Americans'] lives.[47]

It was for this reason he argued that, as he had seen in the United States, religion was the great antidote to untamed materialistic desires and the atomization of society into a set of narcissistic, isolated individuals:

We have to recognize that if religion does not save men in the other world, it is at least very useful for their happiness and importance in this. That is above all true of men who live in free countries. When a nation's religion is destroyed, doubt takes a grip upon the highest areas of intelligence, partially paralyzing all the others. Each man gets used to having only confused and vacillating ideas on matters which have the greatest interest for himself and his fellows. He puts up a poor defense of his opinions or abandons them, and, as he despairs of ever resolving by himself the greatest problems presented by human destiny, he beats a cowardly retreat into not thinking at all. Such a state cannot fail to weaken the soul, strains the forces of the will, and shapes citizens for slavery. Not only do the latter allow their freedom to be taken from them, they often give it up.

This insight from Tocqueville is crucial, for he realized that *all* of human life was a matter of faith, not in the religious or mystical sense, but in the sense that all of us have imperfect knowledge about everything and everyone that surrounds us, and yet, in order to survive and prosper, we must act anyway. Therefore, that which bridged the inevitable gap between knowledge and ignorance, and which thus made action of any kind possible, was faith, for no one can act according to perfect knowledge; none possess such knowledge. This is quite contrary to the much more modern notion that faith is some sort of belief without evidence. On the contrary, faith had always been defined in the Judeo-Christian tradition as justified trust in someone or something. This is why Tocqueville identified God as the anchor for human existence: nothing else can be assumed without Him. The physical and moral parameters of the universe lose all definition if God does not exist, with unavoidable implications for human liberty. He continued:

This constant upheaval in everything brings disquiet and exhaustion. As everything in the domain of their intelligence is shifting, they crave at least for a firm and stable state in their material world. Being unable to recover their ancient beliefs, they find a ruler. In my opinion, I doubt whether man can ever support at the same time complete religious independence and entire political freedom and am drawn to the thought that if a man is without faith, he must serve someone, and if he is free, he must believe. It must be acknowledged that equality, which brings great benefits into the world, arouses in men, as I shall demonstrate, very dangerous instincts. It tends to their isolation from each other in order to persuade them to have concern only for their individual selves. It exposes their souls to an excessive love of material enjoyment. The greatest advantage religions bring is to inspire quite contrary instincts. Every single religion places the object of man's desire beyond and above possessions of this earth, and by its nature lifts his soul toward those regions which are much above the senses. In addition, they impose upon each man certain obligations toward the human race or encourage a shared endeavor, something drawing him away from a contemplation of himself . . . which shows how important it is for men to retain their religion even on achieving equality.[48]

As Tocqueville noted, religion anchored the soul of man in such a way as to make self-government more attainable, and as such, his propensity to seek out a human ruler (i.e., a tyrant) less likely. This is a fascinating and often overlooked aspect of the Founders' views of morality, for they believed it necessitated simplicity. Atheism, they thought, and a dissolution in religious belief in general, would encourage uncontrolled luxury and an excessive love of material abundance, a "nothing is ever enough" type of culture as the values of society became more materialistic and less spiritual in their foundations. Counteracting this kind of moral decay was yet another benefit of religious virtue. "Virtue and simplicity of manners are indispensably necessary in a Republic, among all orders and degrees of men,"[49] Adams had written, and his sentiments were echoed by many other Founders. If one's ultimate security were based on the hereafter, one would not be as disposed to find ultimate contentment in the pleasures of this life.

As several of the Founders had predicted, and all of them had observed, when religion was tossed out by the French revolutionaries, a vacuum was created into which rushed every species of violence, immorality, and oppression, precisely because morality and reason, ironically in the name of reason, were both ripped from their transcendent moorings and fell prey to the passions of fallen men. Such were the dangerous and inevitable consequences of making man, rather than the Creator, the definer of truth. With this loss of self-government, and lacking the spiritual capacity to make up for it, they required a ruler, and that is exactly what the French got with Napoleon. Tocqueville brilliantly articulated how atheism led to such disastrous consequences:

> Whenever among the opinions of a democratic nation you come across some of those evil theories which promote the belief that everything perishes with the body [atheism] you may consider men with such views as natural enemies of the people. I am offended by many views held by materialists [atheists]. Their doctrines appear to me pernicious and their arrogance disgusts me. If their system could be of some use to man, it would be in giving him a modest opinion of himself. But they do not demonstrate such a truth and when they think they have done enough to prove that they are brutish [like animals], they seem as proud as if they had demonstrated that they were gods. In all nations, materialism is a dangerous illness of the mind, but in a democracy, it must be especially feared because it united marvelously well with that defect of the heart most familiar to those peoples. Democracy encourages the taste for physical pleasures which, if excessive, soon persuades men to believe that nothing but matter exists. Materialism in its turn gives them the final impetuous enthusiasm for these very pleasures. Such is the vicious circle into which democratic nations are driven . . . Most religions are only general, simple, and practical channels for teaching men that the soul is immortal. That is the most considerable advantage a democratic nation derives from religious beliefs, and one which makes them more necessary for such a nation than for all others. When, therefore, any religion has put down deep roots in a democracy, be careful not to shake them. Rather, take care to preserve them as the most valuable bequest from aristocratic times.

Do not seek to snatch from men their ancient religious opinions in order to replace them with new ones, lest at the point of exchange their soul finds itself momentarily void of beliefs and the love of physical pleasures spreads to fill it entirely. Certainly transmigration of souls is no more rational a doctrine than materialism. However, if it was absolutely vital for a democracy to choose between the two, I would judge without hesitation that its citizens run less a risk of being brutalized by believing that their souls will pass into the body of a pig than by thinking that their soul is nothing at all.[50]

Religion further combated the nihilism of materialism and atheism by encouraging a deep sense of gratefulness and appreciation for the blessings of life. This is a most curious thing to observe in the Founders' writings: despite their living in a time that did not come close to matching our own in terms of material convenience and prosperity, they complained very little, and oftentimes their sense of appreciation was expressed in theological terms. While a more complete discussion of this topic will take place in chapter 9, suffice it to say here that the Founders, as Tocqueville described, saw religion as the great counterweight to the seeking of mere physical pleasures, which they believed undermined the virtuous life by encouraging a sense of entitlement that merely resulted in misery. It is essential to note this fact, for it is beyond doubt that we in twenty-first-century America, while our physical needs are not only met but exceeded in many ways beyond the Founders' wildest dreams, find it far easier to complain. Whereas today human suffering of any kind is used (sometimes for understandable reasons) to question the existence of God, the Founders found such suggestions preposterous. All things considered, they had every reason to believe that God was good and that this world was, in many respects, a wonderful place, and that to the extent it was not, it was typically the result of human behavior. And when those trials that were beyond man's control inevitably arose? "Murmur not at the ways of Providence" Jefferson wrote to a newly born child.[51] Translation: don't complain or gripe—God is wiser than you.

Jefferson, a man who had lost his wife and numerous children in addition to the various other vicissitudes and trials of life, could barely contain his thankfulness while reflecting with Abigail Adams on what he presumed to be his fast-approaching death and the life he had led, and he did not fail to offer his gratitude to God:

> Our next meeting must then be in the country [heaven] to which they have flown—a country for us not now very distant. . . . Nor is the provision for it more easy than the preparation has been kind. Nothing proves more than this, that the Being who presides over the world is essentially benevolent. . . . On the whole, however, perhaps it is wise and well to be contented with the good things which the master of the feast[52] places before us, and to be thankful for what we have, rather than thoughtful about what we have not. You and I, dear Madam, have already had more than an ordinary portion of life, and more, too, of health than the general measure. On this score I owe boundless thankfulness.[53]

Franklin, a man of many sorrows as well, offered similar thoughts while reflecting on his life in his *Autobiography*:

> And now I speak of thanking God, I desire with all humility to acknowledge that I owe the mentioned happiness of my past life to his kind Providence, which led me to the means I used and gave them success—My belief of this induces me to *hope*, though I must not *presume*, that the same goodness will still be exercised towards me in continuing that happiness, or in enabling me to bear a fatal reverse, which I may experience as others have done, the complexion of my future fortune being known to him only, and in whose power it is to bless to us even our afflictions.[54]

Firmly within the Judeo-Christian tradition, Adams also reflected on the trials of life in religious terms and saw them as a necessary prerequisite to finding true knowledge, wisdom, and happiness, and thus true virtue:

Did you ever see a portrait or a statue of a great man, without perceiving strong traits of pain and anxiety? These furrows were all ploughed in the countenance by grief . . . None were fit for legislators and magistrates but sad men.[55] And who were these sad men? They were aged men who had been tossed and buffeted in the vicissitudes of life, forced upon profound reflection by grief and disappointments, and taught to command their passions and prejudices . . . Grief drives men into habits of serious reflection, sharpens the understanding, and softens the heart; it compels them to rouse their reason, to assert its empire over their passions, propensities and prejudices, to elevate them to a superiority over all human events, to give them the *felicis animi immotam tranquilitatem* [the imperturbable tranquility of a happy heart]: in short, to make them stoics and Christians.[56]

There was a sense of resignation to suffering and setbacks. They were an accepted reality of life, and were not, to the Founders, a legitimate reason to question God's existence. Adams rejected such a nihilistic view of life as nothing but "false philosophy and false Christianity. If it is at any time a vale of tears, we make it such."[57]

This sense of gratefulness, even during life's greatest torments, was also a strong encouragement to the doing of good deeds, for happy, grateful people tend to want to give more to others. Franklin described his "theology" of doing good and bearing suffering this way:

For my own part, when I am employed in serving others, I do not look upon myself as conferring favors, but as paying debts. In my travels and since my settlement I have received much kindness from men, to whom I shall never have any opportunity of making the least direct return; and numberless mercies from God, who is infinitely above being benefited by our services. These kindnesses from men I can therefore only return on their fellow men, and I can only show my gratitude for those mercies from God by a readiness to help his other children and my brethren. For I do not think that thanks, and compliments, though repeated weekly, can discharge our real obligations to each other, and much less those to our Creator . . . Even the mixed imperfect pleasures we enjoy in this world are rather from God's goodness than our merit, how much more such happiness of Heaven? For my own part, I have not the vanity to think I deserve it, the folly to expect it, nor the ambition to desire it, but content myself in submitting to the will and disposal of that God who made me, who has hitherto preserved and blessed me, and in whose fatherly goodness I may well confide, that he will never make me miserable, and that even the afflictions I may at any time suffer shall tend to my benefit.[58]

But this appreciation and love for religion went far beyond theoretical concerns. Rather, it was based in large part on the American story itself. As we have already seen and will continue to see, the Founders were profoundly affected by their Puritan ancestors who had come to the New World to escape persecution in Europe, which to them represented a new, metaphorical exodus of a new Israel (the Puritans) from the slavery of a new Egypt (Europe). This biblically inspired heritage was essential to their understanding of the American narrative and cause.

THE AMERICAN STORY: THE PURITANS AND THE NEW WORLD

The birth of the United States cannot be separated from the religious heritage that informed the principles upon which it was founded. "It is religion which has given birth to Anglo-American societies: one must never lose sight of that. In the United States, religion is thus intimately linked to all national habits and all the emotions which one's native country arouses. That gives it a particular strength." This is how Tocqueville described the culture that eventually led to the rise of the United States in the New World. He also explained the religious heritage that gave rise to the notions of human liberty that would form the foundations of the American Republic:

Most of English America has been peopled by men who, having shaken off the authority of the Pope, acknowledge no other religious supremacy. They brought, therefore, into the New World a form of

Christianity which I can only describe as democratic and republican. This fact will be exceptionally favorable to the establishment of a democracy and a republic in governing public affairs. From the start, politics and religion were in agreement and they have continued to be so ever since.[59]

Adams, writing in a newspaper editorial in the 1760s as "Governor Winthrop" and "Governor Bradford," two of the original Puritan governors of the Massachusetts Bay and Plymouth colonies, reminded his fellow citizens, the posterity of the Pilgrims, what their noble dream had been when they arrived in the New World:

> We have often congratulated each other, with high satisfaction, on the glory we secured in both worlds by our favorite enterprise of planting America. We were Englishmen. We were citizens of the world. We were Christians. The history of nations and of mankind was familiar to us, and we considered the species chiefly in relation to the system of great nature and her all-perfect author. In consequence of such contemplations as these, it was the unwearied endeavor of our lives to establish a society on English, humane, and Christian principles. This . . . we are conscious was our noble aim. We succeeded to the astonishment of all mankind, and our posterity, in spite of all the terrors and temptations which have from first to last surrounded them and endangered their very being, have been supremely happy.

He went on to remind them that "if our posterity have not without interruption maintained the principal ascendency in public affairs, they have always been virtuous and worthy, and have never departed from the principles of the Englishman, the citizen of the world, and the Christian."[60] In a series of magisterial editorials from around the same time, known as *A Dissertation on the Canon and the Feudal Law*, he described the historical context that compelled the Puritans to leave Europe and begin anew in the New World. Their motives were not only profoundly religious but—quite counterintuitively to the modern mind—based on their hatred of the union of church and state and

Europe: "It seems to have been even *stipulated* between them [church and state] that the *temporal* grandees [the state] should contribute every thing in their power to maintain the ascendency of the *priesthood* [the church], and that the spiritual grandees, in their turn, should employ that ascendency over the *consciences* of the *people*, in impressing on their minds a *blind, implicit* obedience to civil magistracy."[61]

This is crucial to remember when we look at what the Founders had to say about the separation of church and state: in Europe, the state had helped support the church, and the church in turn provided the theological basis for greater and ever-increasing state power, encouraging the people to blindly obey the state, regardless of its abuses. The Founders' animosity toward this arrangement was not some eighteenth-century ideal derived from secular intellectuals. It was bequeathed to them by their Puritan ancestors, who were not at all opposed to the church influencing the morality of society (quite the opposite), but did oppose the state, through the church, compelling uniformity of religious doctrine in order to make the people more sheep-like in their obedience. The issue was never one of the state forcing a particular form of morality, for Christian morality, while found in the Bible, had always been predicated on the basis of reason and natural law as well. This is why Montesquieu declared, "Christianity is full of common sense,"[62] for the morality it encouraged was simple and straightforward, and it in fact rarely, if ever, was the direct cause of conflict in Europe. Instead, mostly abstract and esoteric doctrinal issues had been the basis for the religious tyranny and violence so abhorred by the Puritans, issues of baptism and the Eucharist (Mass), salvation being through faith alone or works, whether churches should be organized independent of or according to the dictates of a central authority, and so on. But as Adams narrates, this cozy and mutually beneficial relationship between church and state continued "till GOD, in his benign providence, raised up the champions who began and conducted the *Reformation*."[63] The Reformation of the sixteenth century, led by figures such as Martin Luther, John Calvin, and Ulrich Zwingli, was thus seen by the Founders as one of the direct causes of the Puritan migration in the seventeenth, and thus the American Revolution in the eighteenth century. It was during this time that the Bible first became accessible to common people in their own tongue rather than just to the educated or the clergy. This was why Thomas Paine, in his famously invective pamphlet *Common Sense*, spoke with such contempt to the tyranny of both church *and* state, "king-craft" and "priest-craft" in Europe, not because he disdained religion (at that point), but for "withholding the scripture from the public in Popish [Catholic] countries." Samuel Adams, in a speech delivered just after the signing of the Declaration of Independence, drew the same historical connection: "He who made all men hath made the truths necessary to human happiness obvious to all. Our forefathers threw off the yoke of Popery in religion; for you is reserved the honor of leveling the popery of politics. They opened the Bible to all, and maintained the capacity of every man to judge for himself in religion."[64]

As detailed by John Adams, the Puritans had been determined to inaugurate an entirely new system of government and society:

[T]heir policy . . . was founded in wise, humane and benevolent principles; it was founded in revelation [the Bible], and in reason too . . . But they saw clearly that popular powers must be placed, as a guard, a control, a balance, to the powers of the monarch and the priest, in every government, or else it would soon become the man of sin, the whore of Babylon,[65] the mystery of iniquity, a great and detestable system of fraud, violence, and usurpation. Their greatest concern seems to have been to establish a government of the church more consistent with the scriptures, and a government of the state more agreeable to the dignity of human nature, than any they had seen in Europe . . . as their principles and theory, i.e. as human nature and the Christian religion require it should be, they endeavored to remove from it as many of the feudal inequalities and dependencies as could be spared . . . [They] had an utter contempt of all that dark ribaldry [something scurrilous] of hereditary indefeasible right—the Lord's anointed—and the divine miraculous original of government [the

Divine Right of Kings] with which the priesthood had enveloped the feudal monarch in clouds and mysteries, and from which they have deduced the most mischievous of all doctrines, *that of passive obedience and non-resistance* . . . they thought all such slavish subordinations were equally inconsistent with the constitution of human nature and that religious liberty with which Jesus had made them free.[66]

It is important to note that Adams credits the Puritans, not secular eighteenth-century Enlightenment philosophers, with originating the ideas of separation of powers, checks and balances, separation of church and state (as we shall see), and many other features of what would become the US Constitution, and all of these ideas resulted from their religiously informed ideas of the "dignity of human nature" endowed by God Himself. Rather than leaving Europe because they abhorred religion the Puritans left for precisely the opposite reason: to worship as they saw fit, and construct societies more in keeping with their views of human nature, government, and a free society. It was thus the Puritans who began the great experiment in self-government in the New World. It is no wonder they saw themselves as a new Israel fleeing the slavery of the new Egypt, and it no surprise that this biblical narrative of freedom from slavery was the inspiration behind the original proposal for a new seal for the United States in 1776: "Dr. F[ranklin] proposes a device for a seal," John Adams wrote to his wife "Moses lifting up his wand and dividing the Red Sea, and Pharaoh, in his chariot, overwhelmed with the waters. This motto: rebellion to tyrants is obedience to God. Mr. Jefferson proposed: the children of Israel in the wilderness, led by a cloud by day, and a pillar of fire by night."[67]

Jefferson referred to the same narrative as president of the United States, noting in his second inaugural address, in 1805, "I shall need, too, the favor of that Being in whose hands we are, who led our forefathers, as Israel of old, from their native land, and planted them in a country flowing with all the necessaries and comforts of life."

During the Revolution, many of the British had in fact mocked what they saw as the overly religious Puritan ancestors of their American cousins. Adams addressed their ridicule head-on in a response that could just as easily be made today: "It may be thought polite and fashionable, by many modern fine gentlemen perhaps, to deride the characters of these Persons [the Puritans] as enthusiastical, superstitious . . . but such ridicule is founded in nothing but foppery and affectation, and is grosly [*sic*] injurious and false."[68]

In fact, it was this religious zeal that Adams commended and praised, noting that "no great enterprise, for the honor or happiness of mankind, was ever achieved without a large mixture of that noble infirmity," of being "religious to some degree of enthusiasm."[69] Franklin, though not an orthodox Christian, made the exact same point while in England, acting as a colonial agent to the king. In a newspaper editorial in which he wrote a mock parliamentary speech, he referenced the Puritans' crucial role in overthrowing the tyrannical Stuart dynasty during the English Civil War of the seventeenth century. This led to the English Bill of Rights, which in turn greatly informed the American Bill of Rights, ratified a century later:

> I am an American: In that character, I trust this House will show some little indulgence to the feelings which are excited by what fell this moment from an honorable and military gentleman under the gallery. According to him, sir, the Americans are unequal to the people of this country in devotion to women, and in courage, and in what in his sight seems worse than all, they are religious . . . Sir, they were such religionists that vindicated this country from the tyranny of the Stuarts. Perhaps the honorable gentleman may have some compassionate feelings for that unhappy family: does that sharpen his resentment against the Americans, who inherit from those ancestors not only the same religion, but the same love of liberty and spirit to defend it?[70]

The Founders saw themselves as the heirs of these pious and enterprising Puritans, who were the original defenders of human liberty against the tyranny of kings and the institutionalized church. "It was this struggle" Adams noted, "that peopled America. It was not religion *alone*, as is commonly supposed, but it was a love of *universal Liberty*, and a hatred, a dread, a horror of the infernal confederacy [between church and state], before described, that projected, conducted, and accomplished the settlement of America."[71]

THE AMERICAN STORY: THE REVOLUTION

Largely thanks to the religious fervor of their ancestors, religion and virtue were key elements in not just the Founders' notions of human rights and obligations, but in their justification of the Revolution itself. Jefferson's immortal statement of the rights of humanity being "endowed by their Creator" was not an isolated one, but rather the culmination of more than a century's worth of effort on the part of the original settlers of the American continent. In fact, the ardent love of liberty exhibited by the colonists was directly attributed to this Puritan heritage. Adams overflowed with admiration:

> If ever an infant country deserved to be cherished, it is America: if ever any people merited honor and happiness, they are her inhabitants . . . they have the tender feelings of humanity, and the noble benevolence of Christians. They have the most habitual, radical sense of liberty, and the highest reverence for virtue. They are descended from a race of heroes who, placing their confidence in Providence alone set the seas and skies, monsters and savages, tyrants and devils, at defiance for the sake of Religion and Liberty. And the present generation have shown themselves worthy of their ancestors.[72]

While the issue of "no taxation without representation" was enormously important during the Revolution and the period preceding it, it was only one part of a broader question: Did Parliament have a right to legislate for the colonies at all? Adams answered in profoundly religious terms: "I would ask, by what law the Parliament has authority over America? By the law of GOD in the Old and New Testament, it has none. By the law of nature and nations, it has none. By the common law of England it has none . . . What religious, moral, or political obligation then are we under to submit to Parliament as a supreme legislative? None at all."[73]

Far from being confined to just the question of taxation, the colonists believed that parliament legislating for the colonies *at all* was contrary to the British constitution, the largely unwritten yet centuries-old legal norms and traditions that had made Great Britain and its dominions the freest on earth up to that point. It was, among other things, the arbitrary and lawless manner in which Parliament had violated the sovereignty of the colonial legislatures that was their greatest concern. If it could overrule the acknowledged authority of the people themselves in the colonies, what could it not do? The relatively miniscule tax was not the issue but the ability to tax in the first place. In so doing, Parliament was, the Founders determined, acting according to the false right of force rather than the genuine right of justice under law. This is what Jefferson was referring to when he observed that "the God who gave us life gave us liberty at the same time. The hand of force may destroy, but cannot disjoin them."

These parliamentary encroachments inspired the colonists to inquire into the true source of their rights and liberties. Nearly universally, their conclusion, long before 1776, was that the rights of *all men* were endowed by God, not government, and as such, it was the fundamental duty of government to protect these rights. Adams described this awakening among the colonists and the importance of the pulpits of the day in arousing it: "The people, even to the lowest ranks, have become more attentive to their Liberties, more inquisitive about them, and more determined to defend them than they were ever before known, or had occasion to be . . . their merchants have agreed to sacrifice even their bread to the cause of Liberty, their legislatures have resolved, the united colonies have remonstrated, the presses have everywhere groaned, and the pulpits have thundered."[74]

While the modern tendency is to avoid politics in the pulpit (and to act as if it is American to do so), this was precisely what the churches at the time of the Revolution did *not* do, and the Founders applauded them. They recognized that politics was not an isolated matter, but one that directly affected all aspects of life and was informed by the most profound notions of human nature. Liberty for the Founders could not be properly understood without acknowledging its transcendent roots in the divine. For them, to submit to tyranny was not only morally wrong but also spiritually unacceptable. "Let the pulpit resound with the doctrines and sentiments of religious liberty" Adams roared. "Let us hear the dignity of his [man's] nature, and the noble rank he holds among the works of God! That consenting to slavery is a sacrilegious breach of trust, as offensive in the sight of God as it is derogatory from our own honor or interest or happiness, and that God almighty has promulgated from heaven liberty, peace, and goodwill to man [Luke 2:14]!"[75]

Again, in another ironic twist, those opposed to American independence and freedom discouraged the clergy from preaching against the actions of the British government, a fact that greatly aggravated John Adams, for whom the questions at stake were not just political but also religious: "But if a clergyman preaches Christianity, and tells the magistrates that they were not distinguished from their brethren for their private emolument, but for the good of the people; that the people are bound in conscience to obey a good government, but are not bound to submit to one that aims at destroying all the ends of government—oh sedition! Treason!"[76]

This was precisely what so many of the original Puritan settlers found so disconcerting about the alliance of church and state in Europe: they dreaded it not just because it forced one version of Christianity on everyone, but also because the established church preached absolute obedience to the government, no matter how tyrannical it became, "a *blind, implicit* obedience to civil Magistracy"[77] as Adams described it. This, they believed, was contrary to the Christian duty of pastors and other clergy to preach *against* unrighteousness, whether among the laity or in the government. Christ Himself had made a definite distinction between Caesar and the church, a distinction the Puritans felt was critical to the health of both.

This was, in fact, embraced by the Founders. Adams explained: "It is the duty of the clergy to accommodate their discourses to the times, to preach against such sins as are most prevalent, and recommend such virtues as are most wanted . . . If the rights and duties of Christian magistrates and subjects are disputed, should they not explain them, show their nature, ends, limitations, and restrictions?"[78]

On this point, Adams boasted of the clergy in Massachusetts, describing them as "a virtuous, sensible, and learned set of men, and they don't take their sermons from newspapers but the Bible, unless it be a few who preach passive obedience."[79] Furthermore, they embraced the reading of the Bible (the most common textbook among students of the day) and sermons in order to better understand not only their duties as citizens, but the standards by which they should judge their public servants: "A man who can read will find in his Bible, in the common sermon books that common people have by them and even in the almanac and newspapers rules and observations that will enlarge his range of thought and enable him the better to judge who has and who has not that integrity of heart and that compass of knowledge and understanding which form the statesman."[80]

In addition, clergy were responsible for shedding light on injustices in government. Adams noted that government mismanagement of funds was just as sinful as private mismanagement and should not be above clerical criticism: "Justice is a great Christian as well as moral duty and virtue which the clergy ought to inculcate and explain . . . Should not pastors show that justice was due to the public as well as to an individual, and that cheating the public of four thousand two hundred pounds sterling is at least as great a sin as taking a chicken from a private hen roost, or perhaps a watch from a fob!?"[81]

As the contest with Great Britain continued to escalate, many of the Founders constantly expressed a faith in "Heaven" and "Providence," universally common and accepted terms for God in eighteenth-century America. "God Almighty grant us wisdom and virtue sufficient for the high trust that is devolved upon us . . . Resignation to the Will of

Heaven is our only resource in such dangerous times," Adams mused.[82] In addition, the examples drawn upon for inspiration and instruction were not the French skeptics and European intellectuals, but the heroes of the Bible: "The management of so complicated and mighty a machine as the United Colonies requires the meekness of Moses, the patience of Job and the wisdom of Solomon, added to the valor of Daniel."[83]

The religious tone of most of the rhetoric of the Revolution included constant calls for public virtue, with some of the Founders even ascribing the conflict with Great Britain to the colonists' lack of virtue. It was precisely because they saw the Revolution as a duty imposed on them by God, and motivated by what were at root religious causes (i.e., the violation of divinely endowed rights by a worldly government), that they were aroused to dedicate and sacrifice so much. This combination of religiously inspired virtue and political acumen was essential, they thought, not just to the present crisis in which they found themselves, but to the future of the nation as a whole. Adams wrote as much to his wife, Abigail:

> Does not natural morality and much more Christian benevolence make it our indispensable duty to lay ourselves out to serve our fellow-creatures to the utmost of our power, in promoting and supporting those great political systems and general regulations upon which the happiness of multitudes depends? The benevolence, charity, capacity, and industry which, exerted in private life, would make a family, a parish, a town happy, employed upon a larger scale, in support of the great principles of virtue and freedom of political regulations, might secure whole nations and generations from misery, want, and contempt. Public virtues and political qualities, therefore, should be incessantly cherished in our children.[84]

This religious zeal was critical in inspiring a deep willingness to sacrifice and do without in pursuit of the greater goal of liberty. Adams wrote movingly, "Our lives are not in our own power. It is our duty to submit. The ways of Heaven are dark and intricate, its designs are often inscrutable, but are always wise and just and good . . . But all these must go, and my life too, before I can surrender the right of my country to a free Constitution. I dare not consent to it. I should be the most miserable of mortals ever after, whatever honors or emoluments might surround me."[85]

In another letter to his wife and children, he continued the same theme, this time applied to money and the luxuries of life: "Frugality, my dear, frugality, economy, parsimony, must be our refuge. I hope the ladies are every day diminishing their ornaments, and the gentlemen, too. Let us eat potatoes and drink water, let us wear canvas, and undressed sheepskins, rather than submit to the unrighteous and ignominious domination that is prepared for us."[86]

Many of the Founders knew that their cause would likely impoverish them, but the end in sight was more than worth the means. For them, an independent republic was about more than grievances with Great Britain, but about improving the human condition itself for their posterity, regardless of cost: "But a Republic, although it will infallibly beggar me and my children, will produce strength, hardiness, activity, courage, fortitude, and enterprise, the manly, noble, and sublime qualities in human nature in abundance," Adams wrote.[87]

So, despite deprivation and constant danger, an enduring belief in the justice of their cause and the sovereignty of a just God compelled the colonists to continue the fight, praying, as Abigail Adams did, that God would sustain them: "Almighty God, cover the heads of our countrymen and be a shield to our dear friends! How many have fallen, we know not. The constant roar of the cannon is so distressing that we cannot eat, drink, or sleep. May we be supported and sustained in the dreadful conflict."[88]

The New York legislature, largely under the pen of John Jay (later a coauthor of the *Federalist Papers*), adjured their constituents to "rely upon the good Providence of Almighty God for success, in full confidence that without His blessing all our efforts will evidently fail." In the same address, the Revolution was defended as a righteous reaction to "the calls of liberty, virtue, and religion," required by "the dictates of reason and of nature," as well as part of "the great duties they [the colonists] owe to their God, themselves, and their posterity."[89]

The gathering of the Continental Congress and the lead-up to the Declaration of Independence were equally tinged with great religious overtones. Adams described how the liturgical reading of the Thirty-fifth Psalm (for September 7, 1775) by a Philadelphia clergyman profoundly moved the delegates: "You must remember this was the next morning after we heard the horrible rumor of the cannonade of Boston. I never saw a greater effect upon an audience. It seemed as if Heaven had ordained that Psalm to be read on that morning . . . It has had an excellent effect upon everybody here. I must beg you to read that Psalm."[90]

A palpable and growing sense of destiny preceded the signing of the Declaration of Independence. For the first time in history, a people were volitionally and deliberatively deciding upon their own course, staking their cause on divine claims for the sake of earthly good. Accident and force may have been the lot of the majority of humanity, but in 1776, the people of the American colonies, despite the dangers and the trials that no doubt awaited them, chose a different course, which would have a profound and incalculable effect on human history. Adams, once again in biblically inspired language, wrote of the crescendo to the great event in the following way: "Is it not a saying of Moses, 'Who am I, that I should go in and out before this great people?' [Exodus 3:11]. When I consider the great events which are passed, and those greater which are rapidly advancing, and that I may have been instrumental of touching some spring, and turning some small wheels which have had and have such effects, I feel an awe upon my mind which is not easily described."[91]

Even ministers, far from being remote and distant from this great event, were intimately involved in it: "The clergy here [Philadelphia] of every denomination . . . thunder and lighten every Sabbath. They pray for Boston and Massachusetts. They thank God most explicitly and fervently for our remarkable success. They pray for the American Army. They seem to feel as if they were among you."[92]

It comes as no surprise, then, that upon the actual signing of the Declaration, Samuel Adams described what it meant in undeniably religious terms: "We have this day restored the Sovereign to whom all men alone ought to be obedient. He reigns in Heaven, and with a propitious eye beholds his subjects assuming that freedom of thought, and dignity of self-direction which He bestowed on them. From the rising to the setting sun, may His kingdom come."[93]

Throughout the war, many of the Founders saw countless examples of the providence of God. Battles that should have been lost were miraculously won. In the case of the British siege of New York, a mysterious fog had rolled in, allowing the Continental army to escape undetected. George Washington himself, while often at the head of his men, was never once injured in eight years of war. "The singular interpositions of Providence in our feeble condition," he noted, "were such as could scarcely escape the attention of the most unobserving," a reality he acknowledge to be "little short of a standing miracle."[94] When the peace treaty with Great Britain was concluded, Washington ordered "the Chaplains with the several brigades [to] render thanks to Almighty God for all his mercies, particularly for his overruling the wrath of man to his own glory, and causing the rage of war to cease amongst the nations." But this wasn't just because America had finally achieved victory: this was a standard order from Washington, who placed the highest priority on divine service for the men under his command.

In proclaiming an end to hostilities in 1783, Washington compared the opportunity made available to the American people as the greatest source of hope for mankind since the arrival of Christ. This proclamation, he said, "must afford the most rational and sincere satisfaction to every benevolent mind, as it puts a period to a long and doubtful contest, stops the effusion of human blood, opens the prospect to a more splendid scene, and like another morning star [referring to Jesus; see 2 Peter 1:19; Revelation 2:28; 22:16], promises the approach of a brighter day than hath hitherto illuminated the Western Hemisphere."

In his farewell benediction as commander in chief to the governors of each state, he encouraged them to "demean [them]selves with that charity, humility, and pacific temper of mind which were the character-istics of the Divine Author of our religion [Jesus], and without which a humble imitation of whose example in these things we can never hope to be a happy nation."[95]

Years later, Adams, as an older man, reflected on the Revolution in these terms:

> The general principles on which the fathers achieved independence, were the only principles in which that beautiful assembly of young men could unite . . . And what were these general principles? I answer, the general principles of Christianity, in which all those sects were united, and the general principles of English and American liberty, in which all those young men united, and which had united all par-ties in America, in majorities sufficient to assert and maintain her independence.[96]

RELIGION, MORALITY, AND A FREE SOCIETY

The unmistakable influence of religion on the American Revolution became a constituent element in the Founders' vision of a free society. In his farewell address, Washington went so far as to assert that opposing religion was incompatible with genuine American patriotism:

> Of all the dispositions and habits which lead to political prosperity, religion and morality are indispensable supports. In vain would that man claim the tribute of patriotism, who should labor to subvert these great pillars of human happiness, these firmest props of the duties of men and citizens . . . A volume could not trace all their connections with private and public felicity . . . And let us with caution indulge the supposition that morality can be maintained without religion. Whatever may be conceded to the influence of refined education on minds of peculiar structure, reason and experi-ence both forbid us to expect that national morality can prevail in exclusion of religious principle.

Drawing from the book of Proverbs, he went on to exhort the American people to always exhibit a moral and virtuous example to the world: "It will be worthy of a free, enlightened, and, at no distant period, a great nation, to give to mankind the magnanimous and too novel example of a people always guided by an exalted justice and benevolence . . . Can it be, that Providence has not connected the permanent felicity of a nation with its virtue?"[97] [Proverbs 14:34]

The Founders believed freedom was possible only for a moral and religious people. If one was not capable of governing oneself in a moral fashion, it was logically inconceivable that one could then choose governors who would exhibit any such control. As Jefferson noted to Adams, "If ever the morals of a people could be made the basis of their own government it is our case."[98] This notion was not simply a hangover from the Founders' Puritanical heritage, but a fact made obvious by the study of human history, for, as Montesquieu observed, "in a popular state there must be an additional spring, which is virtue. What I say is confirmed by the entire body of history and is quite in conformity with the nature of things."[99]

For the Founders, there was no separation between private morality and public morality: if a man was not moral in his private dealings, there was no reason to believe he would be moral in his dealings on behalf of the public. Samuel Adams explained:

> There are virtues and vices which are properly called political. "Corruption, dishonesty to one's country, luxury, and extravagance tend to the ruin of States." The opposite virtues tend to their establishment. But "there is a connection between vices as well as virtues and one opens the door for the entrance of another." Therefore "Wise and able politicians will guard against other vices," and be attentive to promote every virtue. He who is void of virtuous attachments in private life is, or very soon will be void of all regard for his country. There is seldom an instance of a man guilty of betraying his country who had not before lost the feeling of moral obligations in his private connections.[100]

The Founders recognized that the imperfect state of human nature necessitated the coercive control of government, while at the same time liberty necessitated as little control as possible. This is why morality was so important to them, for some sort of control on human behavior needed to exist somewhere, and the less there was within (personal morality), the more there needed to be without (government). As Tocqueville noted of the American conception of liberty, "[it] cannot be established without morality."[101] In expressing a sentiment that is ubiquitous throughout the Founders' writings, Samuel Adams avowed "We may look up to armies for our defense, but virtue is our best security. It is not possible that any State should long remain free, where virtue is not supremely honored." He continued:

> [T]he utmost pains [ought to] be taken by the public to have the principles of virtue early inculcated on the minds even of children, and the moral sense kept alive, and that the wise institutions of our ancestors for these great purposes be encouraged by the government. For no people will tamely surrender their liberties, nor can any be easily subdued, when knowledge is diffused and virtue is preserved. On the contrary, when people are universally ignorant, and debauched in their manners [morals], they will sink under their own weight without the aid of foreign invaders.[102]

What was his solution to this problem? Education of the next generation, centered in and founded on morality derived from religious principles:

> Let divines and philosophers, statesmen and patriots, unite their endeavors to renovate the age, by impressing the minds of men with the importance of educating their little boys and girls; of inculcating in the minds of youth the fear and love of the Deity and universal philanthropy, and, in subordination to these great principles, the love of their country; of instructing them in the art of self-government, without which they never can act a wise part in the government of societies, great or small; in short, of leading them in the study and

practice of the exalted virtues of the Christian system, which will happily tend to subdue the turbulent passions of men, and introduce that golden age, beautifully described in figurative language [the Millennium].[103]

It is essential to realize that for the Founders, morality was not something that ultimately sprang from the force of government coercion but was an inner quality of the people and the society itself. This was not a principle they applied only to America, but one whose truth had been confirmed by history, even in their own day. "It is wholly owing to the constitution of the people, and not to the constitution of the government." Paine had observed in Common Sense, "that the crown is not as oppressive in England as in Turkey." Nearly a century later, Tocqueville made the exact same observation: "My aim has been to demonstrate, using America as my model, that laws and, above all, customs [morals/cultural habits] enabled a democratic nation to remain free."[104]

"Punishments will cast out of society a citizen who, having lost his mores [morals], violates the laws," Montesquieu had noted. "But if everyone loses his mores, will punishments reestablish them? Punishments will indeed check many consequences of the general evil, but they will not correct this evil."[105] It was for this reason that liberty, for the Founders, was not simply doing whatever one wished to do, but doing that which was one's duty, "that temperate portion of liberty which does not infer either anarchy or licentiousness [immorality],"[106] as Jefferson put it. They recognized that the most absolute enemy of freedom is freedom that is absolute, and that to frame liberty outside of moral boundaries was to cause it to lose any sense of meaning or usefulness. Liberty was not simply a question of an individual's sphere of action but was a *moral proposition*. For the Founders, the best way for a people to retain as much liberty as possible, and thus negate the need for government coercion, was to behave, as much as possible, as if they did not need a government to control them. The solution was self-government, a self-imposed system of morality, for which religion provided the greatest overall encouragement. Hence Montesquieu's observation that "When a people have good mores [morals], laws become simple."[107] Being able to do whatever one desires at any given point in time flows from an amoral conception of liberty not shared by our Founders, for whom it was moral precisely because it included a set of obligations and duties to one's fellow man for which the individual assumed responsibility without being forced to do so by the state.

As previously discussed, religion was essential to their conception of liberty because it formed a *coherent* framework of moral values, rather than subjecting them to the *ad hoc* whims of personal desires. Religion was thus meant to provide a shared set of moral beliefs that would help bind society together, rather than have every individual deciding entirely for himself what was moral based only on his own desires. Such narcissism and misplaced individualism was never a part of the Founders' conception of liberty, which is why they saw religion as the essential "social glue" of a shared public morality. Tocqueville described it this way:

> No social grouping can prosper without shared beliefs or rather there are none which exist in that way, for, without commonly accepted ideas, there is no common action, and without common action, men exist separately but not as a social unit. For society to exist and all the more so, for such a society to prosper, all the citizens' minds must be united and held together by a few principal ideas. This could not possibly exist unless each of them occasionally draws his opinions from the same source and agrees to accept a certain number of ready-formed beliefs.[108]

This role of religion as a "social glue" was not contrary to religious diversity either, but was rather supported by it. "Christian sects are infinitely varied and endlessly modified," Tocqueville noted. At the same time, "Christianity itself is an established and unassailable fact which no one undertakes either to attack or defend. The Americans, having accepted without question the main teachings of the Christian religion, are obliged to accept in the same way a great number of moral truths which derive from it and hold it together." And yet, within the context of great diversity, "they all agree about the duties that men owe to each other. Each sect adores God in its own particular way, but all sects preach the same morality in the name of God."[109] He described this phenomenon further:

> So Christianity reigns without obstacles by universal consent, so, as I have already said elsewhere, the result is that in the world of morality everything is definite and settled, although the world of politics is given over to debate and human experiment. Thus, the mind of man never beholds an unlimited field in front of itself. However bold he might be, a man senses from time to time that he must halt before insurmountable barriers and test his most audacious ideas against certain formalities which either hold him back or stop him altogether.[110]

Tocqueville then went on to describe how and why the Founders saw religion, within the context of the separation of church and state, as so important to a free society: "Thus, while the law allows the American people to do everything, religion prevents their imagining everything, and forbids them from daring to do everything."[111] In other words, religion taught citizens to steward their appetites, their desires, and their general affairs in a moral fashion, and moral people need neither police nor any form of force to compel them to do those things which should and have already formed a habit of doing. Franklin summarized these habits thus: "To God we owe fear and love; to our neighbors justice and charity; to ourselves prudence and sobriety."[112] It was this tendency of religion to point men outside of themselves and toward their duties (rather than their desires) that made it such a powerful force on the side of morality and thus on the side of liberty. John Adams described it this way:

> It [a republic] is productive of everything which is great and excellent among men. But its principles are as easily destroyed as human nature is corrupted. Such a government is only to be supported by pure religion or austere morals. Public virtue cannot exist in a nation without private, and public virtue is the only foundation of Republics. There

must be a positive passion for the public good, the public interest, honor, power, and glory, established in the minds of the people, or there can be no republican government, nor any real liberty. And this public passion must be superior to all private passions. Men must be ready, they must pride themselves, and be happy to sacrifice their private pleasures, passions, and interests, nay their private friendships and dearest connections when they stand in competition with the rights of society.[113]

In a letter to her son, John Quincy, who was en route to France with his father during the Revolutionary War, Abigail Adams wrote about the supreme importance of the "religious sentiments" that undergirded morality, which for her was far more important than mere knowledge:

Great learning and superior abilities, should you ever possess them, will be of little value and small estimation, unless virtue, honor, truth, and integrity are added to them. Adhere to those religious sentiments and principles which were early instilled into your mind, and remember that you are accountable to your Maker for all your words and actions . . . dear as you are to me, I would much rather you should have found your grave in the ocean you have crossed, or that any untimely death should crop you in your infant years, than see you an immoral, profligate, or graceless child . . . [I hope this war that Britain is waging] may stamp upon your mind this certain truth, that the welfare and prosperity of all countries, communities, and, I may add, individuals, depend upon their morals.[114]

Filling a person's head with mere knowledge did not make him free, but knowledge tempered and controlled by a moral sense based on accountability to his Creator could. For the Founders, this was the only type of education that made sense in a free society. John Quincy's father offered a similar exhortation: "But, my dear boy, above all things, preserve your innocence, and a pure conscience. Your morals are of more importance, both to yourself and the world, than all languages and all sciences. The least stain upon your character will do more harm to your happiness than all accomplishments will do it good."[115]

John Quincy would go on to become, among other things, an ambassador, secretary of state, congressman, and even president of the United States.

Religion, as made clear during the Revolution, was also essential to understanding the rights of man, and thus the role of government and the duties of citizenship. If rights were divinely endowed to men who were created equal in the sight of God, then it was incumbent not just on individuals, but on government itself to respect and protect them, and on the individual to positively utilize them in a virtuous fashion for the benefit of his fellow man. Since government had not bestowed rights, it could not rightfully take them away, nor would a virtuous citizenry allow it to do so. It was for this reason Washington believed our government "can never be in danger of degenerating into a monarchy, an oligarchy, an aristocracy, or any other despotic or oppressive form, so long as there shall remain any virtue in the body of the people."[116]

As Tocqueville noted, "Christianity, which has made all men equal before God, will not flinch to see all citizens equal before the law,"[117] yet another reason the Founders saw religion, specifically the Judeo-Christian kind, as necessary for human liberty. As profound as their thoughts had been, the philosophers of ancient Greece and Rome had never come close to such an idea:

> The deepest and most eclectic minds in Rome and Greece were unable to reach this most general and yet most simple of generalizations, that men were alike and that all of them had equal rights to freedom at birth. They expended great effort to prove that slavery was a feature of nature which would always exist . . . Their minds, although broadened in several directions, were limited in this one, and Jesus Christ had to come into the world to reveal that all members of the human race were similar and equal by nature.[118]

Tocqueville argued that in America, political philosophy was preceded by a Judeo-Christian ethic. It was precisely because of that ethic that human liberty was seen as inviolable, because it was a gift of God, not an allowance from man. Religion could therefore never impose its doctrines or practices upon anyone through force (i.e., government), but was instead meant to inform the conscience, and thus direct all of society, both people and government, toward the moral ends required by liberty. From this sprang what today would be a most startling conclusion:

> Religion, which never interferes directly in the government of Americans, should therefore be regarded as the first of their political institutions, for, if it does not give them the taste for liberty, it enables them to take unusual advantage of it. . . . I do not know whether all Americans put faith in their religion, for who can read into men's hearts? But I am sure that they believe it necessary for the maintenance of republican institutions. This is not an opinion peculiar to any class of citizens or to one party, but to a whole nation. It is found in every rank of society.[119]

This brings us to the infamous and deeply misunderstood phrase "separation of church and state."

SEPARATION OF CHURCH AND STATE: WHAT DOES IT MEAN?

The phrase "separation of church and state" comes from a letter written by President Thomas Jefferson in 1802 to the Danbury Baptists, and has since become perhaps the most misunderstood phrase in American history. For the Founders, separation of church and state was a separation between two institutions. Unfortunately, "separation of church and state" has become, in our own day, the separation of religion from society, a twist the Founders did not, and probably could not, anticipate arising from the idea of institutionally separating the church and the government.

So what does the famous letter from Thomas Jefferson actually say?

> Believing with you that religion is a matter which lies solely between man and his God, that he owes account to none other for his faith or his worship, that the legitimate powers of government reach actions

only, and not opinions, I contemplate with sovereign reverence that act of the whole American people which declared that their legislature should "make no law respecting an establishment of religion, or prohibiting the free exercise thereof," thus building a wall of separation between Church and State.

Jefferson was speaking very particularly about a person's religion, his style of worship, and his opinions regarding each. Nowhere is there any indication whatsoever that he envisioned religion being separated from public life. This is confirmed by the next few lines of the letter, which are rarely quoted:

> I shall see with sincere satisfaction the progress of those sentiments which tend to restore to man all his natural rights, *convinced he has no natural right in opposition to his social duties.* [emphasis added]

Among the natural rights of mankind of which Jefferson was speaking was the right to freedom of religion. But what is most interesting is what he said about those natural rights: they are compatible with man's *social duties*, meaning his actions within society. In other words, Jefferson himself, in the letter made famous for the supposed opposite reason, affirms religion's role in society, while maintaining that, institutionally, church and state are and ought to remain separate. This comes as no surprise, for the Founders constantly reiterated the importance of morality to a free society and what they saw as religion's role in maintaining that morality, while also asserting that the church and the government ought to remain separate institutions.

The Founders were influenced and inspired by many aspects of their Puritan past, and as we have seen, the Puritans were extraordinarily religious people. John Adams pointed out to Jefferson how the separation of church and state, or at least the beginnings of it, was a fundamental principle of these highly religious people: "I agree with you that 'it is difficult to say at what moment the Revolution began.'[120] In my opinion, it began as early as the first plantation of the country. Independence of Church and Parliament was a fixed principle of our predecessors in 1620 [when the Pilgrims arrived at Plymouth Rock], as it was of Samuel Adams and Christopher Gadsden[121] in 1776. And independence of Church and Parliament was always kept in view in this part of the country, and, I believe, in most others."[122]

So it was in fact the very religious settlers of what would become the United States who inspired the idea of separation between church and state (even while not living up to it perfectly or uniformly in the early colonial governments themselves). In other words, separation of church and state was a *religious* idea, based on the teachings of Christ in which He differentiated between the church and Caesar, and in reaction against the "divine right of kings" that was asserted by tyrannical monarchs throughout Europe.

But this is where some historical context is quite fitting. In Europe, the combination of church and state was meant to achieve two things: religious uniformity and obedience to the government. The established church benefited from the spiritual monopoly enforced by the state, and the state benefited from the moral monopoly provided by the established church in preaching blind obedience to the government, no matter how tyrannical the monarch became. Forced religious uniformity and blind obedience were precisely what the Founders sought to avoid. Jefferson confirmed this historical view of the Founders when he asked, "Why subject it [religion] to coercion?" His answer? "To produce uniformity," something he did not believe was inherently desirable. He continued: "What has been the effect of coercion? To make one half the world fools, and the other half hypocrites." The fools were those who naively believed they could, through force, make someone agree with them. The hypocrites were those who "agreed" as a result of that force, but privately continued to believe and sometimes practice otherwise, as had happened for centuries among European Jews who were forced to convert to Catholicism but continued to adhere to and practice their Jewish beliefs in private. And because of his general skepticism of government competence and effectiveness, particularly over religion, Jefferson rather dryly and sarcastically noted that "was the government to prescribe to us our medicine and diet, our bodies would be in such keeping as our souls are now."[123]

James Madison called religion "the duty which we owe to our Creator,"[124] and as such, it could not be infringed upon by earthly force. It was a natural right of mankind to worship God as his conscience dictated, therefore, a particular set of doctrines could not be forced on him by earthly powers. Separation of church and state was therefore about preventing people from being forced to "agree" to a particular set of *religious doctrines*—which pertain to the mind and one's private religious practices—by imposing them legally. As an example, it was meant to prevent the government forcing a Catholic to attend a Protestant church, or a Protestant being forced to partake in a Catholic Mass. It had nothing to do with the law being informed by certain *moral values*. In this sense, separation of church and state was also thought of in terms of applying the law not to opinions of the mind (theology), but to actions of the body (morality). Jefferson addressed this issue quite directly:

> The error seems not sufficiently eradicated that the operations *of the mind*, as well as the *acts of the body*, are subject to the coercion of the laws. But our rulers can have authority over such natural rights only as we have submitted to them. The rights of conscience we never submitted, we could not submit. We are answerable for them to our God. The legitimate powers of government extend to such acts only as are injurious to others. But it does me no injury for my neighbor to say there are twenty gods, or no god. It neither picks my pocket nor breaks my leg.[125]

Jefferson further noted, "It is error alone which needs the support of government. Truth can stand by itself." Thus, the famous line about his neighbor's beliefs neither picking his pocket nor breaking his leg was not a statement about the moral content of laws (as is oftentimes asserted), but was specifically related to compelling belief in a set of religious doctrines.

Upon the threshold of becoming president, Jefferson spoke

caustically of those who still desired the government to establish a national church and enforce religious uniformity on the country. Incidentally, he said nothing about not being able to legislate morality, nothing about the influence of religious people on politics, or any of the sorts of things that have become commonplace today in the name of "separation of church and state." Rather, in avowing his opposition to such schemes, he defended his position with this famous but rarely quoted-in-context line: "For I have sworn upon the altar of God eternal hostility against every form of tyranny over the mind of man."[126] In other words, in defending what he believed to be the essence of the separation of church and state, Jefferson appealed to God, because for him, as well as the other Founders, this separation had nothing to do with religion's influence on societal morality and how that morality was incorporated into legislation. Rather, the crux of the matter was the idea that you could force people to believe a particular set of doctrines and force them to sit in a particular church on Sunday, and then preach that they should blindly obey the government regardless of its abuses (which had been done in Europe under the guise of the "divine right of kings"), all of which would make the people far easier to control and manipulate. The political power of the state would be used to prop up the physical power of the church, and the spiritual and moral power of the church over the consciences of the faithful would be used to reinforce their obedience to the government.

No one had ever objected to laws that enforced a particular moral code (since all laws are meant to enforce some version of morality). The "infernal confederacy" (Adams's name for the alliance between church and state) had *never* been about morality, but about which religious institutions, their associated doctrines, and the government with which they were allied, would be in power and hold sway over the people through force. The Founders did not want all Americans to be forced to conduct religious services in the same way, nor did they want their power of thought and their right to form their own opinions to be infringed upon by a national church that dictated to them the doctrines they would be required to "believe." And since a national church would be an offshoot of a national government, the Founders most of all did not want a tyrannical government to be able to use its clerical lapdogs to manipulate the people into blind obedience or forced adherence to doctrines they had not freely chosen to believe. Adams explained in his *Defense*:

> In the divine theory, upon which most of the governments of Europe still rest, it is not only treason, but impiety and blasphemy, to resist any government whatever. If the sovereignty of a nation is a divine right, there is an end of all the rights of mankind at once; and resistance to the sovereignty, wherever placed, is rebellion against God.[127]

It thus becomes clear why Jefferson called Christianity "reason and verity itself in the opinion of all but infidels," and therefore it was "protected under the wings of the common law from the dominion of other sects, but not erected into dominion over them."[128] These are the true foundations of the "separation of church and state." The "dominion" of which he spoke was doctrinal, not moral.

As much as they believed in the institutional separation of church and state, the Founders were adamantly opposed to the separation of religion and society. Countless times, and uniformly across their writings, they commended religion as being the single best expedient of morality, and separation of church and state as a means to *preserve* this crucial element of religion that made a free society possible while also preventing its corruption by politics. Jefferson himself affirmed this role of religion in society while also defending its institutional separation from government: "Religion is well supported; of various kinds, indeed, but all good enough, all sufficient to preserve peace and order, or if a sect arises whose tenets would subvert good morals, good sense has fair play, and reasons and laughs it out of doors without suffering the state to be troubled with it."[129]

Yet again, in a superb twist of irony, Jefferson praised the "free inquiry" made possible by the separation of church and state as the very same freedom that allowed Christianity to arise in the first place,

and the various ways in which it had been corrupted over the centuries to be purged: "Had not the Roman government permitted free
inquiry, Christianity could never have been introduced. Had not free
inquiry been indulged at the era of the Reformation the corruptions of
Christianity could not have been purged away. If it be restrained now,
the present corruptions will be protected and new ones encouraged."[130]

This brings up another important aspect of separation of church and
state: it was intended to help maintain the purity of both religion and
government, and allow society to unite around the core moral principles
of religion (which the Founders assumed to be Judeo-Christian values)
while avoiding divisive doctrinal issues. If no one sect could impose its
particular religious practices through governmental force, then one of
the single greatest historical dangers to the peace of society was taken off
the table, and instead religion could serve its function of encouraging
morality while avoiding sectarian conflict. As Madison put it, "We are
teaching the world the great truth that governments do better without
Kings and Nobles than with them. The merit will be doubled by the
other lesson that religion flourishes in greater purity without than with
the aid of government."[131] He went further in a letter to another friend:
"Rival sects, with equal rights, exercise mutual censorships in favor of
good morals . . . And no doubt exists that there is much more of religion
among us now than there ever was before the change . . . This proves . . .
that the law is not necessary to the support of religion."[132]

Thomas Paine, in his *Common Sense*, made a similar comment
about religious diversity, again not in secular, but in religious terms:
"For myself, I fully and conscientiously believe that it is the will of the
Almighty that there should be diversity of religious opinions among us.
It affords a larger field for our Christian kindness. . . . I look on the
various denominations among us to be like children of the same family,
differing only in what is called their Christian names."

Later in his life, Madison addressed those states that continued
to have established churches[133] and defended the idea of separation
of church and state, not by contending for a secular, humanistic view

of the world, but by appealing to Christian principles in the form of the famous dichotomy between God and Caesar articulated by Christ Himself in Matthew 22 and Mark 12. In addition, he again reinforced the idea that separation of church and state was about forcing particular religious opinions upon the mind, not "legislating morality": "Ye States of America which retain in your constitutions or codes any aberration from the *sacred principle* of religious liberty by giving to Caesar what belongs to God, or joining together what God has put asunder, hasten to revise and purify your systems and make the example of your country as pure and complete in what relates to the *freedom of the mind* and its allegiance to its maker, as in what belongs to the legitimate objects of political and civil institutions."[134]

This justification of the principle of separation of church and state on *religious* grounds was ubiquitous throughout the writings of the American Founders. It had nothing to do with antipathy for religion, Christianity, or religion's influence on society, but rather the *means* through which religion influenced society: would a particular denomination's doctrines be accepted because of rational inquiry or by the force of government requiring someone to believe something (a chimerical concept at best)? Our Founders chose the former. Nor did it have anything to do with religion's influence on morality, which the Founders constantly encouraged. As Washington said, "No man's sentiments are more opposed to *any* kind of restraint upon religious principles than mine are," and such was the opinion of the Founders as a whole.

It is thus no surprise that, when examining our Founders' actual words, a contemporary American "educated" on the faulty conceptions of separation of church and state that are rampant today would be quite shocked to find, not the separation of religion and society, but the synergy of religion and liberty, of spirituality and political freedom. Both were essential to the Founders' vision of a free society. Tocqueville brilliantly commented on this unique synergy accomplished by the Americans: "This [Anglo-American] civilization is the result (and this is something we must always bear in mind) of two quite distinct ingredients which anywhere else have often ended in war, but which Americans have succeeded somehow to meld together in wondrous harmony, namely the *spirit of religion* and the *spirit of liberty*. . . . Americans," he observed, "show in practice that they feel it necessary to instill morality into democracy by means of religion." He continued, "Liberty looks upon religion as its companion in its struggles and triumphs, as the cradle of its young life, as the divine source of its claims. It considered religion as the guardian of morality, morality as the guarantee of law and the security that freedom will last."[135]

Tocqueville further commented that "Americans so completely identity the spirit of Christianity with freedom in their minds that it is almost impossible to get them to conceive the one without the other." He even provided an anecdote of a judge who refused to hear the testimony of a witness in a trial who refused to affirm a belief in God, the idea being that such a man did not believe he was ultimately responsible to a higher power, but only to himself, and thus his testimony was unreliable. It was this synergy, Tocqueville argued, that made America unique: "America is still the country in the world where the Christian religion has retained the greatest real power over people's souls," he wrote, "and nothing shows better how useful and natural religion is to man since the country where it exerts the greatest sway is also the most enlightened and free."[136]

Indeed, it was this highly religious conception of liberty that Tocqueville argued was at the heart of the separation of church and state. "Religion looks upon civil liberty as a noble exercise for man's faculties and upon the world of politics as a field prepared by the Creator for the efforts of man's intelligence," he noted.[137] Everywhere he went, clergy and layperson, politician and merchant alike, all attributed the great influence of religion on morality, and society in general, to the separation of church and state, the exact same point made by the Founders. At the same time, Europe was witnessing the beginning of the end of a "Christian" order, and yet it was full of established national churches. Why were the Old and New Worlds so different in this regard? Tocqueville explained:

When a religion seeks to base its empire only upon the desire for immortality which torments every human heart equally, it can aspire to universality. But, when it happens to combine with a government, it has to adopt maxims which only apply to certain nations. Therefore, by allying itself to a political power, religion increases its authority over some but loses the hope of reigning over all . . . When it is mixed up with the bitter passions of this world, it is sometimes forced to defend allies who have joined it through self-interest and not through love. It has to repel as enemies men who, while fighting against those allies of religion, still love religion itself . . . In Europe, Christianity has allowed itself to be closely linked with the powers of this world. Today these powers are collapsing, and it is virtually buried beneath their ruins. It has become a living body tied to the dead. If the bonds holding it were cut, it would rise again.[138]

But in the United States, religion was altogether different—it was something believed and engaged in because of conviction, not legal obligation. Not only that, but from the beginning, the earliest settlers of the New World largely came out of religious conviction and a desire to establish a society more consonant with the Scriptures and their religious beliefs. The Exodus narrative of Israel escaping Egypt was deeply ingrained in the American psyche, for Israel had indeed fled into the wilderness to worship God first, and only then formed their body politic.

Benjamin Franklin described not only the lack of nonbelief in America, but the esteem in which sincere religion was held: "Serious religion under its various denominations is not only tolerated, but respected and practiced. Atheism is unknown there, infidelity rare and secret, so that persons may live to a great age in that country without having their piety shocked by meeting with either an atheist or an infidel."[139] Tocqueville observed the exact same phenomenon, noting that "a materialistic [atheistic] philosophy is virtually unknown to [Americans]."[140] So what did the practice of "serious religion" look like in everyday American life?

In the United States on the seventh day of the week, trade and industry seem suspended throughout the nation . . . On this day, places of business are deserted. Each citizen goes to church accompanied by his children and there he listens to strange speech apparently little suited to his ear. He is regaled with the countless evils caused by pride and covetousness. He hears of the need to control his desires, of the subtle pleasures of virtue alone, and the true happiness they bring. Having returned home, he does not hurry back to his business ledgers. He opens the Holy Scriptures and discovers the sublime or touching depictions of the greatness and goodness of the Creator, the infinite magnificence of God's handiwork, the lofty destiny reserved for man, his duties, and his claims to everlasting life . . . he suddenly bursts into an ideal world where all is great, pure, and eternal.[141]

Religion thus did exactly what many of the Founders believed it would and should do: it taught them that they were not the ultimate measure of all things, and they were accountable to a higher power, which served as a powerful regulator of their actions, both private and public. This was where religion's power was most effective, not in particular doctrines being forced down people's throats by law, but in the inculcation of morality and virtue, those great pillars that were necessary to the individual self-government required of citizens who desired to remain free. This was precisely why the Founders justified the separation of church and state on *religious*, not secular grounds. "It cannot, therefore, be said," Tocqueville concluded, "that religion exercises any influence on the laws and on the details of political opinions in the United States, but it does control behavior and strives to regulate the state by regulating the family."[142] But of course, in enunciating this principle, Tocqueville was merely describing what the Founders had already articulated and set into motion. John Adams described it this way:

The foundations of national morality must be laid in private families. In vain are schools, academies, and universities instituted if loose principles and licentious habits are impressed upon children in their earliest years. The mothers are the earliest and most important instructors of youth . . . The vices and examples of the parents cannot be concealed from the children. How is it possible that children can have any just sense of the sacred obligations of morality or religion if, from their earliest infancy, they learn that their mothers live in habitual infidelity to their fathers, and their fathers in as constant infidelity to their mothers?[143]

These "sacred obligations of morality or religion" were what kept families together through the institution of marriage, and were taught and exhibited to the next generation at home, first and foremost. In contrast to Europe, Tocqueville described how the love of order in the United States was a phenomenon that drew its strength not from top-down government enforcement, but the encouragement of religious virtue at home:

> America is certainly the country where the bonds of marriage are most respected and where the concept of conjugal bliss has its highest and truest expression. In Europe, almost all social disorder stems from disturbances at home and not far removed from the marriage bed. These men come to feel scorn for natural ties and legitimate pleasures. There they develop a liking for disorder, a restless spirit, and fluctuating desires . . . the American draws the love of order from his home which he then carries over into his affairs of state.[144]

In further describing Americans' high regard for marriage, he added, "They regard marriage as a contract which, though onerous, must nevertheless be strictly honored in all its clauses because these have all been known beforehand and people have enjoyed the complete freedom not to bind themselves to anything at all."[145]

As Adams had observed, "The influence of example is very great and almost universal, especially that of parents over their children."[146] When families were held together by the sacred institution of marriage, and when parents taught their children moral values supported by the concept of ultimate accountability to God, society prospered; for where self-government reigned, new laws and government agencies were not needed. The family was to be the schoolhouse in which the morality of the nation would be taught and honed for the benefit of all. This is why Tocqueville affirmed "it is just when it [religion] is not speaking of freedom that it most effectively instructs Americans how to be free."[147]

But of course, many today argue that the Founders were hostile toward religion (and Christianity in particular), that they were secularists and humanists, and that at best, they were deists. While the evidence already presented shows such claims to be false, more exists and shows even more clearly how inaccurate they are.

Clearly the Founders did not believe in separation of church and state in the same way it is commonly taught to us today. One need go no further than our first four presidents, all of whom were Founders, who used religious language in their inaugural addresses and throughout their times in office. In 1789 Washington noted in his first inaugural address:

> It would be peculiarly improper to omit in this first official act my fervent supplications to that Almighty Being who rules over the Universe, who presides in the councils of nations, and whose providential aids can supply every human defect, that his benediction may consecrate to the liberties and happiness of the People of the United States, a Government instituted by themselves for these essential purposes . . . In tendering this homage to the Great Author of every public and private good, I assure myself that it expresses your sentiments not less than my own, nor those of my fellow citizens at large less than either: No People can be bound to acknowledge and adore the invisible hand which conducts the affairs of men more than the People of the United States. Every step by which they have advanced to the character of an independent nation seems to have been distinguished by some token of providential agency . . . [which] cannot be compared with the means by which most governments have been established, without some return of pious gratitude along with a humble anticipation of the future blessings which the past seem to presage . . . I shall take my present leave, but not without resorting once more to the benign

Parent of the human race, in humble supplication . . . for the security
of their Union, and the advancement of their happiness.

President Washington also issued the first Thanksgiving
Proclamation, in which he declared, "It is the duty of all nations to
acknowledge the providence of Almighty God, to obey His will, to
be grateful for His benefits, and humbly implore His protection and
favor." He also prayed that God would "pardon our national and other
transgressions," and for the spread of "the knowledge and practice of
true religion and virtue."[148] His farewell address is also full of language
that is both religious and speaks frequently of the importance of religion
to a free society.

Similarly, John Adams, in his 1797 inaugural speech, declared
his "veneration for the religion of a people who profess and call themselves Christians, and a fixed resolution to consider a decent respect for
Christianity among the best recommendations for the public service." He
concluded with a benedictory prayer for the nation: "And may that Being
who is supreme over all, the Patron of Order, the Fountain of Justice,
and the Protector in all ages of the world of virtuous liberty, continue
His blessing upon this nation and its Government and give it all possible
success and duration consistent with the ends of His providence."

As his predecessor had done, and as virtually all of his successors
would do as well, President Adams famously noted the connection
between religion, morality, and the maintenance of the free society his
fellow Americans so cherished: "Our Constitution was made only for a
religious and moral people. It is wholly inadequate for the government
of any other." This was not a merely token phrase of his, for a year earlier, in the midst of growing tensions with France and the possibility of
war, he had called for a day of national fasting and prayer:

I have therefore thought fit to recommend, and I do hereby recommend, that Wednesday, the 9th day of May next, be observed
throughout the United States as a day of solemn humiliation, fasting,
and prayer . . . that all religious congregations do, with the deepest

humility, acknowledge before God the manifold sins and transgressions with which we are justly chargeable as individuals and as a nation; beseeching him at the same time, of his infinite grace, through the Redeemer of the world, freely to remit all our offenses, and to incline us, by his Holy Spirit, to that sincere repentance and reformation which may afford us reason to hope for his inestimable favor and heavenly benediction . . . that the principles of genuine piety and sound morality may influence the minds and govern the lives of every description of our citizens, and that the blessings of peace, freedom, and pure religion, may be speedily extended to all the nations of the earth.[149]

"I adore with you the genius and principles of that religion [Christianity] which teaches us, as much as possible, to live peaceably with all men [Romans 12:18]"[150] President Adams wrote to some correspondents. "Here, and throughout our country, may simple manners, pure morals, and true religion, flourish forever!" he declared elsewhere.[151]

Thomas Jefferson also used similarly religious language as president. In his first inaugural address, in March 1801, he celebrated the fact that America was "enlightened by a benign religion" (Christianity) and that the American people were correct in "acknowledging and adoring an overruling Providence which by all its dispensations proves that it delights in the happiness of man here and his greater happiness hereafter. . . . This," he noted, was part of "the sum of good government." He concluded with a prayer: "And may that Infinite Power which rules the destinies of the universe lead our councils to what is best, and give them a favorable issue for your peace and prosperity."

In his second inaugural four years later, he continued to affirm the Exodus narrative as the foundation upon which the American story was built, while praying for divine guidance for both himself and the nation he led: "I shall need, too, the favor of that Being in whose hands we are, who led our forefathers, as Israel of old, from their native land, and planted them in a country flowing with all the necessaries and comforts of life; who has covered our infancy with his providence, and our riper years with his wisdom and power; and to whose goodness I ask you to join with me in supplications."

James Madison, in his first inaugural address (1809), likewise encouraged his fellow citizens to remain confident "in the guardianship and guidance of that Almighty Being whose power regulates the destiny of nations, whose blessings have been so conspicuously dispensed to this rising Republic, and to whom we are bound to address our devout gratitude for the past, as well as our fervent supplications and best hopes for the future." Like President Adams before him, he also called for a national day of fasting and prayer during what today we call the War of 1812:

I do therefore recommend . . . [a] day to be set apart for the devout purposes of rendering the Sovereign of the Universe and the Benefactor of Mankind the public homage due to His holy attributes; of acknowledging the transgressions which might justly provoke the manifestations of His divine displeasure; of seeking His merciful forgiveness and His assistance in the great duties of repentance and amendment, and especially of offering fervent supplications that in the present season of calamity and war He would take the American people under His peculiar care and protection; that He would guide their public councils, animate their patriotism, and bestow His blessing on their arms; that He would inspire all nations with a love of justice and of concord and with a reverence for the unerring precept of our holy religion [Christianity] to do to others as they would require that others should do to them [Matthew 7:12; Luke 6:31]; and, finally, that, turning the hearts of our enemies from the violence and injustice which sway their councils against us, He would hasten a restoration of the blessings of peace.[152]

Words like these, all from the mouths of men who either wrote or exerted a great deal of influence on the Constitution, are simply not compatible with the modern notions of separation of church and state and the tendency to declare any public religious displays or utterances "unconstitutional." Such a thing could not have been farther from the

Founders' vision. At the Constitutional Convention, Benjamin Franklin called for prayer by the delegates, noting, as had Washington, Adams, Jefferson, and Madison, that the peculiar way in which the American people had been guided by divine providence made acknowledgment of the Creator not just beneficial, but obligatory:

> How has it happened, sir, that we have hitherto once thought of humbly applying to the Father of Lights to illuminate our understandings? In the beginning of the contest with Britain, when we were sensible of danger, we had daily prayers in this room for the Divine protection. Our prayers, sir, were heard—and they were graciously answered. And have we now forgotten that powerful friend, or do we imagine we no longer need its assistance? I have lived, sir, a long time, and the longer I live, the more convincing proofs I see of this truth, *that* GOD *governs in the affairs of men.* And if a sparrow cannot fall to the ground without his notice [Matthew 10:31; Luke 12:7], is it probable that an empire can rise without his aid? We have been assured, sir, in the sacred writings, that "except the Lord build the house, they labor in vain that build it" [Psalm 127:1]. I firmly believe this; and I also believe that without his concurring aid, we shall succeed in this political building no better than the builders of Babel [Genesis 11:1-9]; we shall be divided by our little, partial, local interests, our projects will be founded, and we ourselves shall become a reproach and a byword [Deuteronomy 28:37; Jeremiah 24:9; Ezekiel 22:4; Joel 2:17] down to future ages.[153]

Adams, around the time the Constitution was approved by the Convention, put Christianity at the very heart of the American Revolution in his apologia for the American forms of government: "The experiment is made, and has completely succeeded; it can no longer be called in question, whether authority in magistrates and obedience of citizens can be grounded on reason, morality, and the Christian religion without the monkery [*sic*] of priests, or the knavery of politicians."[154]

By this did he mean to attest that we are a "Christian nation" in any official sense? No. Rather, he affirmed that the ideas upon which our nation was founded, its revolution secured, and its principles defended were based on Judeo-Christian assumptions and beliefs, whose liberation from the rotted institutional structures of the "infernal confederacy" of church and state in Europe allowed for their resurrection in the hearts and minds of the individual citizens of a rising American society intent on being free.

In his retirement, Adams asked, "Religion, morality, Union, Constitution. Who even among the atheists, the despisers and abhorrers of the Constitution . . . would dare publicly to attack such topics?"[155] Jefferson frequently spoke of that "Infinite Power" and Madison of "that Almighty Being." Many contemporary Americans may ask how the men who devised our Constitution and incorporated within it the idea of separation of church and state could have said such things. The answer is quite simple: either they misunderstood what they intended, or we do.

THE FOUNDERS, GOD, AND CHRISTIANITY

It is a common belief today that the Founders were deists. A point of historical context is necessary here—while today *deist* means one who believes in a god who created the universe and then left it alone, a *deist* in the eighteenth century was someone who believed in God without any particular or specific doctrinal commitments included. This could theoretically include a god who created the universe and then let it be, but not a single Founder believed in such a god. The charge is most frequently made against Thomas Jefferson and Benjamin Franklin. But as seen in both this chapter and others, the writings of both evince no such convictions. Would Franklin have called for prayer at the Constitutional Convention if he had believed God was not involved in the affairs of man? "I say there can be no reason to imagine he would make so glorious a Universe merely to abandon it,"[156] he declared, an impossible statement for a supposed deist. Would Jefferson have included prayers or expressions of thanks to God in his public addresses and private letters if he had believed He was completely detached from His creation? The same goes for all of the Founders—despite modern notions to the contrary, not a single one was a deist who believed the Creator had birthed the universe only to leave it alone.

But were all of the Founders Christians? This is a more complex question that could be a book in and of itself, and one which is addressed not just in this chapter, but throughout this entire book. A a brief survey is nonetheless appropriate here.

As we have already seen, the Revolutionary War was replete with religious and often stridently Judeo-Christian rhetoric and arguments put forth in its favor. George Washington himself made many of them. In speaking with a Delaware Indian tribe during the war, he encouraged them to adopt Christianity, exhorting them "You do well to wish to learn our arts and ways of life, and above all, the religion of Jesus Christ. These will make you a greater and happier people than you are."[157] Additionally, biblical allusions and metaphors are ubiquitous throughout his public addresses, speeches, and private letters, many of which have already been quoted. There are strong indications, both from his own writings and the testimony of others, that Washington was indeed a Christian.

John Adams was a bit more nuanced and definitely more philosophical than Washington in his approach. Without a doubt he always considered himself a Christian, even though he did not believe in the Trinity, placing him by default in the category of an unorthodox Christian (with *orthodox* for our purposes being defined by the Nicene Creed, which affirms the Trinity). "The human understanding is a revelation from its maker, which can never be disputed or doubted . . . No prophecies, no miracles are necessary to prove this celestial communication. This revelation has made it certain that two and one make three, and that one is not three nor can three be one," he once argued.[158] And while he considered Christianity itself a divinely revealed religion, he harbored grave doubts as to the divinity of Jesus, registering his consternation with his much more orthodox son: "An incarnate God!!! An eternal, self-existent, omnipotent omnipresent omniscient Author of this Stupendous Universe, Suffering on a Cross!!! My soul starts with horror at the idea, and it has stupefied the Christian world. It has been the source of almost all the corruptions of Christianity."[159]

Even so, Adams continued to believe in what he saw as the essential truths and divine origins of Christianity, as he declared to his friend Benjamin Rush:

> The Christian religion, as I understand it, is the brightness of the glory and the express portrait of the character of the eternal, self-existent, independent, benevolent, all powerful and all merciful creator, preserver, and father of the universe, the first good, first perfect, and first fair. It will last as long as the world. Neither savage nor civilized man, without a revelation, could ever have discovered or invented it. Ask me not, then, whether I am a Catholic or Protestant, Calvinist or Arminian. As far as they are Christians, I wish to be a fellow-disciple with them all.[160]

He frequently expressed a desire to know God's commands, "which," he said, "to the utmost of my power shall be implicitly and piously obeyed."[161] But it is safe to say that while Adams considered himself a Christian, he was by no means afraid of questioning and probing in such a way that would have been deemed unorthodox. His thoughts on Christianity, and religion in particular, were a fascinating mix of belief and doubt. He always expressed certainty in the moral require-ments of true Christianity, even while questioning particular doctrines, not always necessarily out of lack of belief, but more to satisfy the cravings of his inquisitive mind. Along with many other Founders, he felt that some Christians were too often engaged in abstract doctrinal disputes, when what they should have been doing was "observ[ing] the Commandments, and the Sermon on the Mount"[162] (Exodus 20 and Matthew 5–7), since action in the service of others, and the resulting diffusion of morality, was what he saw as religion's most essential role in any society, particularly a free one. He saw no reason to fight over such abstractions, for morality and good works were, for him, the greatest theology of them all. "My religion is founded on the love of God and my neighbor," he told a friend, "on the hope of pardon for my offences;

upon contrition; upon the duty as well as necessity of supporting with patience the inevitable evils of life; in the duty of doing no wrong, but all the good I can, to the creation, of which I am but an infinitesimal part. Are you a dissenter from this religion? I believe, too, in a future state of rewards and punishments."[163]

In another letter, he described the same thing while emphasizing an appreciation for his life, difficult as it had been: "The love of God and his creation—delight, joy, triumph, exultation in my own existence—though but an atom . . . in the universe—are my religion."[164]

In his famous treatise in which he defended the forms of government adopted by the United States, he declared that "moral and Christian, and political virtue, cannot be too much beloved, practiced, or rewarded."[165] He frequently made religious allusions in his letters to both his wife, Abigail, and his children, noting, for example, to his daughter that "our Savior taught the immorality of revenge, and the moral duty of forgiving injuries, and even the duty of loving enemies."[166]

Additionally, he spoke highly of the Bible throughout his life. As a young man he imagined what a nation would be like if it adopted the Bible's moral precepts:

> Suppose a nation in some distant region should take the Bible for their only law-book, and every member should regulate his conduct by the precepts there exhibited! Every member would be obliged, in conscience, to temperance and frugality and industry; to justice and kindness and charity towards his fellow men; and to piety, love, and reverence, towards Almighty God. In this commonwealth, no man would impair his health by gluttony, drunkenness, or lust; no man would sacrifice his most precious time to cards or any other trifling and mean amusement; no man would steal, or lie, or in any way defraud his neighbor, but would live in peace and good will with all men; no man would blaspheme his Maker or profane his worship; but a rational and manly, a sincere and unaffected piety and devotion would reign in all hearts. What a Utopia; what a Paradise would this region be![167]

As an older man in retirement, his conclusion seems to have not just been maintained, but enhanced, as he declared, "The Bible contains the most profound philosophy, the most perfect morality, and the most refined policy that ever was conceived upon earth. It is the most Republican Book in the world, and therefore I will still revere it. The curses against fornication and adultery, and the prohibition of every wanton glance or libidinous ogle at a woman I believe to be the only system that ever did or ever will preserve a Republic in the world."[168]

Writing to Jefferson, he declared that "the Bible is the best book in the world. It contains more of my little philosophy than all the libraries I have seen; and such parts of it as I cannot reconcile to my little philosophy, I postpone for future investigation."[169] Elsewhere, he lamented that the world did not follow Christ's precepts: "We must come to the principles of Jesus. But when will all men and all nations do as they would be done by? Forgive all injuries and love their enemies as themselves?"[170] He continued to espouse his lifelong nonsectarian belief in the importance of Judeo-Christian religion: "I have attended public worship in all countries and with all sects and believe them all much better than no religion, though I have not thought myself obliged to believe all I heard. Religion I hold to be essential to morals."[171]

Despite all of this, hatred for religion is sometimes imputed to Adams, based primarily on this oft-quoted statement: "Twenty times, in the course of my late reading, have I been on the point of breaking out, 'this would be the best of all possible worlds, if there was no religion in it!!!'" Unfortunately, those who cite only this line are forgetting the very next one: "But in this exclamation, I should have been as fanatical as Bryant or Cleverly [skeptics]. Without religion, this world would be something not fit to be mentioned in polite company—I mean hell."[172] In other words, the quote most often cited to "prove" Adams's hostility to religion actually shows the exact opposite if the very next sentence is included. Such is the tragic misuse of many of the Founders' writings.

If Adams cannot be easily put into a box, then Jefferson is even more difficult. Like Adams, Jefferson considered himself a Christian, though certainly not what other Christians would consider an orthodox one. His opinions were "very different from that anti-Christian system imputed to me by those who know nothing of my opinions" (something many today should take note of), and while he considered himself opposed "to the corruptions of Christianity," he was not opposed "to the genuine precepts of Jesus himself." He explained: "I am a Christian, in the only sense he [Jesus] wished anyone to be: sincerely attached to his doctrines, in preference to all others, ascribing to himself every *human* excellence, and believing he never claimed any other."[173]

Jefferson considered himself an adherent of what he called "primitive Christianity, in all the simplicity in which it came from the lips of Jesus,"[174] and he deemed the Sermon on the Mount to be "the central point of union in religion, and the stamp of genuine Christianity (since it gives us all the precepts of our duties to one another)."[175] Like Adams, he believed that a great deal of theological jargon, which he attributed to abstract Platonic philosophy, had been added on to the plain words of Jesus by both the apostles and later theological commentators. Among the theological "add-ons" he despised the most were the Trinity and the general doctrines of Calvinism. The Trinity he referred to as "the metaphysical abstractions of Athanasius," and Calvinism as "the maniac ravings of Calvin," both of which were "tinctured plentifully with the foggy dreams of Plato," which had "so loaded it [Christianity] with absurdities and incomprehensibilities, as to drive into infidelity men who had not time, patience, or opportunity to strip it of its meretricious trappings, and to see it in all its native simplicity and purity."[176] He had harsh words for those teachers who engaged in "sophisticating and perverting the simple doctrines he [Jesus] taught by engrafting on them the mysticisms of a Grecian sophist [Plato], frittering them into subtleties, and obscuring them with jargon until they caused good men to reject the whole in disgust, and to view Jesus himself as an imposter."[177] This is why Jefferson was insistent that it was he who was a true Christian, while many supposed Christians were followers not of Jesus, but of Athanasius and Calvin:

The doctrines of Jesus are simple, and tend all to the happiness of man. 1). That there is one only God, and he all perfect. 2). That there is a future state of rewards and punishments. 3). That to love God with all thy heart and thy neighbor as thyself is the sum of religion . . . But compare with these the demoralizing dogmas of Calvin. 1). That there are three Gods. 2). That good works, or the love of our neighbor, are nothing. 3). That faith is everything, and the more incomprehensible the proposition, the more merit in its faith. 4). That reason in religion is of unlawful use. 5). That God, from the beginning, elected certain individuals to be saved, and certain others to be damned, and that no crimes of the former can damn them, no virtues of the latter save. Now, which of these is the true and charitable Christian? He who believes and acts on the simple doctrines of Jesus? Or the impious dogmatists, as Athanasius and Calvin?[178]

"Had it [Christianity] never been sophisticated by the subtleties of commentators, nor paraphrased into meanings totally foreign to its character," he argued, "it would at this day have been the religion of the whole civilized world."[179] Elsewhere he explained:

The truth is that the greatest enemies to the doctrines of Jesus are those calling themselves the expositors of them, who have perverted them for the structure of a system of fancy absolutely incomprehensible, and without any foundation in his genuine words. And the day will come when the mystical generation of Jesus by the Supreme Being as his father in the womb of a virgin will be classed with the fable of the generation of Minerva in the brain of Jupiter. But we may hope that the dawn of reason and freedom of thought in these United States will do away [with] all this artificial scaffolding and restore to us the primitive and genuine doctrines of this the most venerated reformer of human errors.[180]

Jefferson also spoke frankly of his desire that belief in the Trinity, and other supposed supernatural and mystical elements of Christianity, would eventually die off in the United States: "I rejoice that in this blessed country of free inquiry and belief, which has surrendered its creed and conscience to neither kings nor priests, the genuine doctrine of one only God is reviving, and I trust that there is not a young man now living in the United States who will not die a Unitarian."[181]

He further expressed his hope that Unitarianism would "effect a quiet euthanasia of the heresies of bigotry and fanaticism which have so long triumphed over human reason, and so generally and deeply afflicted mankind."[182]

Speaking of the moral teachings of Jesus, Jefferson opined: "A more beautiful or precious morsel of ethics I have never seen. It is a document in proof that *I* am a *real Christian*, that is to say, a disciple of the doctrines of Jesus, very different from the Platonists who call *me* infidel and *themselves* Christians and preachers of the Gospel, while they draw all their characteristic dogmas from what its author never said nor saw."[183]

"The sum of all religion," he said, "as expressed by its best preacher [Jesus], [was] 'fear god and love thy neighbor' [and] contains no mystery, needs no explanation."[184] He described Jesus' teachings as "the most perfect and sublime that has ever been taught man" because "they went far beyond both [Jews and philosophers] in inculcating universal philanthropy not only to kindred and friends, to neighbors and countrymen, but to all mankind, gathering all into one family, under the bonds of love, charity, peace, common wants and common aids. A development of this head will evince the peculiar superiority of the system of Jesus over all others."[185] Jefferson also believed that Jesus' teachings were superior because they not only spoke of actions, but the heart and thoughts behind actions, "the fountain head" as he called it. Jesus taught that there was a future state of reward or punishment for deeds done in this life, an essential feature of all good religion and morality according to Jefferson: "The precepts of philosophy and of the Hebrew code laid hold of actions only. He pushed his scrutinies into the heart of man, erected his tribunal in the region of his thoughts, and purified the waters at the fountain head. He taught, emphatically, the doctrines of a future state . . . and wielded it with efficacy as an important incentive, supplementary to the other motives to moral conduct."[186]

At the end of the day, the details of Jefferson's religious opinions, like Adams's, seemed to be in flux, not because he was an atheistic skeptic or nonreligious, but because of his insatiable intellectual curiosity and his bedrock principle that religion which doesn't ultimately lead to moral conduct is worthless religion: "Say nothing of my religion. It is known to my God and myself alone. Its evidence before the world is to be sought in my life; if that has been honest and dutiful to society, the religion which has regulated it cannot be a bad one."[187]

Benjamin Franklin also spoke highly of Christianity while making clear that he did not always agree with some of the doctrines of particular denominations (though he rarely specified which ones). He encouraged his daughter, "Be a good girl, and don't forget your Catechise. Go constantly to meeting—or church . . . and live like a Christian."[188] Because he was not part of a particular denomination, some doubted whether he was a Christian or even if he believed in God. Franklin was quick to correct them:

> I am so far from thinking that God is not to be worshipped, that I have composed and wrote a whole book of devotions for my own use; and I imagine there are few if any in the world so weak as to imagine that the little good we can do here can merit so vast a reward hereafter. There are some things in your New England doctrine and worship, which I do not agree with; but I do not therefore condemn them, or desire to shake your belief or practice of them.[189]

The young Franklin summed up his religious beliefs in nearly the exact same way he did as an old man many years later:

> That there is one God, Father of the Universe. That he is infinitely good, powerful, and wise. That he is omnipresent. That he ought to be worshipped by adoration, prayer, and thanksgiving both in public and private. That he loves such of his creatures as love and do good to others: and will reward them either in this world or hereafter. That men's minds do not die with their bodies, but are made more happy

or miserable after this life according to their actions. That virtuous men ought to league together to strengthen the interest of virtue in the world: and so strengthen themselves in virtue. That knowledge and learning is to be cultivated and ignorance dissipated. That none but the virtuous are wise. That man's perfection is in virtue.[190]

In his *Autobiography*, he not only affirmed his belief in a nondeistic God, but in the essential connection between religion and morality, as well as his distaste for divisive religion:

I never was without some religious principles. I never doubted, for instance, the existence of the Deity, that he made the world and governed it by his Providence, that the most acceptable service of God was the doing good to man, that our souls are immortal, and that all crime will be punished and virtue rewarded either here or hereafter. These I esteemed the essentials of every religion, and being to be found in all the religions we had in our country, I respect them all, though with different degrees of respect as I found them more or less mixed with other articles which without any tendency to inspire, promote, or confirm morality, served principally to divide us and make unfriendly to one another.[191]

He once lamented, "How many observe Christ's birthday! How few His precepts! O tis easier to keep holidays than commandments!"[192] Like Adams and Jefferson, Franklin had no use for religion that only argued about doctrines and carried out rituals but didn't produce some good in the world, which he believed was the essential point of Christ's message:

The faith you mention has doubtless its use in the world. I do not desire to see it diminished, nor would I endeavor to lessen it in any man. But I wish it were more productive of good works than I have generally seen it: I mean real good works, works of kindness, charity, mercy, and public spirit; not holiday keeping, sermon reading or hearing, performing church ceremonies, or making long prayers filled with flatteries and compliments despised even by wise men, and much less capable of pleasing the Deity. The worship of God is a duty, the hearing and reading of sermons may be useful; but if men rest in hearing and praying, as too many do, it is as if a tree should value itself on being watered and putting forth leaves, though it never produced any fruit.[193]

Franklin believed that Jesus had more regard "for the heretical but charitable Samaritan" than for "the uncharitable though orthodox priest and sanctified Levite" (see Luke 10:25–37), and "thought much less of these outward appearances and professions than many of his modern disciples. He preferred the doers of the Word to the mere hearers"[194] (see James 1:22). In response to some of his family members who were concerned about the state of his soul, Franklin responded not by appealing to secular arguments, but like many of the other Founders, to the Bible, which he called "that excellent book."[195] "I think vital religion has always suffered when orthodoxy is more regarded than virtue; and the Scriptures assure me that at the last day we shall not be examined for what we thought, but what we did; and our recommendation will not be that we said Lord! Lord! but that we did good to our fellow-creatures. See Matthew 25."[196]

Rather than feeling any sense of disgust for Christianity, Franklin was in fact very much appreciative of Christianity and its influence in society. His writings throughout his life were, like the rest of the Founders', full of biblical allusions, appeals to the example of Christ, and citations of the Bible in support of morality and virtue. For example, in the 1730s he wrote an article in the local newspaper encouraging people to visit the sick during a plague in Philadelphia:

The great Author of our Faith, whose life should be the constant object of our imitation, as far as it is not inimitable, always showed the greatest compassion and regard for the sick . . . This branch of Christian charity seems essential to the true spirit of Christianity, and it should be extended to all in general, whether deserving or undeserving, as far as our power reaches . . . [we] have opportunity enough of exercising that humane and Christian virtue which teaches a tender regard for the afflicted.[197]

At the end of his life, when asked by the president of Yale what his beliefs about Jesus and Christianity in general were, Franklin summed them up this way:

> As to Jesus of Nazareth . . . I think the system of morals and his religion, as he left them to us, the best the world ever saw or is likely to see. But I apprehend it has received various corrupting changes, and I have, with most of the present dissenters in England, some doubts as to his divinity . . . I see no harm, however, in its being believed, if that belief has the good consequence, as probably it has, of making his doctrines more respected and better observed . . . All sects here, and we have a great variety, have experienced my goodwill in assisting them with subscriptions for building their new places of worship. And, as I have never opposed any of their doctrines, I hope to go out of the world in peace with them all.[198]

In other words, Franklin, like several of the most prominent Founders, could not easily be put into a box—he was both an enthusiastic admirer of Jesus and a devout supporter of religion, and Christianity in general (with money and time, not just words). At the same time, he was not particularly concerned about what he saw as abstract Christian doctrines that had little effect on the practice of virtue in society, and about which he harbored doubts as to their accurate transmission through the ages.

CONCLUSION

"Such are the opinions of Americans," Tocqueville noted of their religious beliefs and the way they had been seamlessly incorporated into their society. "But," he observed sarcastically, "their error is obvious, because every day some learned [European] commentator proves to me that everything in America is fine except this religious spirit which I admire."[199] According to these commentators, American society had too much faith. Take it away, replace it with their atheistic and materialistic philosophy, and it would be perfect. "The only reply I can give to that," Tocqueville responded, "is that those who talk like that have not been to America and have no more seen a religious nation than a free one."[200]

He summed up the case for religion's role in a free society in a way that would have made the Founders proud:

> When these men attack religious beliefs, they are following their emo-tions not their interests. Tyranny may be able to do without faith, but freedom cannot. Religion is much more vital in the republic which they advocate than in the monarchy which they are attacking and in democratic republics most of all. How could society avoid destruction if, when political ties are relaxed, moral ties are not tightened? And what can be done with a nation in control of itself if it is not subject to God? . . . They would say that religious zeal had to burn itself out as freedom and education increased. How vexing that the facts are in conflict with this theory. There are certain European populations whose unbelief is matched only by their brutishness and ignorance, whereas in America you see one of the most free and enlightened nations in the world fulfilling all their public religious duties with enthusiasm.[201]

Among the Founders, atheism was nonexistent, deism was rare (if it existed at all), Christianity was venerated and at the very least respected, and the separation of church and state was the product of religious, not secular or humanistic, convictions. While properly dividing power between church and state, they enthusiastically encouraged the inter-action between religion and society, and constantly asserted its role in maintaining the morality they believed was essential to maintaining the liberty of our nation.

Tocqueville was quite right when he drew the following conclu-sion about the American system begun with the religious Puritans and secured by the Founders: "In America, religion leads to wisdom; the observance of divine laws guides men to freedom."[202]

6

KNOWLEDGE AND EDUCATION: LIBERTY'S SENTINELS, PART II

Virtue was the first sentinel of liberty that the Founders insisted was necessary to its survival. The second was knowledge, and the primary means by which they sought to secure it was education. But what constituted "knowledge," and what did they see as its purpose? Essentially, it was not just information, but the wisdom and discernment to understand and act upon that information so as to make wise decisions that would benefit both the individual and society. The Founders constantly expressed a desire that the next generation would be properly educated so they would not only learn the lessons of the past, but also properly apply those lessons to create a better future for themselves and their posterity. The point was not to idolize the past, but to apply its lessons to the future.

The Founders were themselves extremely well-read individuals, and as students of both human nature and history, they could discern with uncommon wisdom the needs, imperatives, and possibilities of the free society they played such a pivotal role in creating. All of this was largely due to their education, not all of which was formal. John Adams once remarked to Jefferson, "I congratulate you upon your 'canine appetite' for reading. I have been equally voracious for several years, and it has kept me alive."[1] Jefferson likewise commented, "Reading is my delight."[2] Both accumulated thousands of volumes in their personal libraries. Other Founders were nearly if not equally well-read, and just as they knew it was only *because* of such knowledge that they were able to construct the American system, so it would be only *by* such knowledge that the system could be maintained. Otherwise, we would be a nation of sheep, unable to determine our best course either as individuals or as a society, and thus constantly susceptible to our own passions as well as the manipulation of those who would seek to dominate us for their own ends. No wonder Washington called education "one of the surest means of enlightening and giving just ways of thinking to our citizens."[3]

The Founders' views on education fall into two overarching categories: *how* it should be done, and *what* it was for. Another way of putting it would be the purpose of education on the micro level and on the macro level—what was its intended purpose in the life of individuals, and what were the intended benefits to society? The Founders believed it was essential to the health of both. In this regard, it must also be noted that for them, "education" was by no means confined to sitting in a classroom and reading books, though this was obviously very important. Some of them, such as Washington and Franklin had no formal education and yet were highly educated men, because "education" for them was *wisdom*, the inculcating of habits of thinking and acting that were conducive to both private and public good. In this regard, the classroom was important, but not all-encompassing. Wisdom required knowledge and virtue, which could be had outside of a classroom as well. Indeed, the Founders emphasized over and over that the purpose of a classroom was to inspire students with a thirst for knowledge and virtue that they would then apply throughout their lives as productive citizens. This for them was the sum of true education and the source of true knowledge.

Let us look first at the education of the individual.

EDUCATION AND THE INDIVIDUAL

No one was capable of being a good citizen who was not educated, or so the Founders believed. This emphasis on education was no doubt yet another holdover from their Puritan ancestors. Samuel Adams wrote:

Our ancestors in the most early times laid an excellent foundation for the security of liberty by setting up in a few years after their arrival a public seminary of learning; and by their laws they obliged every town consisting of a certain number of families to keep and maintain a grammar school . . . Would not the leading gentlemen do eminent service to the public, by impressing upon the minds of the people the necessity and importance of encouraging that system of education, which in my opinion is so well calculated to diffuse among the individuals of the community the principles of morality so essentially necessary to the preservation of public liberty.[4]

His comments get to a critical part of how the Founders viewed education: it *necessarily* included moral education as well. For them, education of the mind was nothing without a like education of the heart. John Adams articulated it this way: "Knowledge is applied to bad purposes as well as to good ones. Knaves and hypocrites can acquire it, as well as honest, candid, and sincere men. It is employed as an engine and a vehicle to propagate error and falsehood, treason and vice, as well as truth, honor, virtue, and patriotism. . . . There is no necessary connection between knowledge and virtue. Simple intelligence has no association with morality."[5]

"There is no connection in the mind between science and [the] passion[s] by which the former can extinguish or diminish the latter,"[6] he had written during his days as vice president. Knowledge was simply not capable, on its own, of enabling a man to exercise his reason in order to control his passions. He would write to his cousin, Samuel Adams, that he had "the honor most perfectly to harmonize in your sentiments of the humanity and wisdom of promoting education in knowledge, virtue, and benevolence [referring to universal education] . . . Human appetites, passions, prejudices, and self-love will never be conquered by benevolence and knowledge alone, introduced by human means."[7] Thus, they saw morality *and* knowledge as essential to education, for both were absolutely essential to the exercise of liberty. John Locke was perhaps the most precise (and concise) in describing this philosophy of education that was to be adopted by the Founders: "The *freedom* then of man and the liberty of acting according to his own will, is grounded on his having reason, which is able to instruct him in that law he is to govern himself by, and make him know how far he is left to the freedom of his own will."[8]

Benjamin Rush, a signer of the Declaration of Independence and the founder of American medicine, wrote, "[Education is for] laying the foundations for nurseries of wise and good men . . . the only foundation for a useful education in a republic is to be laid in Religion. Without this there can be no virtue, and without virtue there can be no liberty, and liberty is the object and life of all republican governments."[9] At the time, most educational institutions were religious in nature, or founded by religious organizations or people. So when the Founders spoke of spreading knowledge, this nearly always meant that there would be some sort of religious and moral instruction involved. We will continue to see this emphasis on and integration of religious moral instruction into education as we proceed.

The Founders also recognized that for any of this education to be effective, it had to begin at home, for the examples put before children would invariably exert a powerful influence on their future conduct. Government may, by criminal sanction, be able to control behavior, but only to a very limited and ultimately superficial degree. They therefore agreed with Montesquieu's observation that "the means for preventing crimes are penalties, [and] the means for changing manners are examples."[10] In this case, "manners" referred to one's morality and habits.

John Adams wrote a particularly impressive set of letters both to his wife and children on this subject. As the conflict with Britain was heating up very quickly, he wrote to his wife, Abigail, of his concern for their children's education:

> The education of our children is never out of my mind. Train them in virtue, habituate them to industry, activity, and spirit. Make them consider every vice as shameful and unmanly; fire them with ambition to be useful—make them disdain to be destitute of any useful or

ornamental knowledge or accomplishment. Fix their ambition upon great and solid objects, and their contempt upon little, frivolous, and useless ones . . . Every decency, grace, and honesty should be inculcated upon them.[11]

Morality and virtue, and particularly the desire "to excel," were essential to their ideas of education: "Let frugality and industry be our virtues, if they are not of any others. And above all cares of this life, let our ardent anxiety be to mold the minds and manners [morals] of our children. Let us teach them not only to do virtuously but to excel. To excel, they must be taught to be steady, active, and industrious."[12]

But it was not just virtue for virtue's sake for Adams. Rather, he saw virtue, the control of one's passions, and the exercise of one's mind as the means to achieve greatness: "Take care that they don't go astray. Cultivate their minds, inspire their little hearts, raise their wishes. Fix their attention upon great and glorious objects, root out every little thing, weed out every meanness, make them great and manly. Teach them to scorn injustice, ingratitude, cowardice, and falsehood. Let them revere nothing but religion, morality, and liberty."[13]

And how did he define greatness? Writing to one of his children, he repeated the constant refrain with which he intended to inculcate them: "greatness" was serving one's fellow man and being as helpful to him as possible:

If you have not yet so exalted sentiments of the public good as have others more advanced in life, you must endeavor to obtain them. They are the primary and most essential branch of general benevolence, and therefore the highest honor and happiness both of men and Christians, and the indispensable duty of both . . . Knowledge in the head and virtue in the heart, time devoted to study or business, instead of show and pleasure, are the way to be useful and consequently happy.[14]

Writing in the midst of the siege on Boston, it was the education of their children, of all things, to which he sought to bring Abigail's attention:

Human nature with all its infirmities and depravation is still capable of great things. It is capable of attaining to degrees of wisdom and of goodness, which, we have reason to believe, appear respectable in the estimation of superior intelligences. Education makes a greater difference between man and man than nature has made between man and brute. The virtues and powers to which men may be trained by early education and constant discipline are truly sublime and astonishing . . . It should be your care, therefore, and mine, to elevate the minds of our children and exalt their courage, to accelerate and animate their industry and activity, to excite in them a habitual contempt of meanness, abhorrence of injustice and inhumanity, and an ambition to excel in every capacity, faulty, and virtue. If we suffer their minds to grovel and creep in infancy, they will grovel all their lives.[15]

Adams believed that this emphasis on education equally applied to himself, and thus he exercised his mind and his actions in its pursuit, for he too owed it to his fellow man and future generations to be useful. He eloquently articulated how he perceived his duties in this regard:

The science of government it is my duty to study more than all other sciences: the art of legislation and administration and negotiation ought to take place indeed to exclude in a manner all other arts. I must study politics and war, that my sons may have liberty to study mathematics and philosophy. My sons ought to study mathematics and philosophy, geography, natural history, naval architecture, navigation, commerce and agriculture, in order to give their children a right to study painting, poetry, music, architecture, statuary, tapestry, and porcelain.[16]

Education, in a holistic sense, was thus the means by which future generations could be enabled to create a better world and a more meaningful existence for their fellow citizens.

In light of this, the Founders believed that education, particularly of the young, was essential to the success of any society, but particularly a free one. Adams wrote that "liberty cannot be preserved without a general knowledge among the people, who have a right from the frame of their nature to knowledge, as their great Creator who does nothing in vain has given them understandings and a desire to know."[17] Benjamin Franklin seemed to agree:

> I think with you, that nothing is of more importance for the public weal, than to form and train up youth in wisdom and virtue. Wise and good men are, in my opinion, the strength of a state, much more so than riches or arms, which, under the management of ignorance and wickedness, often draw on destruction, instead of providing for the safety of the people. And though the culture bestowed on many should be successful only with a few, yet the influence of those few, and the service in their power may be very great. Even a single woman that was wise by her wisdom saved the city.[18]

The inculcation of virtue, Franklin believed, would also be more successful and enduring if it were done while people were still young:

> I think also that general virtue is more probably to be expected and obtained from the education of youth, than from the exhortation of adult persons; bad habits and vices of the mind being, like diseases of the body, more easily prevented than cured. I think, moreover, that talents for the education of youth are the gift of God; and that he on whom they are bestowed, whenever a way is opened for the use of them, is as strongly called as if he heard a voice from heaven; nothing more surely pointing out duty in a public service, than ability and opportunity of performing it.[19]

In a public pamphlet in which he put forth his own plan for educating the youth of his native Pennsylvania, Franklin wrote, "The good education of youth has been esteemed by wise men in all ages, as the surest foundation of the happiness both of private families and of commonwealths . . . whether in business, offices, marriages, or any other things for their advantage, preferably to all other persons whatsoever even of equal merit."[20] This pamphlet, which he titled *Proposals Relating to the Education of Youth in Pennsylvania*, is a treasure trove when it comes to describing the Founders' views on education (as many of them expressed very similar sentiments). He of course recommends that young people be educated in a variety of subjects, but the two he seemed most passionate about were history and morality (in which he included religion).

So why history? Because Franklin believed history contained lessons about all areas of human life and existence. "If history be made a constant part of their reading," he asked, "may not almost all kinds of useful knowledge be that way introduced to advantage, and with pleasure to the student?" He also believed history held perhaps the greatest lessons with regard to virtue and morality, and thus provided the greatest lessons to the young concerning its importance. He described a thorough education in morality as "descanting [lecturing/discussing] and making continual observations on the causes of the rise or fall of any man's character, fortune, power, etc. mentioned in history; advantages of temperance, order, frugality, industry, perseverance, etc." History provided such opportunities for observation in abundance, for "indeed, the general natural tendency of reading good history must be to fix in the minds of youth deep impressions of the beauty and usefulness of virtue of all kinds, public spirit, fortitude, etc."[21]

In connection with this idea, Franklin also believed history proved that religion was absolutely vital to the encouragement of such morality:

> History will also afford frequent opportunities of showing the necessity of a *public religion*, from its usefulness to the public, the advantage of a religious character among private persons, the mischiefs of superstition, etc. and the excellency of the CHRISTIAN RELIGION above all others, ancient or modern. History will also give occasion to expatiate on the advantages of civil orders and constitutions, how men and their properties are protected by joining in societies and establishing government; their industry encouraged and rewarded, arts invented, and life made more comfortable: the advantages of *liberty*, mischiefs of *licentiousness*, benefits arising from good laws and a due execution of justice, etc. Thus may the first principles of sound *politics* be fixed in the minds of youth.[22]

Franklin believed that by a thorough understanding of history, students could better understand what he called "true merit," which was the term he used to refer to the same thing which Adams meant by "greatness" and "benevolence," namely the service of one's fellow man, which Franklin deemed an inherently religious obligation:

> The idea of what is *true merit* should also be often presented to youth, explained and impressed on their minds, as consisting in an *inclination* joined with an *ability* to serve mankind, one's country, friends, and family; which *ability* is (with the Blessing of God) to be acquired or greatly increased by *true learning*, and should indeed be the great *aim* and *end* of all learning. [Franklin's note]: To have in view the *glory* and *service of God*, as some express themselves, is only the same thing in other words. For *doing good to men* is the *only service of God* in our power, and to *imitate his beneficence* is to *glorify him*.[23]

As an aside, let me briefly address this issue of religion and education, for the Founders constantly spoke of the two in the same sentence. For many today, the emphasis many of the Founders placed on integrating religion into education would be most surprising. They nonetheless saw it as essential. Many of the reasons for this were already covered in the previous chapter. However, in addition to those, there were others, including the belief that religion, Christianity in particular, informed people on how to be good citizens, for it taught that all men were equal and ought to be treated with kindness and benevolence. Benjamin Rush, a Founder who had a great impact on American education, explained:

> Such is my veneration for every religion that reveals the attributes of the Deity, or a future state of rewards and punishments, that I had rather see the opinions of Confucius or Mohammed inculcated upon our youth, than see them grow up wholly devoid of a system of religious principles. But the religion I mean to recommend in this place, is that of the New Testament . . . It is foreign to my purpose to hint at the arguments which establish the truth of the Christian revelation. My only business is to declare, that all its doctrines and

precepts are calculated to promote the happiness of society, and the safety and well-being of civil government. A Christian cannot fail of being a republican. The history of the creation of man, and of the relation of our species to each other by birth, which is recorded in the Old Testament, is the best refutation that can be given to the divine right of kings, and the strongest argument that can be used in favor of the original and natural equality of all mankind. A Christian, I say again, cannot fail of being a republican, for every precept of the Gospel inculcates those degrees of humility, self-denial, and brotherly kindness, which are directly opposed to the pride of monarchy and the pageantry of a court. A Christian cannot fail of being useful to the republic, for his religion teacheth him, that no man "liveth to himself." [Romans 14:7] And lastly, a Christian cannot fail of being wholly inoffensive, for his religion teacheth him, in all things to do to others what he would wish, in like circumstances, they should do to him.

He further noted that religion, liberty, and learning "mutually assist in correcting the abuses, and in improving the good effects of each other. From the combined and reciprocal influence of religion, liberty and learning upon the morals, manners and knowledge of individuals, of these, upon government, and of government, upon individuals, it is impossible to measure the degrees of happiness and perfection to which mankind may be raised."[24]

Tocqueville wrote of education in the United States: "It is in mandates relating to public education that, from the outset, the original character of American civilization is revealed in the clearest light . . . The reader will doubtless have noticed the preamble to these enactments: in America religion leads to wisdom; the observance of divine laws guides men to freedom."[25]

Going back to history, Thomas Jefferson, speaking of a law he had helped pass in Virginia, also stressed history and morality as fundamental to the formation of citizens who can properly govern themselves in a free society, particularly with regard to being the sentinels of their rights and liberty against tyranny:

The general objects of this law are to provide an education adapted to the years, to the capacity, and the condition of everyone, and directed to their freedom and happiness. . . . The first elements of morality too may be instilled into their minds, such as, when further developed as their judgments advance in strength, may teach them how to work out their own greatest happiness by showing them that it does not depend on the condition of life in which chance has placed them, but is always the result of a good conscience, good health, occupation, and freedom in all just pursuits. . . . But of all the views of this law none is more important, none more legitimate, than that of rendering the people the safe, as they are the ultimate, guardians of their own liberty. For this purpose the reading in the first stage, where they will receive their whole education, is proposed . . . to be chiefly historical. History, by apprising them of the past, will enable them to judge of the future. It will avail them of the experience of other times and other nations. It will qualify them as judges of the actions and designs of men. It will enable them to know ambition under every disguise it may assume, and knowing it, to defeat its views.[26]

Benjamin Rush likewise emphasized the importance of teaching history to the next generation: "The science of government, whether it relates to constitutions or laws, can only be advanced by a careful selection of facts, and these are to be found chiefly in history. Above all, let our youth be instructed in the history of the ancient republics, and the progress of liberty and tyranny in the different states of Europe."[27]

But while the Founders believed the history of the entire world was important and instructive, they also knew there was a particular benefit to studying the history of America. Noah Webster, later described as the "Schoolmaster of America," explained it this way: "Every child in America should be acquainted with his own country. He should read books that furnish him with ideas that will be useful to him in life and practice. As soon as he opens his lips, he should rehearse the history of his own country; he should lisp the praise of liberty, and of those illustrious heroes and statesmen, who have wrought a revolution in her favor."

He went on to describe the subject matter essential to studying American history: "A selection of essays, respecting the settlement and geography of America; the history of the late revolution and of the most remarkable characters and events that distinguished it, and a compendium of the principles of the federal and provincial governments, should be the principal school book in the United States."[28]

John Adams considered it the duty of the next generation "to make themselves masters of what their predecessors have been able to comprehend and accomplish but imperfectly."[29] Writing to his own children, he called American history "the most interesting chapter in the history of the world."[30]

Along with American history, it was essential to understand American government, for, particularly at that point, the two were inseparable. For this purpose, Madison had his own set of recommendations on what should be the "textbooks" for such education, and incidentally, they were all original source documents from the men who had framed the government of both the United States and Virginia, his home state: "On the distinctive principles of the government of our own state and of that of the United States, the best guides are to be found in—1. The Declaration of Independence . . . 2. The book known by the title of the Federalist . . . 3. The Resolutions of the General Assembly of Virginia in 1799 on the subject of the Alien and Sedition laws . . . 4. The Inaugural Speech and Farewell Address of President Washington, as conveying political lessons of peculiar value."[31]

Toward the end of his life, he continued to affirm the importance of teaching American history and the principles of American government, from *original sources*: "If the abundance and authenticity of the materials which still exist in the private as well as public repositories among us should descend to hands capable of doing justice to them, then American history may be expected to contain more truth and lessons certainly not less valuable than those of any country or age."[32]

The Founders also saw the integration of morality and knowledge as necessary to the formation of a whole person. Only by the integration of these two things could one ever be wise. An education whose goal was ultimately wisdom was best suited to create individuals secure enough in their own opinions and beliefs to withstand the trials of life, manage their own affairs, and contribute to society. In this regard, the Founders left us numerous letters full of advice to young people, many of which contain truly thought-provoking and inspirational thoughts. For example, Franklin wrote to his younger sister on resisting the urges of pursuing popularity, using Jesus as an example:

> Take one thing with another, and the world is a pretty good sort of a world. And tis our duty to make the best of it and be thankful. One's true happiness depends more upon one's own judgment of one's self, on a consciousness of rectitude in action and intention, and in the approbation of those few who judge impartially than upon the applause of the unthinking, undiscerning multitude who are apt to cry Hosanna today, and tomorrow crucify him.[33]

He also had fitting counsel for a young man just beginning his career: "Be studious in your profession, and you will be learned. Be industrious and frugal and you will be rich. Be sober and temperate and you will be healthy. Be in general virtuous and you will be happy. At least you will by such conduct stand the best chance for such consequences."[34]

Washington had sound advice for his nephew when it came to being charitable to others: "Let your *heart* feel for the affliction and distresses of everyone, and let your *hand* give in proportion to your purse, remembering always the estimation of the widow's mite [Mark 12:41–44; Luke 21:1-4]. But that it is not everyone who asketh that deserveth charity, all however are worthy of the enquiry, or the deserving may suffer."[35]

Adams counseled his son on the importance of maintaining his moral integrity: "My dear boy, above all things, preserve your innocence, and a pure conscience. Your morals are of more importance, both to yourself and the world, than all languages and all sciences. The least stain upon your character will do more harm to your happiness than all accomplishments will do it good."[36] Later in life, Adams would write one of his grandsons about the fundamental importance of a virtuous life, a "worthy" life, as he called it. Such a life was to be prized above power, and more zealously pursued than riches:

> Have you considered the meaning of that word "worthy"? Weigh it well. I had rather you should be worthy Sergeants, than unworthy though conquering Generals; worthy Midshipmen than unworthy though conquering Admirals; worthy Attorneys or Solicitors than unworthy Sergeants or Judges or Lords Chief Justices; worthy Ministers of a petty parish, than unworthy Popes, Cardinals, Archbishops, or Bishops; worthy country shopkeepers in America than unworthy Medici, Hopes, or Wheelwrights. I had rather you should be the worthy possessors of one thousand pounds, honestly acquired by your own labor and industry, than of ten millions by banks and funding Tricks. I had rather you should be worthy shoemakers than Secretaries of State or Treasury acquired by libels in newspapers. I had rather you should be worthy makers of brooms and baskets than unworthy Presidents of the United States procured by intrigue, faction, slander, and corruption.[37]

But perhaps some of the greatest material comes from Jefferson, particularly from letters he wrote to his teenage nephew, Peter Carr.[38] His first exhortation was to virtue: "Encourage all your virtuous dispositions, and exercise them whenever an opportunity arises, being assured that they will gain strength by exercise, as a limb of the body does, and that exercise will make them habitual. From the practice of the purest virtue, you may be assured you will derive the most sublime comforts in every moment of life, and in the moment of death."

Continuing, Jefferson encouraged Peter to place moral virtue at the center of his life:

> When your mind shall be well improved with science, nothing will be necessary to place you in the highest points of view but to pursue the interests of your country, the interests of your friends, and your own interests also, with the purest integrity, the most chaste honor. The

defect of these virtues can never be made up by all the other acquire-
ments of body and mind. Make these then your first object. Give up
money, give up fame, give up science, give up the earth itself and all
it contains, rather than do an immoral act. And never suppose that
in any possible situation, or under any circumstances, it is best for
you to do a dishonorable thing, however slightly so it may appear to
you. Whenever you are to do a thing, though it can never be known
but to yourself, ask yourself how you would act were all the world
looking at you, and act accordingly.

Even during the difficulties of life, Jefferson insisted, his nephew
should never sacrifice his integrity:

If ever you find yourself environed with difficulties and perplexing
circumstances out of which you are at a loss how to extricate yourself,
do what is right, and be assured that that will extricate you the best
out of the worst situations. Though you cannot see, when you take
one step what will be the next, yet follow truth, justice, and plain
dealing, and never fear their leading you out of the labyrinth in the
easiest manner possible. The knot which you thought a Gordian one
will untie itself before you. Nothing is so mistaken as the supposition that a person is to extricate himself from a difficulty by intrigue,
by chicanery, by dissimulation, by trimming, by an untruth, by an
injustice. This increases the difficulties tenfold, and those who pursue
these methods get themselves so involved at length that they can turn
no way but their infamy becomes more exposed.

Part of that virtue, he explained in a later letter to Peter, was charity
for your fellow man: "Above all things lose no occasion of exercising
your dispositions to be grateful, to be generous, to be charitable, to be
humane, to be true, just, firm, orderly, courageous, etc. Consider every
act of this kind as an exercise which will strengthen your moral faculties,
and increase your worth."

"An honest heart being the first blessing," Jefferson had said, "a
knowing head is the second." He therefore recommended that Peter

read widely and "to begin to pursue a regular course in it," as well as soberly consider the subject of religion:

> Your reason is now mature enough to examine this object. In the first place divest yourself of all bias in favor of novelty and singularity of opinion. Indulge them in any other subject rather than that of religion. It is too important, and the consequences of error may be too serious. On the other hand, shake off all the fears and servile prejudices under which weak minds are servilely crouched. Fix reason firmly in her seat, and call to her tribunal every fact, every opinion. Question with boldness even the existence of a god, because, if there be one, he must more approve of the homage of reason than that of blindfolded fear.

And where was young Peter to begin in his inquiry into religious subjects?

> You will naturally examine first the religion of your own country [Christianity]. Read the Bible then, as you would read Livy or Tacitus . . . But those facts in the bible which contradict the laws of nature must be examined with more care, and under a variety of faces. Here you must recur to the pretentions of the writer to inspiration from god. Examine upon what evidence his pretensions are founded, and whether that evidence is so strong as that its falsehood would be more improbable than a change in the laws of nature in the case he relates . . . Examine therefore candidly what evidence there is of having been inspired. The pretension is entitled to your inquiry, because millions believe it . . . You will next read the New Testament. It is the history of a personage called Jesus. Keep in your eye the opposite pretensions, 1. Of those who say he was begotten by god, born of a virgin, suspended and reversed the laws of nature at will, and ascended bodily into heaven, and 2. Of those who say he was a man of illegitimate birth of a benevolent heart, enthusiastic mind, who set out without pretensions to divinity, ended in believing them, and was punished capitally for sedition by being gibbeted [hung] according to the Roman law which punished the first commission of that offence by

whipping, and the second by exile or death *in furcâ* [in fork] . . . but keep reason firmly on the watch in reading them all.

Concerning the enterprise of evaluating religion in general, Jefferson concluded:

> Do not be frightened from this inquiry by any fear of its consequences. If it ends in a belief that there is no god, you will find incitements to virtue in the comfort and pleasantness you feel in its exercise, and the love of others which it will procure you. If you find reason to believe there is a god, a consciousness that you are acting under his eye, and that he approves you, will be a vast additional incitement; if that there be a future state [heaven], the hope of a happy existence in that increases the appetite to deserve it; if that Jesus was also a god, you will be comforted by a belief of his aid and love. In fine, I repeat that you must lay aside all prejudice on both sides, and neither believe nor reject anything because any other persons, or description of persons have rejected or believed it. Your own reason is the only oracle given you by heaven, and you are answerable not for the rightness but uprightness of the decision.

What is perhaps most fascinating is the extent to which Jefferson encouraged the young man regarding not *what* to think, but *how* to think. His manifest intent was to prejudice his nephew in no particular direction but that of seeking the truth, a most worthy endeavor for those who are engaged in the practice of educating others, whether formally or informally.

But perhaps the most beautiful piece of wisdom offered by Jefferson to a young person was offered to a newborn child who had been named after him. The boy's mother wrote Jefferson, asking him to offer her son some benedictory life advice. Jefferson, then an old man with barely a few years left to live, wrote this short but memorable charge to the newborn: "Adore God; reverence and cherish your parents; love your neighbor as yourself, and your country more than life. Be just; be true; murmur not at the ways of Providence—and the life into which you have entered will be one of eternal and ineffable bliss."[39]

Other Founders would have no doubt enthusiastically seconded his advice.

But was the Founders' interest in education merely limited to the individual benefits that would accrue by the accumulation of wisdom? Hardly. On the contrary, they believed it was essential to maintaining a free government and society.

EDUCATION AND THE SELF-GOVERNING SOCIETY

When we consider the general civic ignorance and apathy that are prevalent in the United States today—in spite of the fact that it is *we* who live in the so-called Information Age—Tocqueville's observations on the state of civic knowledge and engagement in 1830s America should be shocking and even convicting to many modern Americans:

> I have scarcely ever encountered a single man of the common people in America who did not perceive with surprising ease the obligations entailed in the laws of Congress and those which owe their beginnings to the laws of his own state, nor who could not separate the matters belonging to the general prerogatives of the Union from those regulated by his local legislature and who could not point to where the competence of the federal courts begins and the limitation of the state tribunals ends.[40]

He made similar observations that, although more localized in nature, were nonetheless largely characteristic of the American people as a whole: "In New England, each citizen learns the elementary concepts of human knowledge. Beyond that he is taught the doctrines and evidence of his religion. He undergoes instruction on the history of his country and the principal features of its constitution. In Connecticut and Massachusetts you will seldom find a man who has only an inadequate knowledge of these things, and anyone completely unaware of them is quite an oddity."[41]

That a far larger proportion of American citizens were considerably more familiar with how their government worked and their nation's history in the 1830s than in twenty-first-century America should be sobering. Tocqueville observed that most citizens on the street were quite familiar with the "doctrines and evidence" of their religion (essentially Christian theology and apologetics), American history, and the Constitution. Today, these would probably be the three subjects with which a regular person on the street would be *least* familiar.

The point is, the Founders were absolutely convinced that only a knowledgeable, well-informed, and well-educated people could govern themselves, hold their governors to account, and prevent the encroachment of tyranny. Tocqueville remarked that, because of the great learning that went into creating the Constitution, it was uniquely required of the American people that they be knowledgeable of the system their forefathers had established: "The federal system rests therefore, whatever one does, upon a complicated theory which, in application, demands a daily exercise of rationality from its citizens . . . However, on scrutinizing the Constitution of the United States, the most complete of all known federal constitutions, it is frightening to note how many differences of knowledge and discernment it assumes in those governed."[42]

Notice Tocqueville's use of the word "frightening." This was a typical European reaction to a system that trusted the people and actually relied on their judgment far more than any in Europe had ever dared. Indeed, as Jefferson had noted as president, "As men become better informed, their rulers must respect them the more," a truth that no doubt instilled fear in every absolute monarch in Europe that his people might become too educated or know too much. Education, however, was exactly what prepared citizens for such self-government, for as Jefferson also noted, "Whenever the people are well informed, they can be trusted with their own government; that whenever things get so far wrong as to attract their notice, they may be relied on to set them to rights."[43]

Noah Webster took notice of the same phenomenon: "Information is fatal to despotism…But 'in a republican government,' says . . . [Montesquieu], 'the whole power of education is required.' Here every class of people should know and love the laws. This knowledge should be diffused by means of schools and newspapers; and an attachment to the laws may be formed by early impressions upon the mind."[44]

This was perhaps yet another reason why the French and American revolutions, though ostensibly initiated on similar grounds, were in fact utterly different, and not surprisingly turned out so differently. The French people, up to the revolution, had never experienced self-rule, nor were they the beneficiaries of widespread education, both of which the American colonies were quite familiar, and had been for more than a century. The French had thus fallen into what Adams referred to as a "brutal rage," the fate of any people who sought liberty, but not knowledge.

Adams explained it this way to his fellow colonists as the conflict with Britain headed inexorably toward war, encouraging them to learn the lessons of past republics, as well as the British constitution itself:

> This spirit [of liberty] . . . without knowledge, would be little better than a brutal rage. Let us tenderly and kindly cherish therefore the means of knowledge. Let us dare to read, think, speak, and write. Let every order and degree among the people rouse their attention and animate their resolution. Let them all become attentive to the grounds and principles of government, ecclesiastical and civil. Let us study the law of nature, search into the spirit of the British constitution, read the histories of ancient ages, contemplate the great examples of Greece and Rome.[45]

To ensure that the spirit of liberty would always be combined with education, the Founders wholeheartedly endorsed a system of local public education by which the people would be enlightened and equipped to govern themselves and their country. "Laws for the liberal education for youth, especially of the lower class of people, are so extremely wise and useful, that to a humane and generous mind, no expense for this purpose would be thought extravagant,"[46] Adams wrote. He explained further in his famous *Defence*:

The instruction of the people, in every kind of knowledge that can be of use to them in the practice of their moral duties, as men, citizens, and Christians, and of their political and civil duties, as members of society and freemen, ought to be the care of the public, and of all who have any share in the conduct of its affairs, in a manner that never yet has been practiced in any age or nation. The education here intended is not merely that of the children of the rich and noble, but of every rank and class of people, down to the lowest and the poorest. It is not too much to say, that schools for the education of all should be placed at convenient distances, and maintained at the public expense. The revenues of the state would be applied infinitely better, more charitably, wisely, usefully, and therefore politically, in this way, than even in maintaining the poor. This would be the best way of preventing the existence of the poor. If nations should ever be wise, instead of erecting thousands of useless offices, or engaging in unmeaning wars, they will make a fundamental maxim of this: that no human being shall grow up in ignorance. In proportion as this is done, tyranny will disappear.[47]

Also, in accordance with Franklin's notion of education inculcating "true merit," the Founders hoped that education would not be confined only to those fortunate few who happened to be born into wealthy or privileged families. Rather, believing as they did that merit was the foundation of a free society (whereas privileges granted by the state had been the norm in Europe between monarchs and the nobility, and only very occasionally the "commoner"), it was their desire that any meritorious person, no matter his circumstances, could be educated and consequently become useful to his country. Adams had written as early as the 1760s that "the perseveration of the means of knowledge among the lowest ranks is of more importance to the public than all the property of all the rich men in the country."[48] Likewise, Jefferson was an ardent advocate for universal education, and higher education for those who merited it, asserting that "worth and genius" should be "sought out from every condition of life, and completely prepared by education for defeating the competition of wealth and birth for public trusts."[49] For those who were best suited for it, he suggested the creation of "some institution where science in all its branches is taught, and in the highest degree to which the human mind has carried it." And finally, he advocated that "such a degree of learning [be] given to every member of the society as will enable him to read, to judge, and to vote understandingly on what is passing."[50]

Madison, likewise, summarized a position held by many of the Founders:

> Learned institutions ought to be favorite objects with every free people. They throw light over the public mind which is the best security against crafty and dangerous encroachments on the public liberty. They are the nurseries of skillful teachers for the schools distributed throughout the community. They are themselves schools for the particular talents required for some of the public trusts, on the able execution of which the welfare of the people depends. They multiply the educated individuals from among whom the people may elect a due portion of their public agents of every description, more especially of those who are to frame the laws . . . Without such institutions, the more costly of which can scarcely be provided by individual means, none but the few whose wealth enables them to support their sons abroad can give them the fullest education.[51]

Adams, writing to a certain John Taylor, noted that it was essential that the wealthy of the United States do all they could to support the education of even those at the very bottom of the societal ladder:

> My humble opinion is that knowledge, upon the whole, promotes virtue and happiness. I therefore hope that you and all other gentlemen of property, education, and reputation will exert your utmost influence in establishing schools, colleges, academies, and universities, and employ every means and opportunity to spread information, even to the lowest dregs of the people . . . The conditions of humanity will be improved and ameliorated by its expansion and diffusion in every

direction. May every human being—man, woman, and child—be as well informed as possible![52]

Several of the Founders were also vocal advocates of extending the opportunities of higher education to women as well, which was a rarity in the eighteenth century. Abigail Adams was perhaps the most vocal in this regard:

> I most sincerely wish that some liberal plan might be laid and executed for the benefit of the rising generation, and that our new Constitution may be distinguished for encouraging learning and virtue. If we mean to have heroes, statesmen, and philosophers, we should have learned women. The world perhaps would laugh at me and accuse me of vanity, but you, I know, have a mind too enlarged and liberal to disregard the sentiment. If much depends, as is allowed, upon the early education of youth, and the first principles which are instilled take the deepest root, great benefit arise from literary accomplishments in women.[53]

Her husband, John, was also supportive of such an idea. He once wrote to his daughter "Nabby" about the importance of women to education: "It is by the female world that the greatest and best characters among men are formed. I have long been of this opinion to such a degree that when I hear of an extraordinary man, good or bad, I naturally or habitually inquire who was his mother? There can be nothing in life more honorable for a woman than to contribute by her virtues, her advice, her example, or her address, to the formation of a husband, a brother, or a son to be useful to the world."[54]

Benjamin Rush also supported education for women:

> To qualify our women . . . they should not only be instructed in the usual branches of female education, but they should be taught the principles of liberty and government, and the obligations of patriotism should be inculcated upon them . . . Besides, the first impressions upon the minds of children are generally derived from the women.

Of how much consequence, therefore, is it in a republic that they should think justly upon the great subject of liberty and government![55]

All of these measures were intended to equip Americans to be a self-governing people. Madison had written that even though "liberty and order will never be *perfectly safe*," it is nonetheless essential "that the public opinion of the United States should be enlightened, that it should attach itself to their government as delineated in the *great charters*, derived not from the usurped power of kings, but from the legitimate authority of the people, and that it should guarantee, with a holy zeal, these political scriptures from every attempt to add to or diminish from them [Revelation 22:18–19]." Such knowledge, he argued, was essential if a people intended to be self-governing: "A popular government without popular information or the means of acquiring it is but a prologue to a farce or a tragedy, or perhaps both. Knowledge will forever govern ignorance, and a people who mean to be their own governors must arm themselves with the power which knowledge gives."[56]

To the end of his life, his conviction of the importance of education for a self-governing people never wavered:

> The American people owe it to themselves and to the cause of free government to prove by their establishments for the advancement and diffusion of knowledge that their political institutions . . . are as favorable to the intellectual and moral improvement of man as they are conformable to his individual and social rights. What spectacle can be more edifying or more seasonable than that of liberty and learning, each leaning on the other for their mutual and surest support?[57]

Washington charged his countrymen with the same task in his farewell address, for precisely the same reason: How could a people who intended to have a strong, if not paramount control over the course of their national affairs exercise such a responsibility if they were uneducated, or worse, miseducated? "Promote then as an object of primary importance, institutions for the general diffusion of knowledge. In proportion as the structure of a government gives force to public opinion, it is essential public opinion should be enlightened."[58]

Noah Webster explained the essential connection between an educated people and a self-governing people:

> In our American republics, where [government] is in the hands of the people, knowledge should be universally diffused by means of public schools. Of such consequence is it to society, that the people who make laws, should be well informed, that I conceive no Legislature can be justified in neglecting proper establishments for this purpose . . . When I speak of a diffusion of knowledge, I do not mean merely a knowledge of spelling books, and the New Testament. An acquaintance with ethics, and with the general principles of law, commerce, money and government, is necessary for the yeomanry [common people] of a republican state.[59]

Benjamin Rush was also a strong supporter of educating the people on subjects important to their national welfare, for they needed to be informed about those topics on which their government would be acting: "I wish likewise to see the numerous facts that relate to the origin and present state of commerce, together with the nature and principles of money, reduced to such a system, as to be intelligible and agreeable to a young man . . . I consider its effects as next to those of religion in humanizing mankind, and lastly, I view it as the means of uniting the different nations of the world together by the ties of mutual wants and obligations."[60]

Webster further argued that "wrong measures [of a legislature] generally proceed from ignorance either in the men themselves, or in their constituents. They often mistake their own interest, because they do not foresee the remote consequences of a measure." He then pointed out how essential morality was to an education that allowed men to be free and properly equipped them for the responsibilities of self-government:

> It may be true that all men cannot be legislators; but the more generally knowledge is diffused among the substantial yeomanry [common people], the more perfect will be the laws of a republican state . . .

> Every small district should be furnished with a school . . . This school
> should be kept by the most reputable and well informed man in the
> district. Here children should be taught the usual branches of learning;
> submission to superiors and to laws; the moral or social duties; the
> history and transactions of their own country; the principles of liberty
> and government. Here the rough manners of the wilderness should be
> softened, and the principles of virtue and good behavior inculcated.
> The *virtues* of men are of more consequence to society than their
> *abilities*; and for this reason, the *heart* should be cultivated with more
> assiduity than the *head*.[61]

Jefferson often expressed his belief that knowledge, when attached to
virtue, was the best way to thwart tyrannical designs on the Constitution
and the liberty of the people. Only knowledge among the citizenry could
prevent them from potentially being manipulated by the government
itself into willingly sacrificing their freedom: "I hold it, therefore, certain, that to open the doors of truth, and to fortify the habit of testing
everything by reason are the most effectual manacles we can rivet on
the hands of our successors to prevent their manacling the people with
their own consent," he wrote. He went on to warn that the liberty won
during the revolution would ultimately be temporary if the people
were not properly educated: "Convinced that the people are the only
safe depositories of their own liberty, and that they are not safe unless
enlightened to a certain degree, I have looked on our present state of
liberty as a short-lived possession unless the mass of the people could
be informed to a certain degree."[62]

Jefferson's solution was straightforward:

> Enlighten the people generally and tyranny and oppressions of body
> and mind will vanish like evil spirits at the dawn of day. Although
> I do not, with some enthusiasts, believe that the human condition
> will ever advance to such a state of perfection as that there shall no
> longer be pain or vice in the world, yet I believe it susceptible of much
> improvement, and most of all in matters of government and religion,

and that the diffusion of knowledge among the people is to be the instrument by which it is to be effected.[63]

But more than being able to distinguish between generally constructive or destructive legislation, education was essential if the people were to be the sentinel over their rights, as well as the powers reserved by the Constitution to the federal government and the states respectively. As we saw in chapter 4, the Constitution specifically limited the powers of the federal government, leaving the remainder to the states. In the absence of amendments, that was all the power that the people granted in the Constitution. But the underlying theoretical foundations of the Constitution, while relatively straightforward, are often difficult to apply. Tocqueville therefore argued that education was essential if the American people were to maintain their Constitution: "In all periods of history, education helps to defend men's independence, but this is especially true in times of democracy. . . . Men need great intelligence, knowledge, and skill to manage and sustain subsidiary powers in such circumstances and to create, within the body of independent but individually weak citizens, free associations capable of resisting tyranny without destroying public order."[64]

It was for this reason that he asserted that "in the United States, the education of the people powerfully contributes to the maintenance of the democratic republic. That will always be so, in my view, wherever education to enlighten the mind is not separated from that responsible for teaching morality."[65]

The Founders, likewise, believed it was essential for the American people to be educated to a degree that would allow them to keep both their state and federal governments in their proper places. "Let it be the patriotic study of all," Madison exhorted his countrymen, "to maintain the various authorities established by our complicated system, each in its respectively constitutional sphere, and to erect over the whole one paramount Empire of reason, benevolence, and brotherly affection." He observed elsewhere, "To secure all the advantages of such a system, every good citizen will be at once a sentinel over the rights of the people;

over the authorities of the con-federal government; and over both the rights and the authorities of the intermediate [State] governments."[66]

As a practical example, Jefferson asserted that education was itself a matter which the people should jealously guard and maintain as a local function, as the federal government had not been delegated any authority whatsoever over education. Indeed, even the central governments of each of the states should be prevented from exercising too much direct control over schools, instead leaving it to local authorities: "But if it is believed that these elementary schools will be better managed by the governor and council, the commissioners of the literary fund, or any other general authority of the government than by the parents within each ward, it is a belief against all experience."[67]

In addition to its role in allowing the people to watch over their government, the Founders also believed education must prepare American citizens for "active duty" in their government should the voices of their countrymen ever call them to assume it. As Montesquieu noted, "It is in republican government that the full power of education is needed. . . . Political virtue is a renunciation of oneself, which is always a very painful thing."[68] Likewise, Webster believed in "such a system of education as gives every citizen an opportunity of acquiring knowledge and fitting himself for places of trust,"[69] a "place of trust" referring to public service. Webster called this one of the *sine qua non* ["essential ingredients"] of the American Republic. Similarly, Adams asserted that "our policy must be to improve every opportunity and means for forming our people, and preparing leaders for them in the grand march of politics."[70]

Finally, but no less significantly, the Founders expressed an abiding belief in the importance of a free press to inform the people concerning the actions of their government and political leaders, an idea so critical that they protected it in the First Amendment of the Constitution. To clarify, though, for the Founders, the "press" were not institutionalized journalists and what we would today call "news organizations." Rather, it was quite literally the press, that tool by which ideas could be engraved and mass-produced by ink on paper. The "press" therefore referred to the transmission of ideas using what was, at that time, the single best method at achieving that very thing. Benjamin Franklin, himself a printer, stated his principles with regard to "the press":

> It is a principle among printers that when truth has fair play, it will always prevail over falsehood; therefore, though they have an undoubted property in their own Press, yet they willingly allow that anyone is entitled to the use of it who thinks it necessary to offer his sentiments on disputable points to the public, and will be at the expense of it. If what is thus published be good, mankind has the benefit of it. If it be bad...the more tis made public, the more its weakness is exposed, and the greater disgrace falls upon the author, whoever he be.[71]

Interestingly, many of the Founders were incredibly active writers in the press, even though not a single one of them was a "journalist" (a profession which did not exist in the eighteenth century), and the papers they wrote for frequently included much more than just news, but advice, advertisements, essays, and the like. This is vital if we are to understand what our Founders were actually saying about freedom of the press. It was no less than the freedom of any citizen to speak his mind and have his ideas freely transmitted (assuming there were newspapers who were willing to publish him).

However, even as "the press" grew to become more of a profession, few Founders continued to speak as forcefully in defense of its freedom as Jefferson, who wrote, "No government ought to be without censors, and where the press is free, no one ever will. If virtuous, it need not fear the fair operation of attack and defense. Nature has given to man no other means of sifting out the truth either in religion, law, or politics. I think it is as honorable to the government neither to know, nor notice its sycophants or censors, as it would be undignified and criminal to pamper the former and persecute the latter."[72]

Jefferson asserted a free press was particularly important in mitigating against the oppression of tyrannical governments:

I may err in my measures, but never shall deflect from the intention to fortify the public liberty by every possible means, and to put it out of the power of the few to riot on the labors of the many . . . which we trust will end in establishing the fact that man may be governed by reason and truth. Our first object should therefore be to leave open to him all the avenues to truth. The most effectual hitherto found is the freedom of the press. It is therefore the first shut up by those who fear the investigation of their actions.[73]

A free press, then, was necessary not only to inform public opinion, but also as a means to *express* public opinion to those in power: "The only security of all is in a free press," Jefferson wrote. "The force of public opinion cannot be resisted, when permitted freely to be expressed. The agitation it produces must be submitted to. It is necessary, to keep the waters pure."[74]

For Jefferson, as long as citizens were well educated and they had a free press willing to do its job as the investigative arm of the rights and liberty of the people, tyranny would always be outmatched and outgunned: "The functionaries of every government have propensities to command at will the liberty and property of their constituents. There is no safe deposit for these but with the people themselves; nor can they be safe with them without information. Where the press is free, and every man able to read, all is safe."[75]

In sum, the Founders believed that liberty was ultimately and finally preserved by a virtuous people and an educated citizenry, and that for a free country to maintain itself, the moral and intellectual habits appropriate for a free people ought to be encouraged from every sector of society. "There is no doubt," Adams wrote, "that the schools, academics, and universities, the stage, the press, the bar, pulpit, and parliament, might all be improved to better purpose than they have been in any country for this great purpose." He continued:

The emanations of error, folly, and vice which proceed from all these sources might be lessened, and those of wisdom, virtue, and truth might be increased; more of decency and dignity might be added to the human character in high and low life; manners [morals] would assist the laws, and the laws reform manners; and imposture, superstition, knavery, and tyranny be made ashamed to show their heads before the wisdom and integrity, decency and delicacy of a venerable public opinion.[76]

It comes as no surprise, then, that it was Thomas Jefferson, third president of the United States and the author of her magisterial Declaration of Independence, who perhaps most powerfully and laconically summarized the fundamental issue of knowledge and education in a free society: "If a nation expects to be ignorant and free, in a state of civilization, it expects what never was and never will be."[77]

7

"EVERY MAN UNDER HIS OWN VINE AND
FIG TREE": LIBERTY'S DREAM

We hear often about the "American dream." But what is it? Interestingly enough, this phrase was foreign to our Founders. But they had plenty to say about what they considered essential for Americans to be free, to fully possess their liberty, as it were. Much of it we have already discussed, but many of those threads will come together in this chapter.

George Washington constantly used a particular phrase throughout his whole life to refer to his desire to simply be on his farm, minding his own business, at peace, at liberty, and left to his own affairs: "under my vine and fig tree." He was referring to a verse from the Bible: "But they shall sit every man under his vine and under his fig tree; and none shall make them afraid: for the mouth of the LORD of hosts hath spoken it" (Micah 4:4). The context of the verse is a vision of the "Millennium," the thousand-year messianic rule of God in a world in which men would enjoy peace and security. It turns out this is, in spirit, a good representation of what the Founders believed was the "American dream."

In essence, it was the ability of each man to exercise his liberty, without government interference, in a morally responsible way so as to reap the fruits of his own labor and talents, and thereby contribute to the good of himself and society. Contrary to what had been the status quo for the vast majority of human history, when it was not one's merit but the circumstances of one's birth that dictated one's destiny, the

Founders believed in a society built upon, driven by, and dependent upon merit, and the protection of that merit by government, whether economic, moral, artistic, political, or otherwise. They knew that "Life, Liberty, and the Pursuit of Happiness" began to mean something only once a person discovered his purpose for being on this earth. They believed that America should be a place where that purpose could be attained to whatever extent the individual sought and worked to attain it, unhindered by entrenched power and interests, unchained from the circumstances of his birth. Citizens should be free to associate with one another or not as they pleased in a civil society, and not only should the government place as few obstacles as possible in the way of individuals achieving their dreams, but it was duty-bound to protect their right to benefit from the fruits of those dreams (i.e., their property). As we shall see, this was not a vision of a "cutthroat" society, for it assumed a morally responsible people who, in the context of the civil society, took care of one another (as Americans were famous for doing) as a matter of personal obligation. If they looked to the government at all, they turned to their local authorities, as they were in the best position to respond to local needs and situations. In other words, the "American dream" of the Founders was intended to *unleash the full power of human potential so as to enable human flourishing to the greatest possible extent.*

James Madison said that liberty was "the great end for which the Union was formed."[1] But like the rest of the Founders, he realized that human liberty was not a risk-free business. For them, the choice was between what Jefferson termed "the calm of despotism" or the "boisterous sea of liberty,"[2] and what Samuel Adams called the "tranquility of servitude" or "the animated contest of freedom."[3] In other words, the Founders recognized that inherent to the project of liberty was an unavoidable level of insecurity. And yet, as we shall see, they believed the benefits of liberty were not only worth it, but morally required by virtue of the fact that each person was endowed by the Creator not only with unalienable rights, but with individual gifts and skills.

Upon visiting the United States and closely observing its people over a number of years, an astonished Tocqueville wrote, "It is only fifty years since the United States emerged from the colonial dependence in which England held it . . . Yet no nation of the earth has made such swift progress in trade and industry as the Americans. Today they are the second maritime nation of the world."[4] Tocqueville knew he was witnessing something in America that was very different from what he had left behind in Europe. Yet George Washington had predicted that very thing forty years before: "When, if that property was well secured, faith and justice well preserved, a stable government well administered, and confidence restored, the tide of population and wealth would flow to us from every part of the globe, and, with a due sense of the blessings, make us the happiest people upon earth."[5]

How could Washington know this? The answer is simple but three pronged. First, the Founders recognized that all people had different characteristics and gifts by which they could acquire property and which would affect their standing in human society, and that each had a right to exercise those faculties. The Founders had much to say on this aspect of human nature. John Adams, for example, wrote, "None will pretend that all are born of dispositions exactly alike—of equal weight, equal strength, equal length, equal delicacy of nerves, equal elasticity of muscles, equal complexions, equal figure, grace, or beauty."[6]

Second, because they had unequal faculties by which they obtained property, all things being equal, each individual would earn both different types and amounts of property. Or as Adams put it, "These were all born to equal rights, but to very different fortunes, to very different success and influence in life." He went on to explain how this was a crucial difference between the American and French revolutions:

> That all men are born to equal rights is true. Every being has a right to his own, as clear, as moral, as sacred as any other being has. This is as indubitable as a moral government in the universe. But to teach that all men are born with equal powers and faculties, to equal influence in society, to equal property and advantages through life, is as gross a fraud, as glaring an imposition on the credulity of the people as ever was

practiced by monks, by Druids, by Brahmins, by priests of the immortal Lama, or by the self-styled philosophers of the French Revolution.[7]

For the Founders, it was nonsense to assert that "all men are created equal" meant all men would, and should, be *made* equal in their possessions or the outcomes of their lives. In fact, Madison labeled any scheme "for an equal division of property" as "improper" and a "wicked project."[8]

"No matter what a nation does," Tocqueville commented, "it will never succeed in reaching perfectly equal conditions. If it did have the misfortune to achieve an absolute and complete leveling, there would still remain the inequalities of intelligence which come directly from God and will always elude the lawmakers. The inevitable result of these varying faculties," he explained, was that "natural inequality being very great, fortunes become unequal from the moment each man uses all his talents to get rich."[9] Inequality in conditions was therefore the necessary consequence of the different faculties by which property was obtained.

And finally, because government exists to protect rights, and the right to property is a natural right endowed by the Creator, government exists to *equally protect* the *unequal faculties* by which each person acquires property. Madison elucidated:

> Government is instituted to protect property of every sort . . . This being the end of government, that alone is a *just* government which *impartially* secures to every man, whatever is his *own* . . . Conscience is the most sacred of all property . . . That is not a just government, nor is property secure under it, where the property which a man has in his personal safety and personal liberty, is violated by arbitrary seizures of one class of citizens for the service of the rest.[10]

Under this philosophy, neither could the rich aggrandize themselves at the expense of the poor, nor could the poor aggrandize themselves at the expense of the rich. All were equally entitled to their own property. He continued:

That is not a just government, nor is property secure under it, where arbitrary restrictions, exemptions, and monopolies deny to part of its citizens that free use of their faculties, and free choice of their occupations, which not only constitute their property in the general sense of the word, but are the means of acquiring property strictly so called . . . A just security to property is not afforded by that government under which unequal taxes oppress one species of property and reward another species, where arbitrary taxes invade the domestic sanctuaries of the rich, and excessive taxes grind the faces of the poor, where the keenness and competition of want [a free market] are deemed an insufficient spur to labor, and taxes are again applied, by an unfeeling policy, as another spur. . . If there be a government then which . . . *directly* violates the property which individuals have in their opinions, their religion, their person, and their faculties . . . such a government is not a pattern for the United States . . . If the United States mean to obtain or deserve the full praise due to wise and just governments, they will equally respect the rights of property, and the property in rights.[11]

Benjamin Franklin affirmed the same idea, drawing upon the lessons of history with regard to the unequal application of the law to varying classes of people, whether rich or poor:

History affords us many instances of the ruin of states, by the prosecution of measures ill suited to the temper and genius of their people. The ordaining of laws in favor of one part of the nation, to the prejudice and oppression of another, is certainly the most erroneous and mistaken policy. An equal dispensation of protection, rights, privileges, and advantages, is what every part is entitled to, and ought to enjoy . . . These measures never fail to create great and violent jealousies and animosities between the people favored and the people oppressed; whence a total separation of affections, interests, political obligations, and all manner of connections, by which the whole state is weakened.[12]

The unequal property that resulted from the application of unequal faculties of acquiring it was an inequality the Founders not only accepted, but believed was a positive good, because it was based on merit, not privilege. It was the result of the work one was willing to put in rather than the lucky or unlucky circumstances into which one might have been born. Those who by their own merit prospered the most (and not necessarily based on the size of their bank account) they called the "natural aristocracy." This was in contrast to what they would call the "artificial aristocracy," a privileged group who had become wealthy or powerful by virtue of their connections and proximity to power, not their merit. "Few men will deny that there is a natural aristocracy of virtues and talents in every nation and in every party, in every city and village. Inequalities are a part of the natural history of man,"[13] Adams had written. But as for the "artificial aristocracy," the Founders had quite different sentiments. Jefferson explained:

> There is also an artificial aristocracy, founded on wealth and birth, without either virtue or talents . . . The natural aristocracy I consider as the most precious gift of nature, for the instruction, the trusts, and government of society. And indeed, it would have been inconsistent in creation to have formed man for the social state, and not to have provided virtue and wisdom enough to manage the concerns of the society. May we not even say that that form of government is the best which provides the most effectually for a pure selection of these natural aristoi into the offices of government? The artificial aristocracy is a mischievous ingredient in government, and provision should be made to prevent its ascendency.[14]

European history had largely been the tale of hundreds of artificial aristocracies, those connected to the powerful and who thereby became privileged, regardless of their merit, and used this privilege to oppress other portions of society. The Founders would have none of this for America, which is why they insisted every man be free to earn and manage his property as he saw fit, not according to what a centralized government power saw fit.

"The true foundation of republican government is the equal right of every citizen in his person and property, and in their management," Jefferson wrote.[15] Madison concurred: "The personal right to acquire property, which is a natural right, gives to property, when acquired, a right to protection as a social right."[16] This belief was simply the extension of the principle of merit: that merit, not the circumstances of one's birth, should dictate one's destiny. It also required that the principle be applied to all, meaning that simply because someone had *less* did not mean that someone else deserved to be taxed *more*. As we already saw, Madison was strongly opposed to such an idea, as were the other Founders. They recognized that "'abilities' form a *distinction* and confer a privilege, in fact," as Adams had said, "[but] they give no peculiar rights in society,"[17] except that of benefiting by the fruit of those abilities. "In a Republic," Madison asserted, "personal merit alone could be the ground of political exaltation,"[18] and therefore a rich man deserved nothing by virtue of his being rich, just as the poor man was not entitled to another's property by virtue of his being poor. "American legislators," Tocqueville noted, "seemed to have had some success in opposing the notion of rights to the feelings of envy."[19] In the system envisioned by the Founders, even though they predicted that it would one day happen as tyranny inevitably set in (as it had done to all societies throughout history), arousing the envy of one section of society for the wealth of another was seen as utterly destructive, not only of the rights to property, but of the moral strength of the people. We shall return to this momentarily.

Jefferson espoused the same idea in his second inaugural, in which he declared that the government's goals were "equality of rights maintained," and the protection of "that state of property, equal or unequal, which results to every man from his own industry, or that of his fathers."[20] Madison had in fact noted that unequal property was exactly what one should expect from a government that equally protected the unequal faculties of acquiring property: "A distinction of property results from that very protection which a free government gives to unequal faculties of acquiring it. There will be rich and poor, creditors and debtors, a landed interest, a monied interest, a mercantile interest, a manufacturing interest."[21]

This was yet another manifestation of the Founders applying their knowledge of human nature: they recognized that, regardless of our desires to the contrary, human nature tended to be concerned first and foremost with one's self, one's family, and one's friends before all others. This was not going to be changed by government action or legislation; it simply *is*. People naturally take care of and acquire more property if they are the ones who stand to gain by it, rather than if the fruit of their labor will go to someone else. Conversely, the less someone stands to benefit from his own labor, the less incentivized he will be to work for that benefit. As has been said, if everyone is responsible for everything, no one is responsible for anything. These are the brutal facts of human nature. Don't believe so? Check out a public bathroom.

And yet, the Founders did not believe that man's selfishness should simply run wild (as chapter 5 made completely clear). On the contrary, by *equally* protecting the right of *everyone* to acquire property, all men were thereby incentivized to obtain such property in a way that respected the rights of others. Thus, the human tendency to be selfish could, by equal application of the rule of law, be made to become a means of benefit for all. It was for this reason, as Tocqueville explained, that Americans saw liberty and prosperity as two sides of the same coin:

> Americans alternately display so strong and similar a passion for prosperity and freedom that one must suppose these impulses to be united and mingled in some part of their souls. Americans in fact do regard their freedom as the best tool and surest safeguard of their wellbeing. They love them both, the one as a vehicle for the other. Therefore, they do not consider their concern for public matters to be none of their business. On the contrary, they believe it to be their chief concern to secure for themselves a government which allows them to obtain the good things they want and will not stop them from peacefully enjoying those they already possess.[22]

Americans were of the same general belief as Alexander Hamilton, who noted that "there is good reason to believe that where the laws are wise and well executed, and the inviolability of property and contracts maintained, the economy of a people will, in the general course of things, correspond with its means."[23] Tocqueville explained that Americans believed in "grant[ing] privileges to no one, allowing all equal education and equal independence, and leaving each man to establish his own place in the world for himself," and that they therefore accepted the fact that "natural inequality will soon come to light and wealth pass automatically to the most able." And since the right to benefit from the fruits of one's labor was legally protected, there was a massive incentive to become productive, exercise creativity in the pursuit of further productivity, and thereby increase and enhance overall prosperity, exactly as Washington had predicted and Tocqueville confirmed: "In the United States," he said, "there is no limit to the inventiveness of man to discover ways of increasing wealth and to satisfy the public's needs. The most enlightened inhabitants of each district constantly use their knowledge to make new discoveries to increase the general prosperity, which, when made, they pass eagerly to the mass of the people." It comes as no surprise then that he was convinced that "there is possibly no country on the earth with fewer idle men than America, and where all those who work are so eager to seek out their own prosperity."[24] This was part of the general belief in a free market, as unregulated by government as possible, allowing to each man as much latitude as possible in benefiting from his own industry. It was also part of what Federalist No. 11 referred to as "the adventurous spirit, which distinguishes the commercial character of America," and what Europeans in many instances found distasteful. "What we call the love of gain," Tocqueville remarked, "is often laudable hard work for the Americans," where "nothing stands in the way of the surging spirit of enterprise."[25] This was an essential part of the "American dream" of the Founders.

The effects of this were that all men worked and worked hard, even the rich. "There is no such thing in this country as what would be called wealth in Europe," Jefferson remarked. "The richest are but a little at ease, and obliged to pay the most rigorous attention to their affairs to keep them together."[26] When in Europe, Benjamin Franklin wrote a public newspaper article in which he was giving free advice to those Europeans who sought to immigrate to America. He explained:

> Everyone will enjoy securely the profits of his industry. But if he does not bring a fortune with him, he must work and be industrious to live. . . . Multitudes of poor people from England, Ireland, Scotland, and Germany, have by this means in a few years become wealthy farmers, who in their own countries . . . could never have emerged from the poor condition wherein they were born. . . . If they are poor, they begin first as servants or journeymen; and if they are sober, industrious, and frugal, they soon become masters, establish themselves in business, marry, raise families, and become respectable citizens.[27]

Those who had never been able to move up the social ladder in Europe because of an entrenched "artificial aristocracy" that lived off the hard work of the laboring poor could do it in America if they worked hard, if they wisely stewarded their money, and if they maintained their sobriety (which for the Founders was sometimes a catchword not just for alcoholism, but immorality in general). In America, their merit would count for something. As Franklin had said many decades before as "Poor Richard," in America "In short, the way to wealth, if you desire it, is as plain as the way to market. It depends chiefly on two words: INDUSTRY and FRUGALITY; i.e. waste neither time nor money, but make the best use of both."[28] Tocqueville observed the same thing, noting that "in America, most wealthy people started from poverty; almost all those who now enjoy leisure were busy in their youth."[29] Franklin continued, "Also, persons of moderate fortunes and capitals, who having a number of children to provide for, are desirous of bringing them up to industry, and to secure estates for their posterity, have opportunities of doing it in America, which Europe does not afford."[30]

Not only were there few people in America who could be called "rich" in the European sense; there were also "few people so miserable as the poor of Europe." Instead, Franklin observed that "it is rather a general happy mediocrity that prevails." He concluded, "The almost general mediocrity of fortune that prevails in America, obliging its people to follow some business for subsistence, those vices that arise usually from idleness are in a great measure prevented. Industry and constant employment are great preservatives of the morals and virtue of a nation. Hence bad examples to youth are more rare in America, which must be a comfortable consideration to parents."[31]

In other words, because each person had to make his own way, there were very few people just sitting around doing nothing in America. This in turn helped preserve the moral character of the people, which in turn kept them working hard. It was seen as a duty to provide for oneself. This is why many of the Founders had such a high admiration for farmers, or those who otherwise provided for themselves. Because they were self-sufficient, not only were they not a drain on public money, but they were a net positive to the society by the contribution of their taxes, as well as their ability to help provide for any needs that may have arisen in their community. Madison wrote, "The class of citizens[32] who provide at once their own food and their own raiment [clothing] may be viewed as the most truly independent and happy. They are more: they are the best basis of public liberty, and the strongest bulwark of public safety. It follows that the greater the proportion of this class to the whole society, the more free, the more independent, and the more happy must be the society itself."[33]

GOVERNMENT AND THE ECONOMY

Such a culture had consequences for Americans' views on the government's role in the economy. In general, they believed it should have very little do with it. Its job was to protect each man's right to benefit from his own labor. Beyond this, there was little else to do. Tocqueville made an interesting remark on this front, once again distinguishing America from Europe: "The inhabitants of the United States have never been divided by any form of privilege [i.e., the "artificial aristocracy"], nor have they known the mutual relationship between servant and master and, since they do not fear or hate each other, they have never known the need to call in the supreme power to manage the details of their affairs."[34]

In other words, Americans were generally adept at managing their own day-to-day affairs just fine without government interference. And since they believed the government should be as unobtrusive as possible, they saw no reason for it to constantly get bigger. Rather, they believed it should carry out its allotted functions efficiently and effectively, and that was it. As Tocqueville noted, "It is not the elected official who produces the prosperity of American democracy, but the fact that the official is elected."[35] There is, indeed, a constant emphasis among the Founders on an "efficient government." Washington, for example, wrote, "[A]merica, under an efficient government, will be the most favorable country of any in the world for persons of industry and frugality, possessed of a moderate capital, to inhabit. It is also believed that it will not be less advantageous to the happiness of the lowest class of people because of the equal distribution of property, the great plenty of unoccupied lands, and the facility of procuring the means of subsistence."[36] Such efficiency, from their perspective, should be quite possible given the limited extent of the federal government's powers.

As such, the Founding Fathers were strong advocates of a free market in which the rights of all to the fruit of their labor was the primary concern. "We have abundant reason to be convinced," Washington had written, "that the spirit of trade which pervades these States is not to be restrained. It behooves us therefore to establish it upon just principles."[37] These "just principles" were those we have already enunciated: the equal protection of property. The *Federalist Papers* had indeed urged ratification of the Constitution partially on the grounds that it would enable "an unrestrained intercourse [commerce] between the states themselves,"[38] rather than the states engaging in protectionist policies, as many of them had done. In other words, the commerce clause of the Constitution was intended to foster commerce among the states. Jefferson was also in favor of as little government interference as possible: "Our interest will be to throw open the doors of commerce, and to knock off all its shackles, giving perfect freedom to all persons for the vent of whatever they may choose to bring into our ports, and asking the same in theirs," he wrote. Later, as president, he remained committed to that end: "The path we have to pursue is so quiet that we have nothing scarcely to propose to our legislature. A noiseless course, not meddling with the affairs of others, unattractive of notice, is a mark that society is going on in happiness. If we can prevent the government from wasting the labors of the people under the pretense of taking care of them, they must become happy."[39]

In pursuit of such a goal, it was normal for American governments, including the federal government, to add as few government offices and employ as few government employees as possible. "Of civil offices or employments there are few, no superfluous ones as in Europe," Franklin had informed his European readers, "and it is a rule established in some of the States, that no office should be so profitable as to make it desirable."[40] President Jefferson described the exact same thing to an English counter-part, noting that most government employees, including the president of the United States, had their own professions, and did not rely just on government salaries. "Our public economy also is such as to offer drudgery and subsistence only to those entrusted with its administration, a wise and necessary precaution against the degeneracy of the public servants," Jefferson wrote. "In our private pursuits it is a great advantage that every honest employment is deemed honorable. I am myself a nail-maker."[41]

It was a point of pride with Jefferson that by avoiding the unnecessary growth of government through "the suppression of unnecessary offices, of useless establishments and expenses," his administration was able to "discontinue our internal taxes. These covering our land with officers, and opening our doors to their intrusions, had already begun that process of domiciliary vexation which, once entered, is scarcely to be restrained from reaching successively every article of produce and property . . . it may be the pleasure and pride of an American to ask, what farmer, what mechanic, what laborer, even sees a tax-gatherer of the United States?"[42]

As part of their free market approach, Americans were generally opposed to the extension of any government privileges or exemptions to particular industries or businesses. They figured that if it could be supported by the free market, it would, and if it needed government support, it probably wouldn't make it in the free market, and should therefore not be imposed by the government. This was the natural consequence of the principle that government should treat every man equally, and not favor any over another. That included not favoring particular industries over others. "Whatever is least favorable to vigor of body, to the faculties of the mind, or to the virtues or the utilities of life, instead of being forced or fostered by public authority, ought to be seen with regret as long as occupations more friendly to human happiness lie vacant,"[43] Madison wrote. Franklin confirmed Madison's observations, "The governments in America do nothing to encourage such projects [not supported by the free market]. The people by this means are not imposed on, either by the merchant or mechanic."[44]

Commenting on this system, and the limited nature of the federal government's powers, Tocqueville wrote, "It may almost be said that the people are self-governing, in so far as the share left to the administrators is so weak and so restricted and the latter feel such close ties with their popular origin and the power from which it emanates. The people reign in the American political world like God over the universe."[45]

But perhaps the best description of the "American dream" and how it most differed from Europe, came from Jefferson in a letter to a French government official: "We both consider the people as our children, and love them with parental affection," he wrote. "But you love them as infants whom you are afraid to trust without nurses, and I as adults whom I freely leave to self-government."[46]

THE POOR

So what about the poor? The Founders affirmed every man's right to his own property. "But," Adams said, "it is denied that they have right or that they should have power to take from one man his property to make another easy."[47] So were they just thrown out on the street? On the contrary, the Founders constructed a system in which it was expected an active civil society would largely (though not completely) take care of the poor on its own, almost entirely independent of government funds. All things being equal, the Founders were extremely skeptical of government acting as a charity, or getting in the business of transferring the wealth of some to others in the interests of "equality" or "fairness." The fact that such an action necessarily required confiscating the property of one person only to give it to another was contrary to every notion they had of both.

Jefferson described how the poor were cared for in America. While the intent was obviously to help them, there was a strong emphasis on doing so either by requiring them to work at the same time, or by finding them a job to do as quickly as possible so as to regain their self-sufficiency:

> The poor who have neither property, friends, nor strength to labor are boarded in the houses of good farmers to whom a stipulated sum is annually paid. . . . Vagabonds, without visible property or vocation, are placed in workhouses where they are well clothed, fed, lodged, and made to labor. Nearly the same method of providing for the poor prevail through all our states . . . I never yet saw a native [born] American begging in the streets or highways.[48]

While he was away from home commanding the Continental army, Washington instructed those who were managing his estate to "let the hospitality of the house, with respect to the poor, be kept up. Let no one go hungry away—if any of these kind of people should be in want of corn, supply their necessities, provided it does not encourage them in idleness; and I have no objection your giving my money in charity to the amount of forty or fifty pounds a year when you think it well bestowed."[49] He continued this common practice upon his return from the war.

It is probably safe to say that the Founders had a generally much higher view than most twenty-first-century Americans of what people were capable of achieving when they truly set their minds to something, disciplined themselves, and did what they had to do. They universally believed that to do something for someone that he could do for himself, or to give to people with no expectation of labor from them, was not just immoral (for it precluded the giving of charity to those truly in need), but was ultimately a disservice to those seeking such favors. "Thus," Franklin remarked, "if you teach a poor young man to shave himself and keep his razor in order, you may contribute more to the happiness of his life than in giving him a 1,000 guineas."[50] This was no doubt the distant ancestor of our modern "Better to teach a man how to fish . . ." aphorism.

While in Great Britain, Franklin, who both grew up in poverty and was as an adult an incredibly philanthropic man, had the opportunity of observing their poor. Britain, at that time, was one of the most generous nations in the world when it came to public assistance. However, despite such good intentions, Franklin pointed out (in terms that would likely preclude him from any public office today) that the results had been disastrous:

> I think the best way of doing good to the poor is not making them easy *in* poverty, but leading or driving them *out* of it. In my youth I traveled much, and I observed in different countries that the more public provisions were made for the poor, the less they provided for themselves, and of course became poorer. And, on the contrary, the less was done for them, the more they did for themselves, and became richer. There is no country in the world where so many provisions are established for them . . . Under all these obligations, are our poor modest, humble, and thankful? And do they use their best endeavors to maintain themselves, and lighten our shoulders of this burden? On the contrary, I affirm that there is no country in the world in which the poor are more idle, dissolute, drunken, and insolent. The day you passed that act [likely the *Workhouse Test Act* of 1723], you took away from before their eyes the greatest of all inducements to industry, frugality, and sobriety, by giving them a dependence on

somewhat else than a careful accumulation during youth and health, for support in age or sickness. In short, you offered a premium for the encouragement of idleness, and you should not now wonder that it has had its effect in the increase of poverty. SIX *days shalt thou labor* [Exodus 20:9], though one of the old commandments long treated as out of date, will again be looked upon as a respectable precept; industry will increase, and with it plenty among the poorer people; their circumstances will mend, and more will be done for their happiness by inuring [encouraging] them to provide for themselves, than could be done by dividing all your estates among them.[51]

The Founders recognized that such excessive and gratuitous welfare could at first seem to be the result of a society's goodness and benevolence to those in need, but that it inevitably saps the moral foundations that lead to such welfare in the first place. Once such charity becomes coerced, it stops being charity; and once it is expected, it stops being an act of kindness and becomes, instead, an act of entitled expropriation, incentivizing some people to believe they have an automatic right to the produce of others. Charity then becomes a mere compelled deduction from one's own earnings and enterprise, not a sacrifice induced by moral considerations. Thus, the moral muscle that initially encourages such attempts to lift the burdens of poverty from the shoulders of another atrophies, and forced redistribution is substituted for true charity. The result is then invariably ungenerous givers and ungrateful receivers.

Generous men like Franklin recognized that true charity was the result of a willingness to sacrifice financially, yes, but also emotionally and mentally, on behalf of others. As a man who had run away from home in Boston with only a few coins in his pocket and rose from nothing to become one of the most successful printers in America, Franklin also knew that wealth, like poverty, was more often than not the result of a deliberate set of choices. His writings evince a conviction that poverty, in the vast majority of cases, ultimately came down to a lack of virtuous living (see chapter 5), which is not to say that fortuitous circumstances do not affect the realities of one's life, for Franklin himself had had more than enough unfortunate circumstances to deal with. But it was just such circumstances, and his own eventual mastery of them, which taught him that wealth, actuated by purpose, maintained by discipline, and usually enjoyed only after many years of patience and perseverance, was the fruit of a consistent series of choices to live a virtuous life. He knew that simply distributing money did not cure the conditions that led to poverty, which more often had to do with individual choices than circumstances. On the contrary, such policies tended to encourage poverty, for they often interfered in what Franklin called the "order of God and nature" which provided the true wellsprings of prosperity and personal affluence. By short-circuiting the natural consequences of lifestyle choices which tended to lead to poverty through government welfare, the choices themselves would not be cured, only their immediate effects; and having subsidized such choices in the name of ameliorating poverty, the law of unintended consequences would kick in, ultimately causing more harm than good:

> To relieve the misfortunes of our fellow creatures is concurring with the Deity, tis Godlike; but if we provide encouragements for laziness, and supports for folly, may it not be found fighting against the order of God and nature, which perhaps has appointed want and misery as the proper punishments for, and cautions against, as well as necessary consequences of idleness and extravagancy. Whenever we attempt to mend the scheme of Providence and to interfere in the government of the world, we had need be very circumspect lest we do more harm than good. In New England, they once thought blackbirds useless and mischievous to their corn, [and so] they made laws to destroy them. The consequence was the blackbirds were diminished, but a kind of worms which devoured their grass, and which the blackbirds had been used to feed on increased prodigiously; then finding their loss in grass much greater than their saving in corn, they wished again for their blackbirds.[52]

Perhaps we should again take to heart the words of this man who started from nothing, lost nearly everything on numerous occasions, and was still willing to risk every penny of his hard-earned fortune for the sake of American liberty.

THE CIVIL SOCIETY

But the "American dream" of the Founders was by no means simply the tale of the "rugged individual" who trampled upon the poor or left them behind. This is a myth often foisted upon a twenty-first-century citizenry who are ignorant of their history. On the contrary, it was precisely because each person was able to manage and benefit from the fruits of his own labor that Americans were everywhere and constantly freely associating with one another in civil society. The civil society was that set of relationships, totally independent and separate from government, by which private citizens managed their affairs, whether commercially through businesses, spiritually through religious worship, morally through charitable organizations, or through any other sort of mutual endeavor. Americans were famous for not only addressing the ills of society, but increasing its wealth and prosperity primarily through the means of the civil society. There were artistic, academic, industrial, religious, recreational, charitable, and any other type of associations imaginable. This is why Tocqueville so stridently asserted that "nothing deserves to attract our attention more than the intellectual and moral associations of America."[53]

Today, many assume that if someone doesn't want the government to bother him, he doesn't want *people* to bother them. On the other hand, many for whom lack of government interference is the essence of freedom too often forget the necessity of the civil society. Neither view could be further from the American conception of liberty. Being undisturbed by the state is necessary because the state is force. But the American conception of liberty never limited, and on the contrary depended upon, such ties between citizens, the innumerable webs of relationships that constitute the civil society. Thus, the civil society, under the authority of an efficient and limited free government, would combine the best of both worlds: it would maintain as near as possible the liberty of the state of nature that existed prior to government, while government would at the same time uphold the rights of all so as to elude the barbarism and trepidations of that state. Thus, the Founders believed the civil society and government played distinct but mutually beneficial and essential roles in maintaining a free society.

It was the civil society that Thomas Paine, in his *Common Sense*, contrasted with government, asserting they served completely different purposes:

> Some writers have so confounded society with government as to leave little or no distinction between them, whereas they are not only different but have different origins. Society is produced by our wants, and government by our wickedness. The former promotes our happiness *positively* by uniting our affections, the latter *negatively* by restraining our vices. The one encourages intercourse, the other creates distinctions. The first is a patron, the last a punisher. Society in every state is a blessing, but government, even in its best state, is but a necessary evil, in its worst state an intolerable one.

Commercial relationships, the sense of community, duty to one's neighbor, and the sense that "I am my brother's keeper" came not through the state, but through the civil society. If something needed to be done, Americans would take care of it themselves, in free association with their neighbors. No wonder Tocqueville exclaimed, "I cannot express how much I admire their experience and common sense."[54] Because the government was not seen as a source of charity, Americans looked to one another in times of need, which naturally increased their sense of mutual care for one another. They were famous for their concern for their neighbors, precisely because they were often all their neighbors had, and their neighbors were all they had. Tocqueville described this fascinating phenomenon:

> I must say that I have seen Americans making great and sincere sacrifices for the common good, and a hundred times I have noticed

that, when need be, they almost always gave each other faithful support. The free institutions belonging to the inhabitants of the United States . . . provide a thousand reminders to each citizen that he lives in society. They constantly impress this idea upon his mind, that it is duty as well as self-interest to be useful to one's fellows and, as he sees no particular reason to hate others, being neither their slave nor their master, his heart easily inclines toward kindness.[55]

Because Americans had to rise or fall on their merit in the free market, they learned how to serve other people as well as possible, for if they did not do so in the marketplace, they would not survive or be successful. This trait naturally diffused into every other area of American life. So while many today may assume that, with barely any government social spending, early Americans were dying on the streets left and right, quite the opposite was true. Tocqueville wrote, "When an American seeks the cooperation of his fellows, they seldom refuse him and I have often noticed that their help is both spontaneous and enthusiastic. Should some unforeseen accident occur on the public highway, people run from all sides to help the victim. Should some family fall foul of an unexpected disaster, a thousand strangers willingly open their purses and a goodly number of modest gifts come to aid their distress."[56]

Americans were used to working together, and because they saw little need for the government to intrude on the management of their private affairs, they believed it was absurd to think that government should carry out the duties which they believed they owed to their neighbors.

Whereas, in America, citizens took it upon themselves to champion those causes they believed were important, in France, Tocqueville predicted citizens would likely go to the government to fix the problem instead:

The first time I heard that one hundred thousand men in the United States had committed themselves publicly to give up strong drink, I thought this was more of a joke than a serious proposition and, at first, I did not see very clearly why these overly sober citizens did not content themselves merely with drinking water in the privacy of their own homes. In the end, I realized that these one hundred thousand Americans, alarmed by the spread of drunkenness around them, had wished to give their support to temperance. . . . It is probably true that if these one hundred thousand men had lived in France, each one of them would have made individual representations to the government asking it to keep a close eye on all the taverns throughout the realm.[57]

The civil society was the realm in which the greatest fruits of liberty could be experienced and put to good use. It was the space in which a free people could be truly free.

THE TRUE AMERICAN DREAM

George Washington once expressed his hope that "some day or another, we shall become a storehouse and granary for the world."[58] He, like the other Founders, believed America was a rising colossus. Adams exhorted his countrymen with the thought that if they truly realized how few in history had been blessed with such opportunities, they would "feel the strongest motives to fall upon [their] knees in gratitude to heaven for having been graciously pleased to give [them] birth and education in that country and for having destined [them] to live under her laws!"[59]

Jefferson painted a compelling picture of the totality of the "American dream" in his first inaugural address. It was not, as so many assume today, simply material prosperity. Rather, it was

possessing a chosen country, with room enough for our descendants to the thousandth and thousandth generation; entertaining a due sense of our equal right to the use of our own faculties, to the acquisitions of our own industry, to honor and confidence from our fellow citizens resulting not from birth, but from our actions and their sense of them; enlightened by a benign religion, professed, indeed, and practiced in various forms, yet all of them inculcating honesty, truth, temperance, gratitude, and the love of man, acknowledging and adoring an overruling Providence, which by all its dispensations proves that it delights in the happiness of man here and his greater happiness hereafter—with all these blessings, what more is necessary to make us a happy and a prosperous people? Still one thing more, fellow citizens—a wise and frugal government, which shall restrain men from injuring one another, shall leave them otherwise free to regulate their own pursuits of industry and improvement, and shall not take from the mouth of labor the bread it has earned. This is the sum of good government, and this is necessary to close the circle of our felicities . . . the support of the State governments in all their rights, as the most competent administrations for our domestic concerns and the surest bulwarks against anti-republican tendencies . . . economy in the public expense, that labor may be lightly burdened; the honest payment of our debts and sacred preservation of the public faith; encouragement of agriculture, and of commerce as its handmaid; the diffusion of information and arraignment of all abuses at the bar of the public reason; freedom of religion; freedom of the press, and freedom of person under the protection of the habeas corpus, and trial by juries impartially selected.

He concluded:

These principles form the bright constellation which has gone before us and guided our steps through an age of revolution and reformation. The wisdom of our sages and blood of our heroes have been devoted to their attainment. They should be the creed of our political faith, the text of civic instruction, the touchstone by which we try the services of those we trust; and should we wander from them in moments of error or of alarm, let us hasten to retrace our steps and to regain the road which alone leads to peace, liberty, and safety.[60]

Jefferson hoped his countrymen would never forget just how blessed they were, and how truly special the actual "American dream" was:

My God! How little do my countrymen know what precious blessings they are in possession of, and which no other people on earth enjoy.

I confess I had no idea of it myself. While we shall see multiplied instances of Europeans going to live in America, I will venture to say no man now living will ever see an instance of an American removing to settle in Europe and continuing there. Come then and see the proofs of this . . . in order to satisfy our countrymen how much it is in their interest to preserve uninfected by contagion those peculiarities in their government and manners to which they are indebted for those blessings.[61]

Every man under his own vine and fig tree indeed.

8

SLAVERY: LIBERTY'S HYPOCRISY

To give as fair and unbiased an assessment of the Founders as possible, it is necessary to take an unpleasant but necessary look at the gross sin of slavery. The subject, as a whole, is far too complex and enormous to do total justice to it in one chapter, so the scope will simply be to answer a few basic questions: What did the Founders actually believe about slavery? Were they in favor of it? Did they try to make excuses for it? What did they *actually* say about it? What we will discover is that, contrary to what is often taught, the Founders, to their credit, consistently acknowledged the inhumanity and injustice of slavery and its incompatibility with the ideals of the American Revolution. To one degree or another, every single one of them sought its demise.

The fact that our nation was unable to completely live up to the ideas on which it was founded shows how radical those ideas really were, particularly in historical context. This should be a source of both honest pride and candid reflection. There is no excuse whatsoever for slavery. Nothing can be said in its defense, and no efforts whatsoever should be employed to in any way diminish its inhuman brutality and superlatively cruel injustice. Slavery was beyond any doubt the great hypocrisy of the founding generation. What can and must be done, however, is to place slavery in its historical context, and realize that while the moral case against it is absolute and unquestionable, the realities at work at the time present us with a far more nuanced picture. This historical review is all the more important because this single issue has been used by many to convince Americans that the Founders are not worth bothering with at all. Yet this contention is itself utterly ignorant of both human nature and history.

The plain and simple fact is that today, virtually anybody can *easily* decry slavery, for we did absolutely nothing by way of our own moral reasoning and effort to reach that conclusion, nor did we sacrifice of our time, effort, blood, sweat, and tears to achieve its demise. It was handed down to us as an assumed fact of life: slavery is wrong, always has been, and always will be. The substance of this conclusion, however, was completely won by others, many of whom are nameless to us today. The other quite nefarious assumption that many hold at present is that if they had been born during the eighteenth century, *they* would have opposed slavery and called for its abolition. But is this a realistic assumption? On the contrary, the cold, hard reality is that many of us, had we been raised in similar circumstances, would have likely engaged in the same, if not worse actions than those we so easily denounce. These are the hard facts of human nature with which any honest person must come to grips.

But what if we had been born into a world in which such an assumption was not at all common, and in fact, the opposite tended to prevail? To assume we would be as morally pure as we are today is nothing but unbridled arrogance and downright ignorance of our own human nature. Many of those who most disparage the Founders for slavery today are those who also defend the murder of an unborn child. We are thus presented with a most confusing moral landscape: a generation responsible for the intellectual and moral justification of the murder of the unborn by the millions stands in judgment of the Founding generation, who on multiple occasions affirmed the inhumanity of slavery, recognized it contradicted their ideals, and to varying degrees, took steps to contribute to its downfall through outright emancipation, the banning of the slave trade, and personal activism directed at its abolition. Both evils—slavery and abortion—were and are based on the dehumanization of the human person, except the Founders, in unequivocal terms, acknowledged the evil of their day, whereas many of those who criticize them today refuse to censure the far greater evils of our own. History has been generous in its mercy to those generations who owned up to their hypocrisy, and vengeful in its scorn toward those who didn't.

There is also the issue of nature versus nurture. It is common today to hear criticisms of the Founders from those who believe man is inherently good but is "corrupted" by his surroundings. If this is the case, then do the Founders deserve scorn? On the contrary, if men are made "evil" by their surroundings rather than by their nature, then the Founders should be praised for overcoming the prejudices and societal circumstances into which they were born to the extent that they did. If, on the other hand, human nature is fundamentally flawed, as the Founders believed and as history attests, then we should not be surprised that those who expressed and fought for such ideals had, on occasion, such severe blind spots themselves, and lived in a time in which not all wrongs could be made right all at once.

But that is not the whole story. First, we must recognize that those men commonly termed the "Founders" were only individuals. They did not control all of society, nor did what they said automatically go (although it often had great weight). There were many occasions on which they all expressed horror at what was going on in their own time and country, whether it was slavery or a whole host of other topics, and they felt utterly powerless to do anything about it. Imagine if someone in the future pinned the failures of our own generation on just a few individuals. To do so would be highly irrational and injudicious. The same is true of the Founders.

Second, it is commonly believed that the Founders justified slavery, that they minimized it, or that they did not acknowledge its evil and incompatibility with the principles articulated in the Declaration of Independence. This is simply and utterly false. There are numerous examples of the exact opposite, both from those who owned and those who did not own slaves. For example, Alexander Hamilton wrote during the Revolutionary War in support of a plan to offer freedom to slaves who took up arms with the colonists against the British: "The contempt we have been taught to entertain for the blacks makes us fancy many things that are founded neither in reason nor experience . . . An essential part of the plan is to give them their freedom with their muskets . . . The dictates of humanity and true policy equally interest me in favor of this unfortunate class of men."[1]

He remained an opponent of slavery his entire life.

Likewise, Benjamin Franklin was a lifelong opponent of slavery. Upon visiting a school for free black children, he noted that "their apprehension seems as quick, their memory as strong, and their docility in every respect equal to that of white children." And he was not afraid to ask the piercing questions about the slave trade that needed asking among his contemporaries: "Can sweetening our tea, etc., with sugar be a circumstance of such absolute necessity? Can the petty pleasure thence arising to the taste compensate for so much misery produced among our fellow creatures, and such a constant butchery of the human species by this pestilential, detestable traffic in the bodies and souls of men?"[2]

"Slavery is such an atrocious debasement of human nature that its very extirpation, if not performed with solicitous care, may sometimes open a source of serious evil," he wrote in a public newspaper toward the end of his life. As the head of the "Pennsylvania Society for Promoting the Abolition of Slavery, and the Relief of Free Negroes Unlawfully Held in Bondage," he outlined a plan by which he hoped "to instruct, to advise, to qualify those who have been restored to freedom for the exercise and enjoyment of civil liberty" through what we today would call job training, helping them find employment upon the completion of their training, and educating their children so that they could have a better future.[3]

John Jay, a prominent American diplomat and the first chief justice of the United States, plainly acknowledged the hypocrisy of maintaining slavery: "It is much to be wished that slavery may be abolished . . . To contend for our own liberty, and to deny that blessing to others, involves an inconsistency not to be excused."[4]

Thomas Paine had even stronger words for those who enslaved their fellow human beings: "So monstrous is the making and keeping them slaves at all, abstracted from the barbarous usage they suffer, and the many evils attending the practice; as selling husbands away from wives, children from parents, and from each other, in violation of sacred and natural ties; and opening the way for adulteries, incests, and many shocking consequences for all of which the guilty masters must answer to the final Judge."[5]

Madison also saw slavery as a debasement of human nature. "We have seen the mere distinction of color made in the most enlightened period of time a ground of the most oppressive dominion ever exercised by man over man," he said at the Constitutional Convention. In explaining why the Constitution did not ban slavery outright, he wrote, "The southern states would not have entered into the Union of America without the temporary permission of that trade. And if they were excluded from the Union, the consequences might be dreadful to them and to us . . . Under the Articles of Confederation, it might be continued forever. But by this clause, an end may be put to it after twenty years. There is therefore an amelioration of our circumstances."[6]

The fact that the Constitution allowed Congress to ban the slave trade twenty years after its ratification was actually a major selling point the authors of the *Federalist Papers* used to encourage its ratification. Sure enough, Congress did exactly that, and the law went into effect on January 1, 1808, the very first date allowed by the Constitution for the ban of the slave trade. Jefferson wrote, on the occasion of the bill's passage:

> Whatever may have been the circumstances which influenced our forefathers to permit the introduction of personal bondage into any part of these states, and to participate in the wrongs committed on an unoffending quarter of the globe, we may rejoice that such circumstances, and such a sense of them, exist no longer. It is honorable to the nation at large that their legislature availed themselves of the first practicable moment for arresting the progress of this great moral and political error: and I sincerely pray with you, my friends, that all the members of the human family may, in the time prescribed by the Father of us all, find themselves securely established in the enjoyments of life, liberty, and happiness.[7]

Madison concluded that "great as the evil is, a dismemberment of the Union would be worse. If those states should disunite from the other states for not indulging them in the temporary continuance of this traffic, they might solicit and obtain aid from foreign powers."[8] Even with ostensibly justified reasons for making such a compromise, some Founders were very wary of the dissimilarities between the Northern and Southern states on this point even before the Declaration of Independence. "I dread the consequences of this dissimilitude of character," Adams had written, "and without the utmost caution on both sides, and the most considerable forbearance with one another and prudent condescension on both sides, they will certainly be fatal."[9] As we shall see, a number of the Founders who lived well into the 1800s could see that, far from ending slavery as they had expected would be done, the next generation was strengthening it and taking steps to secure its advance across the continent. Every single one of them looked upon this with dread, and they all predicted that it would likely lead to violence. A few years before his death, Madison had written to an abolitionist, "The magnitude of this evil among us is so deeply felt, and so universally acknowledged, that no merit could be greater than that of devising a satisfactory remedy for it,"[10] and he frankly confessed that he did not know what could be done, and this frightened him, as well as others. The Civil War was to make their worst nightmares come true.

And yet, at the time the Constitution was ratified, Madison contended that the "dismemberment of the Union would be worse." Why? Because the lessons of history had taught the Founders that if the United States were to divide into two or more countries, they would likely turn out like Europe, which, as a collection of various countries in close quarters, were constantly at war with one another for centuries. "To avoid the evil under the last head," even the antislavery John Adams acknowledged, "it will be in danger of dividing the continent into two or three nations, a case that presents no prospect but of perpetual war."[11] For centuries Europe had been the scene of multiple major wars: the wars of religion, the Thirty Years' War, the War of the Spanish Succession, the

Seven Years' War (the first "world war" in history, known as the "French and Indian War" in the New World), and many others. The Founders' fears continued to be justified immediately following the ratification of the Constitution in 1789: Great Britain and France were at war a few years later, a war that became the Napoleonic Wars on continental Europe, and the War of 1812 between Great Britain and the United States. This long history of constant warfare continued throughout the nineteenth century as more and more European nations experienced the convulsions of revolution, and it tragically culminated in World War I at the beginning of the twentieth century. This was followed in quick succession by World War II, which, as the most devastating war ever fought on planet Earth, finally brought a period of relative peace and stability to Europe that has lasted for decades, but even in our own day, not yet a century. From the Founders' perspective, the only way this greater evil could be avoided in the New World was by making a *temporary* compromise on slavery (to maintain the Union) so that all the states would be united under one government instead of being multiple nations prone to engage in constant warfare with each other, just as had happened (and continued to happen) in Europe.

We must understand that at this point in our history, each state was almost like its own country. The extent to which, today, our culture and our national habits have become largely homogenous was definitely *not* the case in early America. Frequently, the Founders referred to their individual states as their "country," as many people tended to identify with their own states before they identified as citizens of the United States. Before ratification of the Constitution, Adams referred to the United States as "large and populous nations,"[12] not one "nation." This is why so many of the Founders, George Washington in particular, constantly encouraged his fellow citizens to first and foremost consider themselves as citizens of the United States, because this was an identity that did not come naturally, and to the extent it did it often played second fiddle to state citizenship. It was common to hear the phrase "The United States *are*" rather than "The United States *is*," as is the case today. This provided even more incentives for the Founders to maintain the Union of the States under one government, to prevent sectional conflict and war. Despite their differences on slavery, which many of the Founders believed was on its way toward extinction, they also believed it was essential to keep North and South together to avoid the greater evil of constant warfare.

But even those Founders who were Southerners decried slavery. In the *Federalist Papers*, Madison called the Southern policy of "considering as property a part of their human brethren . . . [a] barbarous policy." He further argued that "we must deny the fact that slaves are considered merely as property, and in no respect whatever as persons,"[13] even while acknowledging that, at least temporarily, the Constitution saw them somewhat in the light of property rather than as full citizens. But this is a source of yet more confusion today over the infamous Three-Fifths Compromise, by which slaves were counted as "three-fifths" of a normal citizen in determining a state's population and its resulting representation by Congress, which was obviously done to placate the Southern states. However, what is not known is that the three-fifths clause was actually intended to, in the long run, curtail slavery. If slaves had been considered full citizens when determining representation by Congress, then the Southern states would have had their populations that much more artificially inflated, thus increasing their representation in Congress. The great irony of course is that if the Constitution had deemed slaves noncitizens, and thus not countable *at all* in the census in terms of representation (zero-fifths), Southern representation in Congress would have been greatly diminished without the artificial boost provided by their slave populations. With that loss of representation, who knows how the fight to end slavery might have turned out? So while the "three-fifths" clause was no doubt a completely unjust provision of the Constitution, reflective more of the Founders' willingness to compromise in order to avoid what they saw as the greater evil of disunion and perpetual warfare, it was intended to be a temporary expedient, and in fact, it was somewhat helpful in reducing the South's representation in Congress. Anybody who claims the Founding

Fathers said blacks were three-fifths of a person is either misinformed or trying to misinform others. Contrary to popular stereotypes that assert that the "three-fifths" clause was pro-slavery, the reality was quite different.

George Washington, although he owned slaves, never uttered one word in support of slavery itself. Rather, it was a practice he found personally disturbing, as he later reflected:

> The unfortunate condition of the persons whose labor in part I employed has been the only unavoidable subject of regret. To make the adults among them as easy and as comfortable in their circumstances as their actual state of ignorance and improvidence would admit, and to lay a foundation to prepare the rising generation for a destiny different from that in which they were born, afforded some satisfaction to my mind, and could not I hoped be displeasing to the justice of the Creator.[14]

In his will, he emancipated all of his slaves and made sure they would be provided for through his estate:

> Upon the decease of my wife, it is my will and desire that all the slaves which I hold in my own right *shall receive their freedom* . . . that all . . . shall be *comfortably clothed and fed by my heirs while they live* . . . to be *taught to read and write*, and to *be brought up to some useful occupation* . . . And I do moreover most pointedly, and most solemnly enjoin it upon my executors hereafter named . . . to see that this clause respecting slaves, and every part thereof be religiously fulfilled at the epoch at which it is directed to take place, without evasion, neglect, or delay . . . particularly as it respects the aged and infirm; seeing that a regular and permanent fund be established for their support so long as there are subjects requiring it.[15]

It is no wonder that, during his own lifetime, the character of George Washington was so celebrated and admired, as evidenced by Phillis Wheatley, a poet who also happened to be a slave, who wrote of the new commander in chief of the Continental army during the Revolution:

Proceed, great chief, with virtue on thy side,

Thy ev'ry action let the Goddess guide.

A crown, a mansion, and a throne that shine,

With gold unfading, WASHINGTON! Be thine.[16]

Washington in turn praised Wheatley's "great poetical talents" and "genius," and welcomed a meeting with her, which eventually did take place.[17]

John Adams was also vociferous in his disdain for slavery:

The turpitude, the inhumanity, the cruelty, and the infamy of the African commerce in slaves, have been so impressively represented to the public by the highest powers of eloquence, that nothing that I can say would increase the just odium in which it is and ought to be held. Every measure of prudence, therefore, ought to be assumed for the eventual total extirpation of slavery from the United States . . . I have, through my whole life, held the practice of slavery in such abhorrence, that I have never owned a negro or any other slave, though I have lived for many years in times, when the practice was not disgraceful, when the best men in my vicinity thought it not inconsistent with their character, and when it has cost me thousands of dollars for the labor and subsistence of free men, which I might have saved by the purchase of negroes at times when they were very cheap.[18]

During the days of the Revolution, Adams summarized the arguments of his friend James Otis in defense of the rights of the American colonists. "He asserted that these rights were inherent and inalienable," wrote Adams, "that they never could be surrendered or alienated but by idiots or madmen, and all the acts of idiots and lunatics were void and not obligatory by all the laws of God and man." He then added, "Nor were the poor Negroes forgotten. Not a Quaker in Philadelphia or Mr. Jefferson in Virginia ever asserted the rights of Negroes in stronger terms."[19]

Notice his reference to Thomas Jefferson as an advocate of the "rights of Negroes." Adams based his assertion on Jefferson's support of numerous attempts to emancipate the slaves in Virginia. Incidentally, it is Jefferson who provides perhaps the best insight into the historical context concerning the peculiarities of slavery. The question is justly asked today, "Why didn't the Founders just free them?" First of all, many of them did not even own slaves and had always opposed slavery. Among those who were slave owners, though, several did, in fact, emancipate them, but at their deaths. The Founders who did *not* emancipate their slaves (or if they did, only did so at their own deaths) often failed to do so because the law itself in a number of Southern states, particularly Virginia, made outright emancipation a morally complicated proposition in certain situations (as we shall soon see). There were concerns in the South regarding the extent to which the two races could coexist, particularly since one had been enslaved by the other. Founders such as Madison and Jefferson shared this concern, which is why they both favored emancipating the slaves, but in such a way that it could be done gradually and peacefully. Per these concerns, both entertained recolonization schemes for emancipated slaves. Some of these concerns were legitimate, such as the concern that former slaves would, upon obtaining their freedom, turn upon their former masters in revenge for the wrongs perpetrated against them. Others were, certainly by modern standards, racist in nature. These are candid facts that need to be recognized. But we must also recognize that if any of us had been born into such a world, we likely would not have been any better. That is not a justification, but simply a comment on the realities of human nature. The fact that these men held antislavery sentiments *at all* is quite extraordinary given the times in which they lived.

Unbeknownst to most, however, one of Jefferson's most famous quotes, even appearing on his memorial in Washington, DC, was directly connected to slavery, though the quote out of context gives no such indication: "And can the liberties of a nation be thought secure when we have removed their only firm basis, a conviction in the minds of the people that these liberties are of the gift of God? That they are not to be violated but with his wrath? Indeed I tremble for my country when I reflect that God is just, that his justice cannot sleep forever."[20]

Jefferson frequently expressed hopes for total emancipation of the slaves, and on a number of occasions worked legislatively to accomplish this goal, to no avail. His hopes, however, remained: "The spirit of the master is abating," he wrote, "that of the slave rising from the dust, his condition mollifying, the way I hope preparing, under the auspices of heaven, for a total emancipation, and that this is disposed, in the order of events, to be with the consent of the masters, rather than by their extirpation [destruction]."[21]

Perhaps the most revealing of Jefferson's writings on this topic comes from a letter he wrote in response to a request for advice from a certain Edward Coles, a young man from Virginia. Though Coles himself owned a number of slaves, he was nonetheless disgusted by slavery, and was considering selling his slaves and moving out of Virginia. Jefferson's response is fascinating:

> The love of justice and the love of country plead equally the cause of these people, and it is a moral reproach to us that they should have pleaded it so long in vain, and should have produced not a single effort, nay I fear not much serious willingness to relieve them and ourselves from our present condition of moral and political reprobation. From those of the former generation who were in the fullness of age when I came into public life, which was while our controversy with England was on paper only, I soon saw that nothing was to be hoped. Nursed and educated in the daily habit of seeing the degraded condition, both bodily and mental, of those unfortunate beings, not reflecting that that degradation was very much the work of themselves and their fathers, few minds have yet doubted but that they were as legitimate subjects of property as their horses and cattle. The quiet and monotonous course of colonial life has been disturbed by no alarm, and little reflection on the value of liberty. And when alarm was taken by an enterprise on their own, it was not easy to carry them to the whole length of the principles which they invoked for themselves.[22]

Jefferson continued by offering his hopes that the next generation would finish the job:

> I had always hoped that the younger generation receiving their early impressions after the flame of liberty had been kindled in every breast, and had become as it were the vital spirit of every American, that the generous temperament of youth, analogous to the motion of their blood, and above the suggestions of avarice, would have sympathized with oppression wherever found, and proved their love of liberty beyond their own share of it. But my intercourse with them, since my return, has not been sufficient to ascertain that they had made towards this point the progress I had hoped. Your solitary but welcome voice is the first which has brought this sound to my ear. . .Yet the hour of emancipation is advancing in the march of time. It will come. . . . This enterprise is for the young, for those who can follow it up, and bear it through to its consummation. It shall have all my prayers, and these are the only weapons of an old man. But in the meantime are you right in abandoning this property, and your country [Virginia] with it? I think not. My opinion has ever been that, until more can be done for them [slaves], we should endeavor, with those whom fortune has thrown on our hands, to feed and clothe them well, protect them from ill usage, require such reasonable labor only as is performed voluntarily by freemen, and be led by no repugnancies to abdicate them, and our duties to them. The laws do not permit us to turn them loose, if that were for their good: and to commute them for other property is to commit them to those whose usage of them we cannot control.[23]

In short, Coles had two options: sell his slaves or keep them. Jefferson suggested he keep them. How could he recommend such a thing when he was supposedly opposed to slavery? Because as already stated, the laws made outright emancipation a difficult step to take, both legally and morally. Therefore, the only way the young man could rid himself of his slaves was to sell them to someone else. But since he could not possibly know how another master would treat them, and since he himself was a benevolent master who generously provided for his slaves, Jefferson suggested that the most humane option was to keep them and continue providing for them. To do otherwise would have been an abdication of his "duties to them." This is a key point in understanding some of the moral subtleties involved in the slavery question. He concluded:

> [I hope that] on the contrary you will come forward in the public councils, become the missionary of this doctrine truly Christian; insinuate and inculcate it softly but steadily through the medium of writing and conversation; associate others in your labors, and when the phalanx is formed, bring on and press the proposition perseveringly until its accomplishment. It is an encouraging observation that no good measure was ever proposed which, if duly pursued, failed to prevail in the end . . . And you will be supported by the religious precept, "be not weary in well doing" [Galatians 6:9]. That your success may be as speedy and complete, as it will be of honorable and immortal consolation to yourself, I shall . . . fervently and sincerely pray.[24]

Such is the context that is rarely provided in the discussion about slavery and the Founding Fathers. This is by no means meant to excuse slavery. It was a monstrous evil for which no excuse can possibly ever satisfy the righteous indictments against it. At the same time, those who insist upon moral perfection from the Founders, who were part of just as imperfect a world as we are today, are often engaging in the worst sort of hypocrisy. Again, we live in an age in which the murder of millions of unborn children has been officially sanctioned by our Supreme Court as a "constitutional right." Many who argue for such a "right" are dehumanizing the human child in the womb in the same way that many blacks were dehumanized. The latter was used to justify keeping people in slavery, the former to sanction their murder.

Jefferson once noted, "The generation which commences a revolution can rarely complete it." The choice with which many of the

Founders felt they were faced was either (1) the existence of the *United States* with slavery, but with an eventual opportunity to totally abolish it; or (2) the existence of numerous tightly packed "countries" on the same continent, with no chance for abolishing slavery, and the likelihood of perpetual war between them, as had happened in Europe. As with all human attempts to see into the future, they were able to do so only imperfectly. But given their apparent choices, the decisions they made become not justifiable so much as understandable. Among a series of very bad options, they chose what they felt was the lesser evil.

In conclusion, let us consult perhaps one of the most authoritative people on this matter: Frederick Douglass. Douglass was not a Founder, but an ex-slave who escaped to the North from bondage and campaigned against slavery for the rest of his life, even becoming friends with Abraham Lincoln. But far from hating and dismissing the Founders, this great man held them in esteem and awe. In 1852 he delivered a famous speech entitled "What to the slave is the 4th?" referring of course to the Fourth of July, when the Founders declared that "all men are created equal, and endowed by their Creator with certain unalienable rights." This speech is often used to criticize the Founders. However, those who do so have either not read the whole speech, or refuse to quote it in context. This shall, accordingly, be done here:

> Fellow citizens, I am not wanting in respect for the fathers of this republic. The signers of the Declaration of Independence were brave men. They were great men too—great enough to give name to a great age. It does not often happen to a nation to raise, at one time, such a number of truly great men . . . I cannot contemplate their great deeds with less than admiration. They were statesman, patriots, and heroes, and for the good they did, and the principles they contended for, I will unite with you to honor their memory . . . With them, nothing was "*settled*" that was not right. With them, justice, liberty and humanity were "*final*," not slavery and oppression . . . Their solid manhood stands out the more as we contrast it with these degenerate times . . . Their statesmanship looked beyond the passing moment, and stretched away

in strength into the distant future. They seized upon eternal principles, and set a glorious example in their defense. Mark them![25]

He went on to say:

Your fathers have lived, died, and have done their work, and have done much of it well. You live and must die, and you must do your work . . . You have no right to wear out and waste the hard-earned fame of your fathers to cover your indolence . . . It was fashionable, hundreds of years ago, for the children of Jacob to boast, we have "Abraham to our father," when they had long lost Abraham's faith and spirit [Matthew 3:9; John 8:39]. That people contented themselves under the shadow of Abraham's great name, while they repudiated the deeds which made his name great. Need I remind you that a similar thing is being done over this country today? . . . Washington could not die till he had broken the chains of his slaves. Yet his monument is built up by the price of human blood, and the traders in the bodies and souls of man shout—"We have Washington to *our father*."

Notice that Douglass explicitly praised the Founders, Washington in particular, but heaped curses on the generation that *followed* the Founders. He continued: "Standing with God and the crushed and bleeding slave on this occasion, I will, in the name of humanity which is outraged, in the name of liberty which is fettered, in the name of the Constitution and the Bible, which are disregarded and trampled upon, dare to call in question and to denounce, with all the emphasis I can command, everything that serves to perpetuate slavery—the great sin and shame of America!"[26]

Imagine: Douglass, a former slave, heaping praises upon the Founders. How could he do this? In short, because Douglass was historically literate. He knew that though they had done it imperfectly, the Founders had advanced the ball down the field significantly, to use a modern sports metaphor. He concluded his thoughts on the Founders with an exhortation on the Constitution:

But I differ from those who charge this baseness on the framers of the Constitution of the United States. *It is a slander upon their memory*, at least, so I believe . . . interpreted as it *ought* to be interpreted, the Constitution is a GLORIOUS LIBERTY DOCUMENT. Read its preamble, consider its purposes. Is slavery among them? Is it at the gateway? Or is it in the temple? It is neither . . . [I]f it be not somewhat singular that, if the Constitution were intended to be, by its framers and adopters, a slave-holding instrument, why neither *slavery, slaveholding*, nor *slave* can anywhere be found in it . . . Now, take the Constitution according to its plain reading, and I defy the presentation of a single pro-slavery clause in it. On the other hand it will be found to contain principles and purposes entirely hostile to the existence of slavery.[27]

If a former slave could heap such praise on the Founders, what, may I ask, justifies the temerity of those today who heap nothing but curses? It is precisely because many notable former slaves knew American history and the true legacy of the Founders that they loved them, and why (to put it bluntly) in our amnesia many middle-class white kids of the twenty-first century, among others, deem them their moral inferiors.

But the most conclusive, if not utterly disturbing evidence that Douglass was correct about the Founders comes from, of all people, the vice president of the Confederacy, Alexander Stephens, who asserted that the new government of which he was an officer was established on completely different principles than those espoused by the Founders when it came to race:

Those ideas [of the Founders], however, were fundamentally wrong. They rested upon the assumption of the equality of races. This was an error. It was a sandy foundation, and the government built upon it fell when the "storm came and the wind blew." Our new government is founded upon exactly the opposite idea; its foundations are laid, its cornerstone rests, upon the great truth that the Negro is not equal to the white man; that slavery subordination to the superior race is his natural and normal condition. This, our new government, is the first, in the history of the world, based upon this great physical, philosophical, and moral truth.[28]

Need more be said?

Many of the great figures of history owned slaves, supported slavery, or remained silent as to its existence. Greek philosophers, Pharaonic kings, Roman statesmen, and others from all corners of the earth whom today we consider great and noble souls did nothing to advance its demise, and in many cases even stunted it. And yet it is the Founders alone who are actively and vociferously criticized. It is the Founders alone upon whom we inflict vituperative and delegitimizing scorn. It is the Founders alone upon whom we maintain a singular gaze of judgment and condemnation, and against whom we render our verdicts of "guilty" with torturous repetition.

Why?

Because the Founders, for the first time in history, discovered that most resplendent gold known as self-government, and the United States was the first nation to build its foundations upon this precious cornerstone. Having wrenched it from the bowels of the earth upon which it had always been accessible but cynically dismissed, they handed it to us, their posterity, with dirt and mud upon it. But they handed it to us nonetheless. Never before had a nation been bequeathed such a gift from its inception; this is why, as we are seeing, the great danger in dismissing or despising the Founders for handing us an imperfect Union is the danger of unjustifiably despising not persons, but the very gold they handed us in the first place. For in the final analysis, the only reason we today criticize slavery with such righteous invective is because a few imperfect men in an imperfect time in the midst of imperfect circumstances dared to declare and defend that which, since time immemorial, had been merely an ephemeral dream in human affairs: that "all men are created equal."

9

TYRANNY OF THE HEART, SOUL, MIND, AND STRENGTH: LIBERTY'S DEATH

When the past is irrelevant to, or even worse, despised by a society, that society has a way of convincing itself that everything it does is new and innovative, and that it is on an inevitable path of progress. The truth of the matter is that in doing so, it is doing nothing but playing yet another variation on the same old tune that has echoed through time since the beginning of human existence. How could it know better, after all?

The Founders attempted, albeit imperfectly, to create a free society based on the realities of human nature and thousands of years' worth of human experience. And yet today, many in our society seem to be under the impression that the last couple of centuries have somehow undone all or most of that. They have thus consigned the Founders to the historical oblivion known as "old-fashioned." If the Founders are indeed "irrelevant," then, as has been said, extraordinary claims require extraordinary evidence.

One of the great secrets the Founders knew was that tyranny need not always arise from the will of one who seeks to be a tyrant or in a society that deliberately seeks one out. The worst tyrants had rarely been those who specifically set out to become tyrants, and rarely had a society slipped into tyranny's grasp by conscious volition. Rather, the greatest danger tended to be those men, and those societies, who had greater faith in their good intentions than in their own fallibility, and in their ability to cheat the realities of human nature than in the lessons of human history.

This is why the Founders' prophecies concerning the rise of tyranny are perhaps the most sobering, precisely because any honest perusal of their contents will make any dismissal of the Founders on the grounds that they are "old-fashioned" seem laughable. This chapter shows their predictions concerning what would occur to any nation, particularly the United States, if any of the principles we have examined became distorted, lost, or otherwise abandoned. Their words are stunning in their accuracy. If they are old-fashioned and irrelevant to our own time, then they should have little or no meaning or application to our society today. But, if these words *do* continue to have meaning and apply to us today, then we must with great honesty and humility reevaluate the wisdom and warnings of our Founders, for they knew the great truth as articulated by Montesquieu, that "in a government that lasts a long time, one descends to ills by imperceptible degrees, and one climbs back to the good only with an effort."[1]

But first, we turn to a "prophecy" uttered, once again, by Alexis de Tocqueville. This comes from the end of his masterpiece, *Democracy in America*, and it lays out his predications of what tyranny could look like in the American future. These words were penned in the 1830s, and there remain few, if any, I have ever read that have struck me as forcefully as these with their prescience and accuracy.

THE PROPHECY

I had noted in my stay in the United States that a democratic state of society similar to the American model could lay itself open to the establishment of despotism with unusual ease . . . If despotism were to be established in present-day democracies, it would probably assume a different character. It would be more widespread and kinder. It would debase men without tormenting them . . .

I wish to imagine under what new features despotism might appear in the world: I see an innumerable crowd of men, all alike and equal, turned in upon themselves in a restless search for those petty, vulgar pleasures with which they fill their souls. Each of them living apart is almost unaware of the destiny of all the rest. His children and personal friends are for him the whole of the human race. As for the remainder of his fellow citizens, he stands alongside them but does not see them; he touches them without feeling them; he exists only in himself and for himself; if he still retains his family circle, at any rate he may be said to have lost his country.

Above these men stands an immense and protective power which alone is responsible for looking after their enjoyments and watching over their destiny. It is absolute, meticulous, ordered, provident, and kindly disposed. It would be like a fatherly authority if, father-like, its aims were to prepare men for manhood, but it seeks only to keep them in perpetual childhood. It prefers its citizens to enjoy themselves provided they have only enjoyment in mind. It works readily for their happiness, but wishes to be the only provider and judge of it. It provides their security, anticipates and guarantees their needs, supplies their pleasures, directs their principal concerns, manages their industry, regulates their estates, divides their inheritances. Why can it not remove from them entirely the bother of thinking and the troubles of life? Thus it reduces daily the value and frequency of the exercise of free choice: it restricts the activity of free will within a narrower range and gradually removes autonomy itself from each citizen . . .

Thus, the ruling power, having taken each citizen one by one into its powerful grasp, and having molded him to its own liking, spreads its arms over the whole of society, covering the surface of social life with a network of petty, complicated, detailed, and uniform rules through which even the most original minds and the most energetic of spirits cannot reach the light in order to rise above the crowd. It does not break men's wills but it does soften, bend, and control them. Rarely does it force men to act, but it constantly opposes what actions they perform. It does not tyrannize but it inhibits, represses, drains, snuffs out, dulls so much effort that finally it reduces each nation to nothing more than a flock of timid and hardworking animals with the government as shepherd. I have always believed that this type of organized, gentle, and peaceful enslavement just described could link up more easily than imagined with some of the external forms of freedom and that it would not be impossible for it to take hold in the very shadow of the sovereignty of the people . . . they [democratic peoples] feel the need to be directed as well as the desire to remain free. Since they are unable to blot out either of these hostile feelings, they strive to satisfy both of them together. They conceive a single, protective, and all-powerful government, but one elected by the citizens. They combine centralization with the sovereignty of the people. That gives them some respite. They derive consolation from being supervised by thinking that they have chosen their supervisors. Every individual tolerates being tied down because he sees that it is not another man nor a class of people holding the end of the chain, but society itself. Under this system, citizens leave their state of dependence just long enough to choose their masters [i.e., through voting] and then they return to it . . . Many people very easily fall in with this type of compromise between a despotic administration and the sovereignty of the people, and they think they have sufficiently safeguarded individual freedom when they surrendered it to a national authority. That is not good enough for me. The character of the master is much less important to me than the fact of obedience . . .

I see quite clearly that, in this way, individual intervention in the most important affairs [i.e., elections] is preserved, but it is just as much suppressed in small and private ones. We forget that it is, above all, in the details that we run the risk of enslaving men. For my part, I would be tempted to believe that freedom in the big things of life is less important than in the slightest, if I thought that we could always be guaranteed the latter when we did not possess the former. Subjection in the minor things of life is obvious every day and is experienced indiscriminately by all citizens. It does not cause them to lose hope but it constantly irks them until they give up the exercise of their will. It gradually blots out their mind and enfeebles their spirit . . .

It will be useless to call upon those very citizens who have become so dependent upon central government to choose from time to time the representative of this government. This very important but brief and rare exercise of their free choice will not prevent their gradual loss of the faculty of autonomous thought, feeling, and action, so that they will slowly fall below the level of humanity. I may add that they will soon lose the capacity to exercise the great and only privilege open to them.

The democratic nations which introduced freedom into politics at the same time that they were increasing despotism in the administrative sphere have been led into the strangest paradoxes. Faced with the need to manage small affairs where common sense can be enough, they reckon citizens are incompetent. When it comes to governing the whole state, they give these citizens immense prerogatives [voting]. They turn them by degrees into playthings of the ruler or his masters, higher than kings or lower than men. Having exhausted all the various electoral systems without finding one which suited them, they look surprised and continue to search, as if the defects they see had far more to do with the country's Constitution than with that of the electorate.

It is, indeed, difficult to imagine how men who have completely given up the habit of self-government could successfully choose those who should do it for them, and no one will be convinced that a liberal, energetic, and prudent government can ever emerge from the voting of a nation of servants . . .

The vices of those who govern and the ineptitude of those governed would soon bring it to ruin and the people, tired of its representatives and of itself, would create freer institutions or would soon revert to its abasement to one single master.[2]

Tocqueville thus predicted, with stunning accuracy, many of the very same things our Founders predicted would happen in our society as we abandoned our founding principles:

1. There would be a decline in education, knowledge, and the rise of a generally ignorant citizenry.

2. There would be a loss of morality and a resulting rise in cultural narcissism.

3. Society would develop an excessive love of material pleasures and prosperity, which both result from and further exacerbate the decline of morality.

4. The Constitution would be intentionally misinterpreted so as to avoid the difficult process of amending it; thus, the limits it placed on the government would become essentially meaningless by the arbitrary redefinition of words.

5. Once these false interpretations of the Constitution gained ground, the government would continue to grow faster and faster, as it would no longer be confined by its previous boundaries.

6. Political parties would encourage and stoke the latent divisions in society to maintain and increase their own power.

7. With the expansion of the state beyond its constitutionally mandated boundaries, there would be a rise in administrative tyranny. This occurs as government becomes more corporatized and amalgamated with financial institutions, incentivizing the devaluation of our currency through fiat money printed by banks.

8. All of the previous points combine to create a monumental problem of debt as government expenses would rise in response to both the need to pay off its allies and sycophants, as well as the greater and greater demands on the public treasury by the citizenry itself.

So what did the Founders say about each of these things?

THE DECLINE OF EDUCATION AND THE RISE OF IGNORANCE

The Founders were certain that an ignorant people were incapable of being free, and at the same time, that a free people were perhaps the most prone to such ignorance. "Almost all mankind have lost their liberties through ignorance, inattention, and disunion," Adams wrote sorrowfully. This made a nation ripe for tyranny. He warned his countrymen before the Revolution that "the jaws of power are always opened to devour, and her arm is always stretched out if possible to destroy the freedom of thinking, speaking, and writing." And that was exactly what the British were attempting to do. They hoped to distract the people from their attempts to tax them so they could fund more government offices and officials in America: "It seems very manifest . . . that a design is formed to strip us in a great measure of the means of knowledge by loading the press, the colleges, and even an almanac and a newspaper with restraints and duties, and to introduce the inequalities and dependences of the feudal system by taking from the poorer sort of people all their little subsistence and conferring it on a set of stamp officers, distributors, and their deputies."[3]

The Founders were perhaps most concerned that, with a rise in ignorance, there would be a proportional rise in apathy toward public affairs. And if the people were unaware of, or kept from knowing what their elected officials were up to, fertile soil for corruption and tyranny would be tilled, as Jefferson warned: "Withdrawn such a distance from the eye of their constituents, and these so dispersed as to be inaccessible to public information, and particularly to that of the conduct of their own representatives, they will form the most corrupt government on earth, if the means of their corruption be not prevented."[4]

"In a nation which is ignorant as well as democratic," Tocqueville remarked, "there is soon bound to be a gigantic difference between the intellectual capacity of the sovereign power and that of each of its subjects." As the knowledge gap increases between the masses and their rulers, "this completes the easy concentration of all power in its hands. The administrative function of the state constantly increases because the state alone is capable of administration."[5]

If such ignorance were to take root, the Founders worried that the people would gradually become less governable, and thereby require a stronger and stronger state. Hamilton warned, "When the minds of these [the "unthinking populace"] are loosened from their attachment to ancient establishments and courses, they seem to grow giddy and are apt more or less to run into *anarchy*."[6]

Perhaps most presciently, the Founders warned that the press could be made an instrument by which the freedom of speech was *reduced*, a very counterintuitive notion, but one that had been (and continues to be) proved by experience. Adams warned about collaboration between the government and a supposedly "free" press during the tense days of the Revolution: "License of the press is no proof of liberty," he wrote. "When a people is corrupted, the press may be made an engine to complete their ruin: and it is now notorious that the ministry [the British government] are daily employing it to increase and establish corruption, and to pluck up virtue by the roots."[7]

Similarly, Jefferson warned that the press could be made into an instrument by which the people were kept in ignorance, rather than informed and up-to-date on those matters most important to their national and civil life: "It is a melancholy truth that a suppression of the press could not more completely deprive the nation of its benefits than is done by its abandoned prostitution to falsehood . . . I really look with commiseration over the great body of my fellow citizens who, reading newspapers, live and die in the belief that they have known something of what has been passing in the world in their time."[8]

Can the men who made such stunningly accurate observations be irrelevant?

THE DECLINE OF VIRTUE AND THE RISE OF LICENTIOUSNESS

Even more than ignorance, the Founders were most concerned about a decline in religion and morality. They would much have preferred a virtuous, simpler society to a more "knowledgeable," sophisticated one.

While reflecting on the notion that America lagged behind Europe, particularly France, in science, Jefferson shot back (within the context of the Napoleonic wars initiated by revolutionary France) with this: "If science produces no better fruits than tyranny, murder, rapine and destitution of national morality, I would rather wish our country to be ignorant, honest and estimable, as our neighboring savages are."[9] In other words, he would have preferred to live with few if any of the benefits of civilization than have those benefits accrue to an immoral country.

"Society is endangered not by the great corruption of the few, but by the laxity of all," Tocqueville had noted, and on this he was in complete agreement with the Founders. "Have you ever found in history one single example of a nation thoroughly corrupted, that was afterwards restored to virtue?" Adams inquired. "It is the manners [morals/cultural habits] and spirit of a people which preserve a republic in vigor. A degeneracy in these is a canker which soon eats to the heart of its laws and constitution,"[10] Jefferson had said. Washington had correspondingly warned that "at the last stage of corrupted morals and political depravity . . . when a people shall have become incapable of governing themselves and fit for a master, it is of little consequences from what quarter he comes."[11] They felt the Revolution had proven the truth of this principle with regard to Great Britain. Adams reflected on the lessons: "Whoever was acquainted with the national history must have been convinced how completely their [Britain's] government was corrupted, and the persons concerned in it lost to all the ties of honor, virtue, and religion—ties which once restrained the nation; ties which alone can restrain any people from robbing and plundering all whom they think in their power."[12]

As previously discussed, the Founders did not believe liberty was doing whatever you wanted, but being empowered to do *as you ought* according to laws that both respected your rights and that you had a voice in making. Jefferson referred to this idea as "that temperate portion of liberty which does not infer either anarchy or licentiousness."[13] The Founders frequently warned of "licentiousness," or a general decline in moral virtue, particularly in the realm of sexuality. Washington observed,

"Liberty, when it degenerates into licentiousness, begets confusion, and frequently ends in tyranny or some woeful catastrophe . . . We are a young nation, and have a character to establish. It behooves us therefore to set out right for first impressions will be lasting, indeed are all in all."[14] Adams offered a similar warning, affirming the universally held opinion among the Founders that the Constitution was simply not capable of governing an immoral people: "[We must] guard ourselves against those principles in government, and those manners, which are so opposite to our own Constitution, and to our characters as a young people, called by Providence to the most honorable and important of all duties, that of forming establishments for a great nation and a new world."[15]

"Our rulers will become corrupt, our people careless,"[16] Jefferson feared. Should that ever happen, there would be an inevitable and potentially disastrous decline in public affairs, as Adams warned: "When public virtue is gone, when the national spirit is fled, when a party is substituted for the nation and faction for a party, when venality [bribery] lurks and skulks in secret, and, much more, when it impudently braves the public censure, whether it be sent in the form of emissaries from foreign powers, or is employed by ambitious and intriguing domestic citizens, the republic is lost in essence, though it may still exist in form."[17]

As president, Adams warned his countrymen that if American society ever "assumes the language of justice and moderation while it is practicing iniquity and extravagance . . . this country will be the most miserable habitation in the world, because we have no government armed with power capable of contending with human passions unbridled by morality and religion." This was the precursor to perhaps his most famous line: "Our Constitution was made only for a moral and religious people. It is wholly inadequate to the government of any other."[18]

American government was limited because it was predicated upon the foundation of a religious and moral people. If that foundation were removed, the government could no longer survive in such a form, as coercive powers would become necessary to fill the vacuum left by moral decrepitude.

Both to warn America and to mock European intellectuals who deplored America's religiosity, Tocqueville commented on the decline of religion in Europe, as well as its effects: "What remains today of those barriers which once held tyranny in check? Since religion has lost its sway over men's souls, the most obvious boundary between good and evil has been overthrown. In the realm of morality, everything seems doubtful and uncertain: kings and nations go forward at random and no one can say where the natural limits of despotism and the boundaries of license are to be found."[19]

In other words, the decline of religion had brought with it moral confusion. Who could say what was right and wrong anymore? If *no one* could, then how could they know when they were being oppressed or tyrannized, or if they themselves were in the right or the wrong? Montesquieu straightforwardly addressed the typical arguments of the European intellectuals who despised religion and argued that it was all but useless because it was susceptible to abuse (a common argument made today as well):

> To say that religion gives no motive for restraint because it does not always restrain is to say that the civil laws are not a motive for restraint either. It is to reason incorrectly against religion to collect in a large work a long enumeration of the evils it has produced without also making one of the good things it has done. If I wanted to recount all the evils that civil laws, monarchy, and republican government have produced in the world, I would say frightful things. Even if it were useless for subjects to have a religion, it would not be useless for princes to have one and to whiten with foam the only bridle that can hold those who fear no human laws.[20]

The Founders, of course, held the same view: religion was by no means a cure-all, and was just as susceptible as anything else to corruption (and had been throughout history), but when left free and not interfered with by the state (as it had been in those historical circumstances that informed the Founders' views), it offered the single best antidote to the decay of public morality.

Likewise, the Founders believed that immorality produced fertile soil for tyranny, and this is precisely what distinguished America from Europe. Based on his time in Europe as a diplomat, Adams reflected: "Oh mores [morals]! I said to myself. What absurdities, inconsistencies, distractions and horrors would these manners [in Europe] introduce into our republican governments in America: no kind of republican government can ever exist with such national manners [morals] as these."[21]

In fact, it was the Founders' experiences in Europe that caused them to be concerned with the phenomenon of urbanization. Jefferson was particularly famous for his antipathy for cities, which were apparently crime-ridden in the eighteenth century, just as they are today: "I view great cities as pestilential to the morals, the health, and the liberties of man," he wrote. "True, they nourish some of the elegant arts, but the useful ones can thrive elsewhere, and less perfection in the others, with more health, virtue and freedom, would be my choice."[22]

Madison shared his view: "A great proportion of the vices which distinguish crowded and thin settlements [cities] are known to have their rise in the facility of illicit intercourse between the sexes on one hand, and the difficulty of maintaining a family on the other."[23]

The Founders also commented fairly frequently on sexual morality. Adams wrote specifically on the role of women in this aspect of public virtue:

> From all that I had read of history and government, of human life and manners, I had drawn this conclusion that the manners of women were the most infallible barometer to ascertain the degree of morality and virtue in a nation. All that I have since read and all the observations I have made in different nations have confirmed me in this opinion. The manners of women are the surest criterion by which to determine whether a republican government is practicable in a nation or not. The Jews, the Greeks, the Romans, the Swiss, the Dutch, all lost their public spirit, their republican principles and habits, and their republican forms of government, when they lost the modesty and domestic virtues of their women . . . I was astonished

that there should be any modesty or purity remaining in the kingdom [of France] . . . Could there be any morality left among such a people where such examples were set up to the view of the whole nation?[24]

Notice that he said that women were a *barometer* of sexual morality in a nation. In other words, Adams was arguing that women, who he felt were often far superior to men in many regards, had a duty to not lower their sexual standards simply because men's tended to be far more lax. If women *did* lower their standards to accommodate such behavior, then society would certainly be on a path to quick decline: "National Morality never was and never can be preserved without the utmost purity and chastity in women," he insisted, "and without national Morality a Republican Government cannot be maintained. Therefore my dear Fellow Citizens of America, you must ask leave of your wives and daughters to preserve your Republick [*sic*]."[25]

Montesquieu had come to the same conclusion, noting that a complete change in sexual morality tended to be one of the last indications that a once-free country was no longer in the moral position to remain free.[26]

"It is not only crimes that destroy virtue," he wrote, "but also negligence, mistakes, a certain slackness in the love of the homeland, dangerous examples, the seeds of corruption, that which does not run counter to the laws but eludes them, that which does not destroy them but weakens them." And quite contrary to the timeless tendency of older generations to blame such a decline on the younger generation, Montesquieu argued it was the opposite: "It is not young people who degenerate. They are ruined only when grown men have already been corrupted."[27] That is why the Founders argued so vehemently for a proper education and moral instruction of the young, for it was by seeing their elders act improperly that they too would fall into moral decline.

Montesquieu brilliantly described how with moral decline, the character of things once seen as right would be changed to the point that they were not only no longer adhered to, but openly rejected, and what had once been right would become not just old-fashioned, but wrong:

When that virtue ceases, ambition enters those hearts that can admit it, and avarice enters them all. Desires change their objects: that which one used to love, one loves no longer. One was free under the laws, one wants to be free against them. . . . What was a *maxim* is now called *severity*; what was a *rule* is now called *constraint*; what was *vigilance* is now called *fear*. There, frugality, not the desire to possess, is avarice. Formerly the goods of individuals made up the public treasury. The public treasury has now become the patrimony of individuals. The republic is a cast-off husk, and its strength is no more than the power of a few citizens and the license of all.[28]

Again, these views were based on the realities of historical experience, not merely theoretical propositions. Speaking of the Chinese, Montesquieu noted that "virtue, care, and vigilance . . . were present at the beginning of the dynasties, and missing at the end." The same had been true of the Romans: "Because the [Roman] people were virtuous they were magnanimous. Because they were free, they scorned power. But when they had lost their principles, the more power they had, the less carefully they managed it, until finally, having become their own tyrant and their own slave, they lost the strength of liberty and fell into the weakness of license."[29]

Jefferson likewise looked to the example of the Romans with regard to the importance of virtue:

No government can continue good, but under the control of the people; and their people were so demoralized and depraved, as to be incapable of exercising a wholesome control . . . Their minds were to be informed by education what is right and what wrong; to be encouraged in habits of virtue, and deterred from those of vice by the dread of punishments, proportioned indeed, but irremissible; in all cases, to follow truth as the only safe guide, and to eschew error, which bewilders us in one false consequence after another, in endless succession. These are the inculcations necessary to render the people a sure basis for the structure of order and good government . . . tell us by what process these great and virtuous men could have led so unenlightened and vitiated [impaired] a people into freedom and good government.[30]

For the Founders, virtue was the great preservative of free countries, and when it was lost, the country it preserved would eventually follow suit.

LUXURY

One of the most important, and yet often untold facts about the beliefs of the Founders was their great concern for what excessive material prosperity—"luxury" as they called it—would do to American virtue, and in like fashion how the decline of virtue would fuel the rise of materialism among the American people. They were by no means against prosperity, but were at any rate very concerned about the effects it would have on those so blessed with it. As "Poor Richard" (Benjamin Franklin) noted, "When *prosperity* was well mounted, she let go the bridle, and soon came tumbling out of the saddle."[31] Such had been the testimony of history. Reflecting upon the same problem, Tocqueville made the following observation:

> But while man takes delight in this worthy and legitimate search for prosperity, the fear is that he will finally lose the use of his most sublime faculties, and that, in his desire to improve his environment, he may debase himself. Therein lies the real danger, not elsewhere. Legislators and all worthy and enlightened men living in democracies must therefore work tirelessly to lift men's minds towards heaven . . . to diffuse throughout these societies the taste for the infinite, the appreciation of greatness, and the love of spiritual pleasures.[32]

"Human nature, in no form of it, could bear prosperity," John Adams had observed.[33] His beliefs were no doubt informed by his more puritanical upbringing, but also his experiences in Europe:

> My dear countrymen! How shall I persuade you to avoid the plague of Europe? Luxury has as many and as bewitching charms on your

side of the ocean as on this, and luxury, wherever she goes, effaces from human nature the image of the Divinity [Genesis 1:26-28]. If I had power, I would forever banish and exclude from America all gold, silver, precious stones, alabaster, marble, silk, velvet, and lace . . . Aye, my dear girls, these passions of yours which are so easily alarmed, and others of my own sex which are exactly like them, have done and will do the work of tyrants in all ages. Tyrants different from me, whose power has banished, not gold indeed, but other things of greater value: wisdom, virtue, and liberty.[34]

He believed that luxury caused a people to become soft in the sense that, once accustomed to luxury, they would judge their national happiness merely by the extent to which they were enjoying their physical pleasures. Adams described the problem this way: "Whenever vanity and gaiety, a love of pomp and dress, furniture, equipage [a carriage and horse with attendants], buildings, great company, expensive diversions, and elegant entertainments get the better of the principles and judgments of men or women, there is no knowing where they will stop, nor into what evils, natural, moral, or political, they lead us."[35]

This is exactly what Adams saw occurring among the people of England, and one of the examples he used to dissuade his, at the time, fellow colonists from submitting wholesale to Parliament:

But where luxury, effeminacy, and venality [bribery] are arrived at such a shocking pitch in England, when both electors and elected are become one mass of corruption, when the nation is oppressed to death with debts and taxes, owing to their own extravagance and want of wisdom, what would be your condition under such an absolute subjection to Parliament? You would not only be slaves, but the most abject sort of slaves to the worst sort of masters![36]

He predicted that "riches, grandeur, and power will have the same effect upon American as it has upon European minds"[37] if the American people were not vigilant in resisting the corruptions of luxury. He called this effect "the spirit of commerce," not because he was opposed to commerce, but because he was concerned that commerce would train people to love nothing *but* material or financial gain. It was this corruption "which even insinuates itself into families and influences holy matrimony, and thereby corrupts the morals of families as well as destroys their happiness." This, he feared, would sap "that purity of heart, and greatness of soul which is necessary for a happy Republic."[38] Writing to Jefferson, Adams laid out his concerns about the corrupting influence of luxury: "Will you tell me how to prevent riches from becoming the effects of temperance and industry? Will you tell me how to prevent riches from producing luxury? Will you tell me how to prevent luxury from producing effeminacy, intoxication, extravagance, vice and folly? When you will answer me these questions, I hope I may venture to answer yours."[39] He saw such luxury as incompatible with the sort of robust qualities he believed were necessary to a republic: hard work, sobriety, frugality, simplicity, and perseverance. Luxury served to undermine all of these things by fueling a craving for material pleasures only, apart from the hard work that had produced them. Once introduced, it would cause laziness to set in, as those who had luxury would no longer desire to work; and those who were less fortunate, seeing the luxury around them, would seek to use public funds to subsidize their desires for a level of luxury they felt entitled to. As Montesquieu had warned, "Every lazy nation is grave, for those who do not work regard themselves as sovereign of those who work."[40] Adams opined:

> The numbers of men in all ages have preferred ease, slumber, and good cheer to liberty, when they have been in competition. We must not then depend alone upon the love of liberty in the soul of man for its preservation. Some political institutions must be prepared, to assist this love against its enemies. Without these, the struggle will ever end only in a change of impostors. When the people, who have no property, feel the power in their own hands to determine all questions by a majority, they ever attack those who have property, till the injured men of property lose all patience, and recur to finesse, trick, and stratagem, to outwit those who have too much strength, because

they have too many hands to be resisted any other way. Let us be impartial, then, and speak the whole truth. Till we do, we shall never discover all the true principles that are necessary.[41]

Once corrupted by luxury and materialism, the effects were quite alarming:

When nations are corrupted and grown generally vicious, when they are intoxicated with wealth or power, and by this means delivered over to the government of the baser passion of their nature, it is very natural that they should act an irrational part. They are really as a body in a state of drunkenness. They neither act nor think like men in sound health, and in possession of their senses. Ambition, avarice and pleasure, when they prevail among the multitude of a nation to a certain degree, produce the appearance of a general delirium and intoxication.[42]

With such cravings for material pleasures in place, sexual norms would no doubt change along with them, as described earlier by Adams. Montesquieu had made the same point: "We have spoken of public incontinence [inability to restrain sexual appetites] because it is joined to luxury. It is always followed by luxury, and always follows luxury. If you leave the impulses of the heart at liberty, how can you hamper the weaknesses of the spirit?"[43]

This is why many of the Founders saw simplicity as a "republican" virtue. They wanted to distinguish themselves from Europe as humble leaders serving at the behest of the people, rather than gaudy, ornately arrayed monarchs ruling over a people whether they liked it or not. Nor did they want to imitate the nobility of Europe, who, though not monarchs, lived in extreme luxury while the people lived in squalor. Such was not the American vision. George Washington, for example, attended his first inauguration in a plain brown suit and avoided ostentation at the precise moment when most leaders would have been enamored with it. "A plain, genteel dress is more admired and obtains more credit than lace and embroidery in the eyes of the judicious and sensible" he once remarked. He was also an advocate of a "plain manner" of living, and much preferred "the simplicity of rural life" to life in a city.[44] Washington believed this was the only proper example a leader in a free society could offer. "This simple government attire does not stem simply from a peculiar twist of the American character," Tocqueville would later write, "but from the basic principles of their society."[45]

Tocqueville summarized well the Founders' position on this very important but often overlooked issue:

> When the taste for physical pleasures in such a nation grows more speedily than education or the habit of liberty, a time occurs when men are carried away and lose self-control at the sight of the new possessions they are ready to grasp. Intent only on getting rich, they fail to perceive the close link between their own private fortunes and general prosperity. There is no need to wrench their rights from such citizens, they let them slip voluntarily through their fingers. The exercise of their political duties seems to them a tiresome nuisance which diverts them from industry. When they are required to elect their representatives to offer help to government, to share in the business of the community, they have no time . . . Whenever working citizens refuse to attend to public affairs and the class which might have devoted its leisure hours to such concerns no longer exists, there is a virtual void in the place of government. If a clever and ambitious man happens to seize power at such a critical moment, he discovers an open path to any encroachment.[46]

Many of our Founders, while by no means opposed to prosperity, recognized that excessive prosperity for prosperity's sake would nearly always overcome human nature and propel it toward excessive hedonism: the seeking of pleasure for pleasure's sake. This would, in turn, undermine the production of the very prosperity which had led to it. They realized that hedonism of the body, uninhibited by morality, eventually leads to hedonism of the mind: individuals feel entitled to their "own truth," the ultimate outworking of the selfish mentality in which the individual becomes the center of his own universe. Notions of public spirit and civic duty die, to the delight of voracious politicians for whom power is the ultimate aphrodisiac. All that matters is the pursuit of pleasure, and selfishness begins to take over the operations of both mind and body. This naturally breaks the mutual bonds of affection that ought to bind citizens together. Once the ravenous heart for whom the answer to "how much will be enough?" is "just a little bit more" took over society, cultural cohesion would break down. We would become atomized, and the culture of associations that has always been so strong in the United States would break down, leaving the government as the last "association" we all "belong to," and thus be called upon to fill the vacuum created by our own excessive love of a good thing. The death of liberty would be the result. Hence the Founders' constant emphasis on the virtues of both hard work *and* contentedness. This was the only solid foundation of both individual and national happiness. Without it, no nation deserved to be happy, and would indeed become the victim of its own good fortune. Would a generation obsessed with pleasures and their own creature comforts have achieved what the founding generation did? Perhaps Franklin, speaking again as "Poor Richard," put it most pithily: "To be content, look backward on those who possess less than yourself, not forward on those who possess more. If this does not make you content, you don't deserve to be happy."[47]

THE DECLINE OF THE CONSTITUTION

With the decline of education and morality and the likely infatuation with luxury and materialism that would result, the Founders were very apprehensive that such a citizenry would want their government to give them things that before they had had to earn for themselves. In other words, they the American people would want "free" stuff from their government.

But the Constitution was of such a character and design that it would not allow that to happen unless either (1) it was properly amended via the process outlined in Article V, *or* (2) it was purposely misinterpreted and its words redefined or ignored so as to fit the proclivities of the citizenry. The former would occur by the Founders' own design, to allow society to alter the Constitution in a way most conducive to their happiness, for they by no means believed that their work was perfect for all of time. The latter, however, was something they very stridently and explicitly warned their posterity against.

As alluded to in chapter 3, two of the greatest limitations placed on the power of the federal government were its enumerated powers and federalism. The first was the list of those subjects on which the federal government could legislate (found in Article I, Section 8), and it was a rather short list indeed. The second was the balance of power between the federal and state governments so each could check and balance the other. The Founders agreed with Tocqueville that knowledge would be required for a free people to properly understand their Constitution, as well as when it was being abused. There was a lot more to it than just the three branches, which, unfortunately, is the extent of most people's knowledge today. The reasons for this were simple, as Madison explained: "As compacts, charters of government [i.e., the Constitution] are superior in obligation to all others, because they give effect to all others. As trusts, none can be more sacred, because they are bound on the conscience by the religious sanctions of an oath."[48]

As the supreme charter of government, it behooved the people of the United States to be familiar with the Constitution, what powers it delegated to the federal government, what powers to the state governments, and how the two interacted.

Over and over again, the Founders emphasized these two fundamentals (enumerated powers and federalism) as essential to the preservation of the Constitution. They were meant to be the great stopgaps of tyranny. Montesquieu had warned that "the corruption of each government almost always begins with that of its principles," and "once the principles of the government are corrupted, [even] the best laws become bad and turn against the state." In other words, no laws could reverse the decline unless the foundational principles which informed them were reasserted. The truth of this observation was particularly applicable to a republic. Once it is corrupted, he said, "None of the ills that arise can be remedied except by removing the corruption and recalling the principles. Every other correction is either useless or a new ill."[49]

The Founders, however, were under no illusions that the Constitution would last forever. They knew that the people, as all people throughout history had done, would eventually become tainted, and thereby require a tyrannical state to govern them. Franklin, in his last speech at the Constitutional Convention, expressed this sentiment: "I believe . . . that this [the Constitution] is likely to be well administered for a course of years, and can only end in despotism, as other forms have done before it, when the people shall become so corrupted as to need despotic government, being incapable of any other."[50]

Incidentally, the greatest fear the Founders had with regard to the undoing of the Constitution was how it was to be interpreted. Already, in their own day, there were those who argued that the meaning of the words in the Constitution needed to be understood differently than when they were first penned, in order to meet the needs of the times. The parallels with the modern-day notion of a "living Constitution" are stunning.[51] And yet the Founders themselves were absolutely opposed to such a scheme of interpretation, or "construction," as they referred to it, for they foresaw that its tendency would be to change a government of limited, enumerated powers into one of unlimited, limitless powers. Likewise, once the federal government went beyond its enumerated powers in a manner other than a constitutional amendment, they believed it would destroy federalism by aggrandizing more and more of the powers that belonged to the states to the federal government. Therefore, in their view, the *only* legitimate way to increase the powers of the federal government was through constitutional amendment. In his farewell address, Washington told his countrymen, "If in the opinion of the people, the distribution or modification of the Constitutional powers be in any particular wrong, let it be corrected by an amendment in the way which the Constitution designates." He then strongly warned his countrymen against augmenting the power of the federal government merely by changing the meaning of words or ignoring them, "for though this, in one instance, may be the instrument of good," he wrote, "it is the customary weapon by which free governments are destroyed. The precedent must always greatly overbalance in permanent evil any partial or transient benefit which the use can at any time yield."[52]

He went on to exhort his fellow Americans to "[always remember] that facility in changes [to the Constitution] upon the credit of mere hypotheses and opinion exposes to perpetual change, from the endless variety of hypotheses and opinion." Until the Constitution was actually *changed* "by an explicit and authentic act of the whole People" (rather than simply applying a "new interpretation"), it was "sacredly obligatory upon all." If the words of the Constitution could mean anything, they would become meaningless, and if meaningless, then "not one, more than another, can be binding, if the spirit and letter of the expression is disregarded."[53]

Madison, the "Father of the Constitution" himself, offered strident words in support of Washington's position: words have meanings, and once the plain meaning of the words of the Constitution were simply changed to whatever people wanted them to mean (as opposed to amending the Constitution), then a government of limited powers could thereby, with great facility, become one of unlimited powers, and there would be no security for "a consistent and stable, more than for a faithful exercise of its powers."[54] Therefore, he believed in "resorting to the sense in which the Constitution was accepted and ratified by the nation."

Madison argued that the Constitution could never be interpreted correctly if it was removed from its historical context: "The intention of the parties to it [the Constitution] ought to be kept in view . . . as far as the language of the instrument will permit, this intention ought to be traced in the contemporaneous expositions." He even recommended a particular set of documents to help in this process, the *Federalist Papers*, which he deemed "the most authentic exposition of the text of the federal Constitution, as understood by the body which prepared and the authority which accepted it."[55]

In a newspaper editorial in which the title asked the question "The

Union: Who are its real friends?" Madison quite forcefully identified those who were *not* its friends: "Not those who study, by arbitrary interpretations and insidious precedents, to pervert the limited government of the Union into a government of unlimited discretion, contrary to the will and subversive of the authority of the people."[56]

Jefferson was particularly wary of making words meaningless when it came to the Constitution and its potential to transform a limited government into an unlimited one by destroying not only the concept of enumerated powers but federalism as well: "The same party takes now what they deem the next best ground, the consolidation of the government; the giving to the federal member of the government, by unlimited constructions of the Constitution, a control over all the functions of the States, and the concentration of all power ultimately at Washington."[57] This is why he expressed his attachment to the Constitution as it was originally understood, "according to its obvious principles, and those on which it was known to be received."[58] For him, there were only two options: "the preservation of State rights as reserved in the constitution, or by strained constructions of that instrument, to merge all into a consolidated government."[59]

Jefferson was horrified by judges who, even in his own day, were perverting the plain meaning of the Constitution: "The steady tenor of the courts of the U.S. to break down the constitutional barrier between the coordinate powers of the States, and of the Union . . . give[s] uneasiness . . . We commit honest maniacs to bedlam [asylums]," he wrote, "so judges should be withdrawn from their bench whose erroneous biases are leading us to dissolution. It may indeed injure them in fame or in fortune, but it saves the republic, which is the first and supreme law."[60]

Washington perhaps put it best when he not only warned his countrymen, but asserted that it was their responsibility to maintain the spirit and the letter of the Constitution against such arbitrary encroachment:

> It is important, likewise, that the habits of thinking in a free country should inspire caution in those entrusted with its administration, to

confine themselves within their respective Constitutional spheres; avoiding in the exercise of the powers of one department to encroach upon another. The spirit of encroachment tends to consolidate the powers of all the departments in one, and thus to create whatever the form of government, a real despotism . . . The necessity of reciprocal checks in the exercise of political power by dividing and distributing it into different depositories, and constituting each the guardian of the public weal against invasions by the others, has been evinced by experiments ancient and modern . . . To preserve them must be as necessary as to institute them.[61]

THE DECLINE OF LIMITED GOVERNMENT

"An *advisory* government is a contradiction in terms," Madison once said. And his point was simply this: once government started exercising power in any sphere, whether legitimate or illegitimate, it would not be *advising* people, but *forcing* them to act or not act in particular ways. This was why maintaining the limits imposed by the Constitution (in the absence of an amendment) was so important, because once the government could exercise *force* in an area of policy in which it was not authorized, it might continue to use force to expand its power further. "In Europe," he wrote, "charters of liberty have been granted by power. America has set the example . . . of charters of power granted by liberty."[62] The Constitution was seen as a charter, and as such, the government operating under that charter was obligated to abide by it, to remain within its limits, and to go no further.

Interestingly enough, this was one of the primary issues of the Revolution that most of us do not hear about. The colonies had long admitted Parliament's *very limited* right to legislate for them. However, in 1766, it had passed the "Declaratory Act," in which it asserted an *unlimited* right to legislate for the colonies. This was a major turning point in what would become the Revolution. Nearly a decade later, Congress referred to this act as one of the stepping stones to war, announcing, "By one statute it is declared that Parliament can 'of right make laws to bind us IN ALL CASES WHATSOEVER.' What is to defend us against so enormous, so unlimited a power?"[63] Parliament was, quite simply, unwilling to stay within its appropriate and accepted boundaries, wanting instead to legislate on *any subject whatsoever*, whereas the colonists recognized its rights to do so only in a particular number of areas. Jefferson affirmed this in his pamphlet "A Summary View of the Rights of British America": "When the representative body have lost the confidence of their constituents, when they have notoriously made sale of their most valuable rights, when they have assumed to themselves powers which the people never put into their hands, then indeed their continuing in office becomes dangerous to the state, and calls for an exercise of the power of dissolution."[64]

This is precisely why, among other reasons, the Founders incorporated enumerated powers into the Constitution: the federal government was intended to be able to legislate only a particular set of subjects.

As an example of the importance of this principle, we turn to Alexander Hamilton, who was perhaps the "biggest government" advocate among the Founders. In Federalist No. 84, he argued *against* a bill of rights. But contrary to the belief that he did so because he wanted the government to have more power, his argument was exactly the opposite:

> They [a list of rights] would contain various exceptions to powers not granted, and on this very account would afford a colorable pretext to claim more than were granted. For why declare that such things shall not be done which there is no power to do? Why, for instance, should it be said that the liberty of the press shall not be restrained when no power is given by which restrictions may be imposed? . . . It would furnish, to men disposed to usurp, a plausible pretense for claiming that power.[65]

In other words, since the Constitution nowhere authorized the federal government to do anything related to the press, there was no point in telling it that it could not do what it was already not authorized to do. To do so would provide a pretext for those who preferred "big," unlimited government to use such a clause to claim they had the right to somehow regulate something in order to "maintain" it. Who knows whether Hamilton would have been right historically, but it is interesting to note just how many federal agencies we have today that play some role in determining what we can and cannot say in particular forums. The point is, even the Founder who believed in the most expansive government argued that a Bill of Rights would be superfluous because the federal government was *already so limited* that it could not encroach on the rights some proposed to include.

But the Founders intended for the federal government to remain limited from a very practical viewpoint as well. Jefferson explained:

> Our country is too large to have all its affairs directed by a single government. Public servants at such a distance, and from under the eye of their constituents, must, from the circumstances of distance, be unable to administer and overlook all the details necessary for the good government of the citizens, and the same circumstance, by rendering detection impossible to their constituents, will invite the public agents to corruption, plunder, and waste.[66]

The people closest to the source of the problems were surely those best fit to solve them, Jefferson contended. To expect a central government to effectively manage the minutiae of daily life, particularly over a large population in an enormous country like the United States, was simply chimerical. Inevitably, Madison predicted, "the incompetency of one legislature to regulate all the various objects belonging to the local governments would evidently force a transfer of many of them to the executive department."[67]

Has not this prediction come true?

According to Madison, as Congress went beyond its enumerated powers, it would be less and less capable of managing the affairs to which it had assigned itself responsibility. This would necessarily require the executive branch to pick up the slack, and therefore concentrate power in administrative agencies, just as Tocqueville's "prophecy" predicted.

That is because the Founders believed Congress should legislate on *general* problems in accordance with the powers it was granted. To do this, Congress must have majorities sufficient to the task of passing laws. Today, that would mean at least 218 representatives and 51 senators—269 people—would be required to agree on the laws that would bind, now, more than 300 million people. Now if the laws were general, and applied to only a particular set of issues, such an arrangement could be practicable. But once Congress goes beyond its enumerated powers into other realms, it necessarily must write laws that are more and more detailed, some today stretching into thousands of pages. This itself was a problem for Madison, who considered "the facility and excess of law-making . . . to be the disease to which our governments are most liable."[68] The implications of this problem were profound: "It will be of little avail to the people that the laws are made by men of their own choice if the laws be so voluminous that they cannot be read,[69] or so incoherent that they cannot be understood."[70]

Here is the crux: society is dynamic and fluid. Conditions change, people change, and things are always in flux. If Congress passed a law that proved ineffective or that was found to be unreadable or incoherent, that would again require *at least* several hundred people to agree on a change to the law. But given political realities, this would in any age be very difficult to achieve. Hence why Congress for decades, as the power of the federal government has continued to expand, has granted the executive branch broad discretion in enforcing the laws, in which administrative agencies are given enormous latitude to apply the law as *they* see fit, in many cases essentially making law themselves through administrative edicts and regulations. Some of this would no doubt be necessary even if Congress stayed within the boundaries of its enumerated powers. But the extent to which this has progressed today is *precisely* what Madison predicted would happen if Congress went far beyond its enumerated powers. Congress would be simply *unable* to manage such detailed affairs across such an enormous country, and would have to pass on the task to others who were not directly accountable to the people. Adams had asserted the same: "Society can be governed only by general rules," he wrote. "Government cannot accommodate itself to every particular case, as it happens, nor to the circumstances of particular persons. It must establish general, comprehensive regulations for cases and persons. The only question is which general rule will accommodate most cases and most persons."[71]

Jefferson sarcastically commented on the same sort of government overreach: "Were we directed from Washington when to sow, and when to reap, we should soon want bread."[72] Adams wrote more ominously of the consequences: "But a constitution of government, once changed from freedom, can never be restored. Liberty, once lost, is lost forever. When the people once surrender their share in the legislature, and their right of defending the limitations upon the government, and of resisting every encroachment upon them, they can never regain it."[73]

Jefferson had likewise warned that all corrupt leaders and interests would manifest "their dispositions to get rid of the limitations imposed by the constitution on the general legislature, limitations, on the faith of which, the states acceded to that instrument [the Constitution]."[74] Such leaders would have no other choice, for the Constitution would blind them too much.

"But," some will argue, "what about the 'general welfare' clause? Didn't that allow Congress to pass whatever laws it desired so long as they were for the 'general welfare' of the country?" Madison had a direct answer to this, as the issue had been raised even in his own day: "With respect to the words 'general welfare,' I have always regarded them as qualified by the detail of powers connected with them. To take them in a literal and unlimited sense would be a metamorphosis of the Constitution into a character which there is a host of proofs was not contemplated by its creators."[75]

The principle he enunciated is basic: the "general welfare" clause is at the beginning of Article I, Section 8. And yet it is followed by numerous other clauses outlining the areas on which Congress could pass laws. If "general welfare" could cover anything, why would they have included the detailed list afterward? That would have been plainly absurd. Madison made this exact point in Federalist No. 41:

> It has been urged and echoed, that the power "to lay and collect taxes, duties, imposts, and excises, to pay the debts, and provide for the common defense and general welfare of the United States," amounts to an unlimited commission to exercise every power which may be alleged to be necessary for the common defense or general welfare. No stronger proof could be given of the distress under which these writers labor for objections, than their stooping to such a misconstruction . . . But what color can the objection have, when a specification of the objects alluded to by these general terms immediately follows, and is not even separated by a longer pause than a semicolon? If the different parts of the same instrument ought to be so expounded, as to give meaning to every part which will bear it, shall one part of the same sentence be excluded altogether from a share in the meaning; and shall the more doubtful and indefinite terms be retained in their full extent, and the clear and precise expressions be denied any signification whatsoever?[76]

Madison would go on to defend this contention in Congress, eerily predicting many of the very things the federal government is doing today (often at the behest of the American citizenry) in the name of the "general welfare":

> [This] construction would not only give Congress the complete Legislative power…it would do more—it would supersede all the restrictions understood at present to lie on their power…[F]or if the clause in question really authorizes Congress to do whatever they think fit, provided it be for the general welfare, of which they are to judge, and money can be applied to it, Congress must have power… to pass laws and apply money, providing in any other way for the general welfare…If Congress can apply money indefinitely to the general welfare, and are the sole and supreme judges of the general welfare, they may take care of religion into their own hands; they may establish teachers in every State, county, and parish, and pay them out

of the public Treasury; they may take into their own hands the education of children, establishing in like manner schools throughout the Union; they may undertake the regulation of all roads, other than post roads. In short, everything, from the highest object of State legislation, down to the most minute object of police, would be thrown under the power of Congress; for every object I have mentioned would admit the application of money, and might be called, if Congress pleased, provisions for the general welfare.[77]

Some today have gone even further, arguing that the "necessary and proper" clause is what allows the federal government to legislate on anything. Not only does this run into the exact same problem the "general welfare" clause had (why list the other powers, then?) but was in fact intended to be a statement of the obvious just in case the obvious was ever questioned, particularly in a time in which the states were more prone to question and infringe upon rightful federal authority. Hamilton explained in Federalist No. 33: "If there is anything exceptionable, it must be sought for in the specific powers upon which this general declaration [i.e., "necessary and proper"] is predicated. The declaration itself, though it may be chargeable with tautology or redundancy, is at least perfectly harmless." And yet, he noted that "it may be affirmed with perfect confidence that the constitutional operation of the intended government would be precisely the same, if these clauses were entirely obliterated, or if they were repeated in every article."

Madison said it even more straightforwardly: "The terms necessary and proper gave no additional powers to those enumerated."[78] In other words, the men who framed the government insisted the "necessary and proper" clause was for all intents and purposes meaningless on its own. In an age in which the states had never been under the leadership of a central federal government, they simply desired to make it absolutely clear that *with respect to the powers delegated to it*, Congress was empowered to legislate that which was "necessary and proper."

Tocqueville had warned, as the Founders had, that persistent usurpations of the Constitution would merely provide the pretext for further usurpations, which would continue *ad infinitum*: "What power will customs retain in a nation which has completely changed in character and continues to change," he asked, "in which there is a precedent for every act of tyranny and an example for every crime and in which nothing is so ancient that people are afraid of destroying it and nothing is no new that they have not the nerve to try it? What resistance do customs offer when they have already proved so yielding?"[79]

The point at which national customs were no longer able to make up for the usurpations of the Constitution was certainly the point that could "only end in despotism," as Franklin had said, "when the people shall become so corrupted as to need despotic government, being incapable of any other,"[80] because by then, the customs themselves would have changed. It is no wonder, then, that Madison gave even more vehement warnings to his countrymen to safeguard the Constitution. As a member of Congress, he wrote, "Every public usurpation is an encroachment on the private right not of one, but of all. The citizens of the United States have peculiar motives to support the energy of their constitutional charters . . . They must be anxious to establish the efficacy of popular charters, in defending liberty against power, and power against licentiousness."[81]

In his post-presidency retirement, he wrote:

Every deviation from it [the boundaries between the local and national governments] in practice detracts from the superiority of a Chartered over a traditional government and mars the experiment which is to determine the interesting problem whether the organization of the political system of the U.S. establishes a just equilibrium, or tends to a preponderance of the national or the local powers, and in the latter case, whether of the national or of the local.[82]

Finally, and perhaps most eerily, several of the Founders, particularly Jefferson, noted toward the end of their lives how the work they had sacrificed so much to achieve was being distorted and undermined. What is particularly ominous about it, however, is that those who sought to undermine the Constitution then were using the same exact arguments that many do today; they justified their position by using two specific clauses: the "general welfare" clause and the commerce clause—precisely the ones under which federal power has been so augmented in our own time. Jefferson wrote:

> I see, as you do, and with the deepest affliction, the rapid strides with which the federal branch of our government is advancing towards the usurpation of all the rights reserved to the States, and the consolidation in itself of all powers, foreign and domestic; and that, too, by constructions which, if legitimate, leave no limits to their power . . . Under the power to regulate commerce, they assume indefinitely that also over agriculture and manufactures, and call it regulation to take the earnings of one of these branches of industry, and that too the most depressed, and put them into the pockets of the other, the most flourishing of all . . . and aided by a little sophistry on the words "general welfare," a right to do, not only the acts to effect that, which are specifically enumerated and permitted, but whatsoever they shall think, or pretend will be for the general welfare.

He concluded:

> Their younger recruits, who, having nothing in them of the feelings or principles of '76, now look to a single and splendid government of an aristocracy, founded on banking institutions, and moneyed incorporations under the guise and cloak of their favored branches of manufactures, commerce and navigation, riding and ruling over the plundered ploughman and beggared yeomanry. This will be to them a next best blessing to the monarchy of their first aim, and perhaps the surest stepping-stone to it.[83]

It is to the role of such financial institutions and interests as Jefferson refers that we shall turn next.

BANKS, SPECIAL INTERESTS, AND THE RISE OF THE CORPORATE STATE

As Jefferson made clear, the Founders were far more prescient when it came to the infiltration of financial interests into the government than many of us may realize. Their concern amounted to this: once the federal government went beyond those powers specifically enumerated in the Constitution, it would become far easier for powerful people and interests to manipulate that power to their own advantage, as well as to the government's.

"What an augmentation of the field for [stock] jobbing, speculating, plundering, office-building and office-hunting would be produced by an assumption of all the state powers into the hands of the general government."[84] So predicted Jefferson, should the federal government take upon itself those powers the Constitution reserved for the states. As the government grew bigger, it would become easier and easier for less-than-honorable "public servants" to conduct nefarious business behind closed doors, and with the greater powers at their disposal, offer favors, exemptions, monopolies, and other privileges to powerful interests. This was exactly the "artificial aristocracy" the Founders most feared and had experienced often during the Revolution, during which, as Franklin anecdotally reported, their "hereditary governors . . . with incredible meanness instructed their deputies to pass no act for levying the necessary taxes unless their vast estates were in the same act expressly excused."[85]

Banking was perhaps the Founders' greatest area of concern, as it could be particularly enticing to the government for several reasons: First, banks could make funding government debt far easier through the proliferation of fiat currency, money not backed by anything except the word of the bank and the government (rather than gold, silver, or some other tangible asset). Second, with a greater ability to expand debt, the immediate need for taxation to fund the debt would be avoided and shifted to the future, and the people would be enticed to incur greater and greater debt that they themselves would not have to pay but would nonetheless benefit from. And third, the additional money expended through debt could be used in ways not intended by the Constitution, but would instead help those in power to secure that power.

Alexander Hamilton, our nation's first treasury secretary, summarized the problem of fiat (paper) money:

> The emitting of paper money by the authority of government is wisely prohibited to the individual states by the national Constitution. And the spirit of that prohibition ought not to be disregarded by the government of the United States. Though paper emissions under a general authority might have some advantages . . . yet they are of a nature so liable to abuse, and it may even be affirmed so certain of being abused, that the wisdom of the government will be shown in never trusting itself with the use of so seducing and dangerous an expedient . . . The stamping of paper is an operation so much easier than the laying of taxes that a government in the practice of paper emissions would rarely fail in any such emergency to indulge itself too far in the employment of that resource to avoid as much as possible one less auspicious to present popularity. If it should not even be carried so far as to be rendered an absolute bubble, it would at least be likely to be extended to a degree which would occasion an inflated and artificial state of things incompatible with the regular and prosperous course of the political economy.[86]

In other words, through fiat currency, government could expend more money simply by printing it rather than taxing the people directly (which would be unpopular). However, printing money in this way would devalue the currency in the long run, making each individual dollar worth less and less as time went along and causing prices to rise through the process of inflation. Thus, the people were taxed, but in a far less conspicuous fashion than if Congress had simply passed an act raising taxes. Adams explained the mechanics:

> Our medium [currency] is depreciated by the multitude of swindling banks, which have emitted bank bills to an immense amount beyond the deposits of gold and silver in their vaults, by which means the price of labor and land and merchandise and produce is doubled, tripled, and quadrupled in many instances. Every dollar of a bank bill that is issued beyond the quantity of gold and silver in the vaults, represents nothing, and is therefore a cheat upon somebody.[87]

Hence why he called the actions of such banks "an enormous tax upon the people for the profit of individuals," and decried "the injustice, impolicy, and inhumanity of paper money."[88] To manage one's currency in such a way that a "common measure of value" was impossible (the value of the currency remained stable, and what you deposited today would be worth the same tomorrow) was, according to Adams, "to deliver up our citizens, their property, and their labor passive victims to the swindling tricks of bankers."[89] He had seen the same process at work during the Revolution when Congress and state legislatures printed reams of paper money to "pay" their bills: "The rapid translation of property from hand to hand, the robbing of Peter to pay Paul distresses me beyond measure," he wrote. "The man who lent another 100 pounds in gold four years ago and is paid now in paper cannot purchase with it a quart part in pork, beef, or land of what he could when he lent the gold. This is fact, and facts are stubborn things."[90]

But, he declared, a stable currency was the only moral—and wise— choice in the long term: "A depreciating currency we must not have. It will ruin us. The medium of trade ought to be as unchangeable as truth, as immutable as morality. The least variation in its value does injustice to multitudes, and in proportion it injures the morals of the people, a point of the last importance in a republican government."[91]

"Our Financial System and our Banks are a species of fraudulent oppression upon the Community," declared John Adams. "There is no remedy but to return to a circulating medium of gold and silver only."[92] If that didn't happen, then banking would soon become the source of the artificial aristocracy he most feared, the very antithesis of a system based on merit: "Our whole system of banks is a violation of every honest principle of banks . . . An aristocracy is growing out of them that will be as fatal as the feudal barons if unchecked in time . . . There is no honest money but silver and gold. Think of the number, the offices, stations, wealth, piety, and reputations of the persons in all the States who have made fortunes by these banks, and then you will see how deeply rooted the evil is."[93]

Jefferson recognized the very same thing, emphasizing its tendency to increase government debt because of the temptations it encouraged to grasp at easy money: "I hope a tax will be preferred [to printing money] because it will awaken the attention of the people, and make reformation and economy [i.e., frugality] the principles of the next election. The frequent recurrence of this chastening operation can alone restrain the propensity of governments to enlarge expense beyond income."[94]

The Founders were also opposed to monopolies for precisely the same reasons mentioned earlier: they were, almost by nature, the result of privilege bestowed by government because of connections and power, not merit. Madison explained: "[Monopolies] are justly classed among the greatest nuisances in government. . . . Monopolies are sacrifices of the many to the few. Where the power is in the few it is natural for them to sacrifice the many to their own partialities and corruptions."[95]

Jefferson, likewise, was fully aware of the threat posed by such institutions: "I hope we shall take warning from the example and crush in its birth the aristocracy of our monied corporations which dare already to challenge our government to a trial of strength and bid defiance to the laws of our country."[96]

It was just such a banking monopoly, in bed with the government, that the Founders most feared, for as Adams noted, such combinations "ha[d] in all times made wild work with elections, but it never invented so artful a scheme of corruption for that purpose as our American banks."[97] Elsewhere he wrote: "I have never had but one opinion concerning banking . . . and that opinion has uniformly been that the banks have done more injury to the religion, morality, tranquility, prosperity, and even wealth of the nation, than they can have done or ever will do good."[98]

In exasperation, Adams had a harsh but truthful warning for his countrymen: "All the perplexities, confusions, and distresses in America arise, not from defects in their constitution or confederation, not from a want of honor or virtue, so much as from downright ignorance of the nature of coin, credit, and circulation."[99]

In short, the Founders were fully aware of the dangers of what today we might call "crony capitalism," or the infiltration of "special interests" into the government, and they knew this would most likely occur through the collusion of financial and political power. Such a development would compromise the integrity of public officials as the power of government increased beyond its constitutional limits. The powerful have always congregated around power, whether it be the banks of today lobbying congressmen, or the nobles of the past engaging in palace intrigue for the aggrandizement of their own private interests. As the power of a centralized government increased, so would its attractive influence on such ominous forces.

Franklin made this exact point to an Englishman during the Revolutionary War:

> The expense of our [Americans'] civil government we have always borne, and can easily bear, because it is small. A virtuous and laborious people may be cheaply governed. Determining, as we do, to have no offices of profit, nor any sinecures or useless appointments, so common in ancient or corrupted states, we can govern ourselves a year, for the sum you pay in a single department, or for what one jobbing contractor, by the favor of a minister, can cheat you out of in a single article.[100]

As its ability to dispense favors increased, and it became easier to do so behind the closed doors of a sprawling, labyrinthine, extraconstitutional state, away from the people's attentive gaze, the more favors would be dispensed. The temptations aroused by avarice and greed would prove too irresistible, and government would become a tool for the few and the connected, who would in turn become tools of the government—a mutually symbiotic and incestuous relationship that would sap the foundations and eventually destroy the Constitution premised on the authority of "We the People." All of this the Founders foresaw centuries in advance, and they left their posterity with clear warnings.

Perhaps we should take these warnings seriously again.

DEBT AND BRIBING THE PEOPLE

Needless to say, the Founders were extremely opposed to government debt, not only because it was an unwise handling of public money in and of itself, but because, as we have seen, they knew that which had so often aided and abetted it: banks and other financial interests getting into bed with government, for the benefit of both, at the expense of the people.

At the end of the day, the Founders knew excessive debt would inevitably lead to the death of liberty. "There does not exist an engine so corruptive of the government and so demoralizing of the nation as a public debt. It will bring on us more ruin at home than all the enemies from abroad against whom this army and navy are to protect us," Jefferson had warned.[101] In asking who were the friends of the Union, Madison answered, "Not those who promote unnecessary accumulations of the debt of the Union, instead of the best means of discharging it as fast as possible, thereby increasing the causes of corruption in the government, and the pretexts for new taxes under its authority, the former undermining the confidence, the latter alienating the affection of the people."[102] Washington had exhorted his countrymen to avoid debt at all costs: "As a very important source of strength and security, cherish public credit. One method of preserving it is to use it as sparingly as possible . . . avoiding likewise the accumulation of debt, not only by shunning occasions of expense, but by vigorous exertions in time of peace to discharge the debts which unavoidable wars may have occasioned, not ungenerously throwing upon posterity the burden which we ourselves ought to bear."[103]

And Paine had advised, "[Since] we are running the next generation into debt, we ought to do the work of it, otherwise we use them meanly and pitifully."[104]

Such collusion between government and banks was what had made debt so dangerous in the past. The banks would obviously have their biggest customer with a national government. But what about the government? How would it benefit? We touched on that briefly in the previous section, but it comes down to the fact that often, as the Founders knew from history, such debt was used by governments to basically bribe their people by offering them more and more benefits, money, or services for "free." This was a recurrent historical phenomenon that the Founders desperately sought to avoid for the United States, for it sapped the very foundations of society, encouraging indolence and apathy for public affairs. All the people would begin to care about was what the government would give them, which would fundamentally shift their attention away from the liberty that government could *not* give, but which was the very reason it existed. Thus, a government intended to protect the liberty it could not bestow would be transformed into a mechanism by which various interests would seek to protect the material benefits that it could.

"The worst Roman emperors were those who gave the most,"[105] declared Montesquieu. Cicero corroborated his assertion: "We must remember the saying—repeated in Rome so often that it has become proverbial: bounty is a bottomless pit. For how can it be anything else when those who have got accustomed to being subsidized are bound to want more, and persons who have never been at the receiving end want to get there?"[106]

Historically, Montesquieu argued, republics had fallen around the time "the people have been corrupted by silver. They become cool, they grow fond of silver, and they are no longer fond of public affairs, without concern for the government or for what is proposed there, they quietly await their payments." He described the gradual decline this way:

> The people fall into this misfortune when those to whom they entrust themselves, wanting to hide their own corruption, seek to corrupt the people. To keep the people from seeing their own ambition, they speak only of the people's greatness. To keep the people from perceiving their avarice, they constantly encourage that of the people. Corruption will increase among those who corrupt, and it will increase among those who are already corrupted. The people will distribute among themselves all the public funds, and, just as they will join the management of business to their laziness, they will want to join the amusements of luxury to their poverty. But given their laziness and

their luxury, only the public treasure can be their object. One must not be astonished to see votes given for silver. One cannot give the people much without taking even more from them. But, in order to take from them, the state must be overthrown. The more people appear to take advantage of their liberty, the nearer they approach the moment they are to lose it. Petty tyrants are formed having all the vices of a single one. A single tyrant rises up, and the people lose everything, even the advantages of their corruption.[107]

Jefferson predicted that as the people became more and more dependent upon "bounty" from the government, it would make them that much more susceptible to the schemes of would-be tyrants: "Dependence begets subservience and venality, suffocates the germ of virtue, and prepares fit tools for the designs of ambition." Why? Because, according to Adams, "the vicious and unprincipled always follow the most profligate leader, him who bribes the highest and sets all decency and shame at defiance. It becomes more profitable, and reputable too, except with a very few, to be a party man than a public-spirited one."[108]

Before the Constitution was even ratified, Madison had predicted precisely such an outcome to Jefferson, arguing that the greatest threat to liberty would not be the federal government oppressing the people purely on its own, regardless of any popular support. Rather, the greatest threat would be a federal government that violated the rights of the few in the name of enacting the will of the many, which would in the long run undermine the interests of both: "Wherever the real power in a government lies, there is the danger of oppression. In our governments the real power lies in the majority of the community, and the invasion of private rights is *chiefly* to be apprehended not from acts of government contrary to the sense of its constituents, but from acts in which the government is the mere instrument of the major number of the constituents."[109]

Per the Founders' arguments, Tocqueville warned that such a turn of events would likely be the result of a "degenerate taste for equality among the people[,] which inspires the weak to bring the strong down to their own level and reduces men to prefer equality in a state of slavery to inequality in a state of freedom." He predicted that this would occur at the same time that individual rights were being diminished and a nebulous "right of society" was being put in its place, fundamentally altering the role of government: "The idea of a right belonging to certain individuals is rapidly disappearing from men's minds to be replaced by the all-powerful and, so to speak, unique right of society itself. . . . Everyone portrays government as a unique, simple, caring, and creative force."[110]

As a result of such change, a leader need only declare his love of "equality," and he would be not only elected, but granted new powers: "The chief and, in a sense, the only condition one needs in order to reach a centralized public power in a democratic society is to love equality or to make men believe you do. Thus, the art of despotism, which was formerly so complicated, is now quite simple: it is reduced, as it were, to a single principle."

The result was a foregone conclusion for Tocqueville—a once-great Republic would become a nation of "supplicants" seeking only benefits from the government. "Whatever the efforts of its leaders," he wrote, "they could never satisfy such a people and the fear always exists that the constitution of the country might finally be overturned . . . It would have been a safer and more honest course to teach every one of their subjects the skill of providing for themselves."[111]

Naturally, by that time, the government would have likely developed an attitude Franklin had warned against long before: "The King's cheese is half wasted in parings. But no matter, 'tis made of the people's milk."

But of course, whatever the government had given to one group of people had to be taken from another group of people, thereby violating their right to their property. This was precisely why the Founders had such a palpable fear of debt, for it would introduce an appetite among the people for things that were not theirs, and this would require more and more confiscations from some in order to give to others. Adams provided perhaps the most graphic warning of the consequences of such a diminution of the principle of private property:

[A] great majority of every nation is wholly destitute of property, except a small quantity of clothes and a few trifles of other movables . . . if all were to be decided by a vote of the majority, the eight or nine millions who have no property would not think of usurping over the rights of the one or two millions who have? Property is surely a right of mankind as really as liberty. Perhaps, at first, prejudice, habit, shame or fear, principle or religion, would restrain the poor from attacking the rich, and the idle from usurping on the industrious. But the time would not be long before courage and enterprise would come and pretexts be invented by degrees to countenance the majority in dividing all the property among them, or at least in sharing it equally with its present possessors. Debts would be abolished first, taxes laid heavy on the rich, and not at all on the others, and at last a downright equal division of everything be demanded and voted. What would be the consequence of this? The idle, the vicious, the intemperate would rush into the utmost extravagance of debauchery, sell and spend all their share, and then demand a new division of those who purchased from them. The moment the idea is admitted into society that property is not as sacred as the laws of God, and that there is not a force of law and public justice to protect it, anarchy and tyranny commence. If "Thou shalt not covet" and "Thou shalt not steal" were not commandments of Heaven [Exodus 20:17, 15], they must be made inviolable precepts in every society before it can be civilized or made free.[112]

Per Adams's prediction, as the people demanded more and more, there would be an increase in the "blind, undistinguishing reproaches against the aristocratical [rich] part of mankind, a division which nature has made, and we cannot abolish, [reproaches which] are neither pious nor benevolent. They are as pernicious as they are false. They serve only to foment prejudice, jealousy, envy, animosity, and malevolence. They serve no ends but those of sophistry, fraud, and the spirit of party. It would not be true, but it would not be more egregiously false, to say that the people have waged everlasting war against the rights of men."[113]

Likewise, in the most prophetic of tones, Jefferson warned that perpetual debt would lead to a war of one portion of society against the other as each sought to be the beneficiaries of government largesse at the other's expense:

> And to preserve their [the people's] independence, we must not let our rulers load us with perpetual debt. We must make our election between *economy and liberty*, or *profusion and servitude*. If we run into such debts as that we must be taxed in our meat and in our drink, in our necessaries and our comforts, in our labors and our amusements . . . as the people of England are . . . we must live as they now do, on oatmeal and potatoes, have no time to think, no means of calling the mis-managers to account, but be glad to obtain subsistence by hiring ourselves to rivet their chains on the necks of our fellow-sufferers . . . This example reads to us the salutary lesson that private fortunes are destroyed by public as well as by private extravagance. A departure in principle in one instance becomes a precedent for a second; that second for a third, and so on, till the bulk of society is reduced to be mere automatons of misery, and to have no sensibilities left but for sinning and suffering. Then begins, indeed, the *bellum omnium in Omnia* ["war of all against all"] which some philosophers observing to be so general in this world have mistaken it for the natural, instead of the abusive state of man. And the fore horse of this frightful team is public debt. Taxation follows that, and in its train wretchedness and oppression.[114]

Such were the ominous consequences of excessive debt as predicted by our Founders. But perhaps most alarming was the type of leaders that would arise at such a perilous time.

PARTIES

The Founders offered one last set of predictions to complete their prophetic circle of tyranny, and they were related to those who would administer the federal government itself. The danger the Founders foresaw on this front was that of the spirit of party, which was not what we mean today when we say "party." Rather, the spirit of party, for them, was the taking of a particular side of a political issue, not because you believed it was best for your constituents or for the country, but because it was what would most effectively keep you in power. In other words, the party spirit was the sacrifice of the national interests to the personal interests of politicians, and the party interests of particular groups.

Abigail Adams, wife of John Adams, had piercing words for this way of conducting public affairs:

> Party spirit is blind, malevolent, uncandid, ungenerous, unjust, and unforgiving . . . yet upon both sides are characters who possess honest views, and act from honorable motives. . . . Party hatred by its deadly poison blinds the eyes and envenoms the heart. It is fatal to the integrity of the moral character. It sees not that wisdom dwells with moderation . . . Thus blame is too often liberally bestowed upon actions which, if fully understood, and candidly judged, would merit praise instead of censure.[115]

Her husband had no love for the party spirit either, writing to his friend Thomas Jefferson, "Both parties have excited artificial terrorism, and, if I were summoned as a witness to say, upon oath, which party had excited, Machiavillialy [sic], the most terror, and which had really felt the most, I could not give a more sincere answer than in the vulgar style, 'put them in a bag and shake them, and then see which will come out first.'" Such a spirit, he believed, was animated entirely by selfish interests and would make rational political discussion impossible: "Parties and factions will not suffer improvements to be made. As soon as one man hints at an improvement, his rival opposes it. No sooner has one party discovered or invented any amelioration of the condition of man, or the order of society than the opposite party belies it, misconstrues it, misrepresents it, ridicules it, insults it, and persecutes it."[116]

Jefferson felt similarly. Even though he was speaking about parties in Britain in the following excerpt, he was speaking of them in the context of politics in America as an illustrative example of the destructive nature of the party spirit:

The nest of office being too small for all of them [the parties] to cuddle into at once, the contest is eternal, which shall crowd the other out. For this purpose, they are divided into two parties, the Ins and the Outs, so equal in weight that a small matter turns the balance. To keep themselves in, when they are in, every stratagem must be practiced, every artifice used which may flatter the pride, the passions, or power of the nation. Justice, honor, faith, must yield to the necessity of keeping themselves in place. The question whether a measure is moral is never asked, but whether it will nourish the avarice of their merchants . . . or produce any other effect which may strengthen them in their places.[117]

It was precisely this will to stay in power, and to aggrandize to themselves more power by any means necessary, that disgusted the Founders the most. While Jefferson spoke with relatively vague language, Adams stunningly predicted, with near-perfect accuracy, how parties would maintain themselves in power, even into our own day:

[Politicians] will bestow all offices, contracts, privileges in commerce, and other emoluments on . . . their connections, and throw every vexation and disappointment in the way of the former, until they establish such a system of hopes and fears throughout the state as shall enable them to carry a majority in every fresh election of the house. The judges will be appointed by them and their party and, of consequence, will be obsequious enough to their inclinations. The whole judicial authority, as well as the executive, will be employed, perverted, and prostituted to the purposes of electioneering. . . . Capital characters among the physicians will not be forgotten, and the means of acquiring reputation and practice in the healing art will be to get the state trumpeters on the side of youth. . . . Even the theatres and actors and actresses must become politicians and convert the public pleasures into engines of popularity for the governing members of the house.[118]

Notice how Adams described how politicians drunk with the party spirit would not only award people offices, but would presumably bestow privileges of particular commercial interests and other benefits on their allies. His comment about politicians recruiting well-known "physicians," "youth," and even "actors and actresses" to achieve their ends is simply stunning, particularly in light of the politics of our own time.

Washington therefore predicted that parties "are likely, in the course of time and things, to become potent engines, by which cunning, ambitious and unprincipled men will be enabled to subvert the power of the people, and to usurp for themselves the reins of government; destroying afterwards the very engines which have lifted them to unjust dominion." He concluded:

> The alternate domination of one faction over another, sharpened by the spirit of revenge natural to party dissention, which in different ages and countries has perpetrated the most horrid enormities, is itself a frightful despotism. But this leads at length to a more formal and permanent despotism. The disorders and miseries, which result, gradually incline the minds of men to seek security and repose in the absolute power of an individual: and sooner or later the chief of some prevailing faction more able or more fortunate than his competitors, turns this disposition to the purposes of his own elevation, on the ruins of public liberty.[119]

Could they have made it clearer? Jefferson, a public official for most of his life, could only hope that Americans would at all times be wary of the dangers of a government loosed from the constitutional leash which alone kept it tame: "The spirit of resistance to government is so valuable on certain occasions that I wish it to be always kept alive. It will often be exercised when wrong, but better so than not to be exercised at all."[120]

FINAL THOUGHTS

At some point, it becomes necessary for us to ask: How could these men, most of whom have been dead for at least two centuries, have predicted with such stunning accuracy so many of the problems we are dealing with today? Perhaps even more pointedly, how did they talk about them in a more articulate and insightful way than most of those alive even today? Either the Founders were incredibly lucky in their analysis, or they were men of exceptional wisdom. If, upon examination, we determine it was the latter, perhaps we should begin listening to their voices again, voices that have been kept secret from us for so long, often because of our own willingness to be ignorant. Are we willing to once again do the hard work of rediscovering the source and heritage of our liberty? Are we content to remain in the dark any longer?

Perhaps one last warning from John Adams in the midst of the revolutionary crescendo will convince us we can no longer remain satisfied with remaining ignorant of the principles of our liberty:

> Nip the shoots of arbitrary power in the bud, is the only maxim which can ever preserve the liberties of any people. When the people give way, their deceivers, betrayers and destroyers, press upon them so fast that there is no resisting afterwards. The nature of the encroachment upon the American constitution is such as to grow everyday more and more encroaching. Like a cancer, it eats faster and faster every hour. The revenue creates pensioners, and the pensioners urge more revenue. The people grow less steady, spirited, and virtuous, the seekers more numerous and more corrupt, and every day increases the circles of their dependents and expectants, until virtue, integrity, public spirit, simplicity, frugality, become the objects of ridicule and scorn, and vanity, luxury, foppery [excessively concerned with nice things], selfishness, meanness, and downright venality swallow up the whole society.[121]

If we disregard such admonitions, surely what Franklin said about the downfall of nations will become true of our own: "Providence will bring about its own ends by its own means, and if it intends the downfall of a nation, that nation will be so blinded by its pride and other passions as not to see its danger, or how its fall may be prevented."[122]

CONCLUSION

LIBERTY'S RESURRECTION

History is so important because it teaches us this vital lesson: Human liberty is not the result of a battle won, and its demise is not the outcome of a battle lost. Neither is there any moment at which it can be definitely declared to have been secured forever. On the contrary, liberty that endures beyond the transitory moment of its birth, should it be born at all, is the result of one thing only: vigilance.

History also shows each of us how relatively unoriginal we are in the grand scheme of the human story. Truth, liberty, and justice have always been endangered possessions, even when relatively safe. They never reach a point of perfect security. Therefore, those who best secure these blessings are those who teach the succeeding generations the lessons of the past, not to crudely imitate it, but to prevent them from succumbing to the delusion that they are immune to the forces of their own human nature and the inevitable hubris that comes with such a belief. Thus, a knowledge of history paradoxically provides us with *justified* pride in our achievements, and at the same time prevents us from the *delusional* pride that would undo them. It anchors us in the eternal, unchangeable truths of the human condition, yet empowers us to apply those truths in ever more creative and innovative ways so as to improve the human experience.

This is the responsibility our Founders recognized had been bestowed upon the American people, who "have now the best opportunity and the greatest trust in their hands that Providence ever committed to so small a number since the transgression of the first pair [Adam and Eve]," said John Adams. "If they betray their trust, their guilt will merit even greater punishment than other nations have suffered, and the indignation of Heaven."[1]

And yet, we find ourselves at a point in our history where so much that we hold dear seems at risk, and perhaps most distressingly, the danger comes largely from within. Wherever one looks—our political systems, our culture, and the state of our morals and education—the immediate picture is disconcerting. We no longer know who we are, and we have largely lost the heritage from which we came. We have forgotten how to answer the "why?" of our liberty.

Even so, it is precisely such moments of distress and turpitude that awaken the energies, sharpen the minds, and inspire the actions of those who *insist* on being free. Such a people at such a time can indeed regain the answers to the "why?" of their liberty. As Adams said, "Calamities are the caustics and cathartics of the body politic. They arouse the soul. They restore original virtues. They reduce a constitution back to its first principles."[2] That has been the purpose of this book, to rediscover that original fountain from which this great and noble experiment in human liberty sprang; to remove the dust which has for too long obscured our heritage and shrouded it in secrets; to do nothing less than arouse the soul, restore original virtues, and by the lips of those who spoke it into existence, resurrect from the dead those principles that first gave us life. I am under no illusions that such a task can be completed, let alone initiated, by one book. But I hope that this one will have played its proper part.

"Indeed, I do not believe that Providence has done so much for nothing," Washington wrote. "It has always been my creed that we should not be left as an awful monument to prove 'that Mankind, under the most favorable circumstances for civil liberty and happiness, are unequal to the task of governing themselves, and therefore made for a master.'"[3] This from a man who had seen both the best and worst of human nature, who witnessed the greatest victories as well as the most dire defeats of the cause to which he had sacrificed his life. "[I] will not believe our labors are lost," Jefferson exclaimed. "I shall not die without a hope that light and liberty are on steady advance . . . In short, the flames kindled on the 4th of July 1776 have spread over too much of the globe to be extinguished by the feeble engines of despotism. On the contrary, they will consume those engines and all who work them."[4]

Such confidence can again be ours, if only we insist that the secrets of our liberty be secrets no longer. May we arise from our stupor of ignorance and apathy; dare to read, write, converse, and think like statesmen; and like our Founders, study politics and war, that our children may study poetry and music. May we, under God and before all the world, once again demonstrate the greatest of all of liberty's secrets: that it is won and secured by those who care least for the exigencies of the moment, and most for the future of their posterity, even if purchased by the sweat of their brow and the blood of their veins. For in the words of Washington, uttered to his countrymen and ours, for that day and this, "This is the moment when the eyes of the whole world are turned upon them, this is the moment to establish or ruin their national character forever . . . it is yet to be decided whether the Revolution must ultimately be considered as a blessing or a curse: a blessing or a curse not to the present age alone, for with our fate will the destiny of unborn millions be involved."[5]

Liberty is difficult work. It is fraught with risks, with dangers, with tempests and storms. It is a boisterous endeavor, an effort for the brave and the enterprising, the courageous and the responsible, the steadfast and the moral. It is not for the lazy, the apathetic, the fainthearted, or the profligate. It offers nothing to a man unwilling to assume the duties commensurately imposed upon him by the very rights he claims to contend for. To such a man, liberty is a curse, a byword, useless. It becomes his source of slavery and ruin. To a society of such men who disfigure liberty, liberty becomes its undoing.

But to those who seek to shoulder their burdens and meet their responsibilities; to those who would steward this divine blessing and nurture its fruits; to those for whom a right is an honor, not a rhetorical panacea, it offers the adventure that has made the greatest displays of human greatness possible, and can do so again. It offers no guarantees except the hope and the possibility of extending the limits of our genius and ingenuity to their greatest potential, beginning with the individual, and for the good of all, an endeavor that, for all its faults, America has carried out since the days of its founding.

"The preservation of the sacred fire of liberty, and the destiny of the republican model of government, are justly considered as *deeply*, perhaps as *finally* staked on the experiment entrusted to the hands of the American people,"[6] Washington observed. We either pass it on to our posterity as it was passed down to us, or it dies here and now. We either assume its risks and keep it, or eschew those risks and lose it forever. The choice is ours.

May we choose well.

NOTES

INTRODUCTION

1. Neil Postman, Amusing Ourselves to Death: Public Discourse in the Age of Show Business (New York: Penguin Books, 2006), xix–xx.
2. Gerald E. Bevan, trans., Democracy in America and Two Essays on America (New York: Penguin Books, 2003), 85.
3. John Rhodehamel, ed. *Washington: Writings* (New York: The Library of America, 1997), 726.
4. Charles Francis Adams, ed., The Works of John Adams, Second President of the United States, Vol. VI (Boston: Little, Brown and Company, 1851), 169.
5. John Adams to John Quincy Adams (September 8, 1790).
6. George A. Peek, Jr., ed., *The Political Writings of John Adams* (New York: The Liberal Arts Press, Inc., 1954), 135.

CHAPTER 1

1. Alexis de Tocqueville, *Democracy in America and Two Essays on America,* trans. Gerald E. Bevan (New York: Penguin, 2003), 326.
2. George A. Peek Jr., ed., *The Political Writings of John Adams* (New York: Liberal Arts Press, 1954), 163.
3. John Rhodehamel, ed., *Washington: Writings* (New York: Library of America, 1997), 606.
4. Adams, letter to Benjamin Rush, 7 September 1808, in *The Works of John Adams, Second President of the United States,* vol. 9 (Google ebook) (Best Books on, 1856), 602.
5. Philip B. Kurland and Ralph Lerner, eds., *The Founders' Constitution, vol. 1* (Chicago: University of Chicago, 2000), chap. 11, doc. 16, http://press-pubs.uchicago.edu/founders/documents/v1ch11s16.html.
6. Frank Shuffelton, ed., *The Letters of John and Abigail Adams* (New York: Penguin, 2004), 279.
7. J. A. Leo Lemay, ed., *Franklin: Writings* (New York: Library of America, 2005), 1393.
8. Merrill D. Peterson, *Jefferson: Writings* (New York: Library of America, 1984), 1386.
9. Adams to Roger Sherman, 18 July 1789, in Kurland and Lerner, *The Founders' Constitution*, chap. 4, doc. 29, http://press-pubs.uchicago.edu/founders/documents/v1ch4s29.html.
10. Gordon Wood, ed., John Adams: *Revolutionary Writings 1775–1783* (New York: Library of America, 2011), 379.
11. Peek, The Political Writings of John Adams, 150.
12. Gordon Wood, ed., *John Adams: Revolutionary Writings 1755–1775* (New York: Library of America, 2011), 88.

13. Lemay, Franklin, 1275.
14. Wood, John Adams: Revolutionary Writings 1755–1775, 209–10.
15. Lester J. Cappon, ed., *The Adams–Jefferson Letters* (Univ. of North Carolina Press, 1988), 435.
16. Jack N. Rakove, ed., *Madison: Writings* (New York: Library of America, 1999), 794.
17. Peek, The Political Writings of John Adams, 161–62.
18. Cappon, The Adams–Jefferson Letters, 338.
19. Abigail Adams to John Quincy Adams, 26 May 1781, in Abigail Adams and John Adams, Familiar Letters of John Adams and His Wife Abigail Adams During the Revolution with a Memoir of Mrs. Adams (n.p.: Mundus, 2010).
20. Peek, The Political Writings of John Adams, 142.
21. Wood, John Adams: Revolutionary Writings 1775–1783, 451.
22. Adams to John Taylor, letter 10, in John Adams, *The Works of John Adams*, vol. 6 (public domain).
23. John Adams, Novanglus Essay No. 3, February 6, 1775.

CHAPTER 2

1. Frank Shuffelton, ed., *The Letters of John and Abigail Adams* (New York: Penguin Books, 2004), 268-69.
2. Gerald E. Bevan, trans., *Democracy in America and Two Essays on America* (New York: Penguin Books, 2003), 54-55.
3. Ibid., 43.
4. Thomas Paine, *Common Sense* (1776).
5. Jack Rakove, ed., *Founding America: Documents from the Revolution to the Bill of Rights* (New York: Barnes & Noble Books, 2006), 53, 58.
6. John Adams, "A Dissertation on the Canon and the Feudal Law," no. 2, August 19, 1765, in *Founding Families: Digital Editions of the Papers of the Winthrops and the Adamses*, ed. C. James Taylor (Boston: Massachusetts Historical Society, 2015), http://www.masshist.org/publications/apde2/view?&id=PJA01dg2.
7. Tocqueville, *Democracy in America*, 326.
8. John Adams, Draft of "A Dissertation on the Canon and the Feudal Law" (August[?] 1765), in Taylor, *Founding Families*.
9. John Adams, "Defence of the Constitutions of Government of the United States," in *The Founders' Constitution*, vol. 1, eds. Philip B. Kurland and Ralph Lerner (Chicago: University of Chicago, 2000), chap. 15, doc. 34, http://press-pubs.uchicago.edu/founders/documents/v1ch15s34.html.
10. Paine, *Common Sense*.
11. John Adams, "A Dissertation on the Canon and the Feudal Law," no. 1 (August 12, 1765), in Taylor, *Founding Families*.
12. Jack Rakove, ed., Founding America: Documents from the Revolution to the Bill of Rights (New York: Barnes & Noble Books, 2006), 55.
13. Henry P. Johnson, ed. *The Correspondence and Public Papers of John Jay*, Vol. I (New York: G.P. Putnam's Sons, 1890), 159.
14. John Adams, "The Earl of Clarendon to William Pym," no. 3, January 27, 1766.
15. Peter Laslett, ed., *Locke: Two Treatises of Government* (Cambridge: Cambridge University Press, 1988), 306.
16. Anne M. Cohler et al., eds., *Montesquieu: The Spirit of the Laws* (Cambridge: Cambridge University Press, 1989), 155.

17. John Adams, "Clarendon to Pym," no. 2, January 20, 1766, at National Archives, Founders Online, http://founders.archives.gov/documents/Adams/01-01-02-0009-0005#DJA01d365n1.
18. John Adams, "A Dissertation on the Canon and the Feudal Law," no. 1, October 21, 1765, in Taylor, *Founding Families*.
19. Samuel Adams, "The Rights of the Colonists," in Kruland and Lerner, The Founders' Constitution, vol. 5, Amendment 1, doc. 15, http://press-pubs.uchicago.edu/founders/documents/amendI_religions15.html.
20. John Adams, "A Dissertation on the Canon and the Feudal Law," no. 3 (September 30, 1765), in Taylor, *Founding Families*.
21. Alexander Hamilton, Federalist No. 1.
22. Washington, letter to James Warren, March 31, 1779.
23. Paine, *Common Sense*.
24. Ibid.
25. Samuel Adams, speech in Philadelphia, August 1, 1776.
26. Paine, *Common Sense*.
27. George Washington, "Circular Letter to the States" (June 8, 1783) in *The U.S. Constitution: A Reader*, ed. Hillsdale College Politics Faculty (Hillsdale, MI: Hillsdale College Press, 2012).
28. John Adams, letter to Arthur Lee, March 24, 1779.
29. John Adams, letter to Abigail Adams, October 13, 1775.
30. Samuel Adams, speech in Philadelphia, August 1, 1776.
31. George Washington, letter to John Armstrong, April 25, 1788.
32. John Adams, letter to Abigail Adams, February 11, 1776.
33. John Adams, letter to John Quincy Adams, April 18, 1776.
34. John Adams, letter to John Quincy Adams, July 27, 1777.
35. John Adams, *A Defence of the Constitutions of Government of the United States of America*, vol., 3, chap. 4, in John Adams, *The Works of John Adams*, 10 vols., vol. 6, ed. Charles Francis Adams (Boston: Charles C. Little and James Brown, 1851), Online Library of America, http://oll.libertyfund.org/titles/2104.
36. John Adams, letter to Abigail Adams, April 15, 1776.
37. John Adams, letter to William Cushing, June 9, 1776.
38. Second Continental Congress, Declaration on the Causes and Necessity of Taking Arms.
39. Benjamin Franklin, letter to David Hartley, October 3, 1775.
40. John Adams, letter to Abigail Adams, July 3, 1776.
41. John Adams, second letter to Abigail Adams, July 3, 1776.
42. John Adams, letter to William Cushing, June 9, 1776.
43. "Letters from a Distinguished American," no. 5 (July 22, 1780), at National Archives, Founders Online, http://founders.archives.gov/documents/Adams/06-09-02-0312-0010.
44. George Washington, Farewell Address to the Armies of the United States, November 2, 1783.
45. George Washington, Farewell Address, September 19, 1796.
46. John Adams, letter to Hezekiah Niles, February 13, 1818.

CHAPTER 3

1. Thomas Paine, *Common Sense* (1776).
2. John Adams, *Defence of the Constitutions of Government of the United States of America* [hereinafter, *Defence*], vol., 3, chap. 1, in John Adams, The Works of John Adams, 10 vols. [hereinafter, *Works*], vol. 6, ed. Charles Francis Adams (Boston: Charles C. Little and James Brown, 1851), Online Library of America, http://oll.libertyfund.org/titles/2104.

3. George Washington, Rules of Civility (1744).

4. Michael Grant, trans., *Cicero: On the Good Life* (New York: Penguin Books, 1971), 183.

5. John Locke, Second Treatise of Civil Government, chap. 9.

6. James Madison, speech in the Virginia Constitutional Convention, December 2, 1829.

7. Adams, *Defence*, vol. 3, chap. 1.

8. James Madison, speech in the Virginia Constitutional Convention: December 2, 1829.

9. Alexander Hamilton, letter to John Jay, November 26, 1775.

10. Paine, *Common Sense.*

11. Federalist No. 51.

12. Anne M. Cohler, et al., eds., *Montesquieu: The Spirit of the Laws* (Cambridge: Cambridge University Press, 1989), 4.

13. John Adams, "Thoughts on Government" (April, 1776), in Adams, *Works*, vol. 4, http://oll. libertyfund.org/titles/2102.

14. Second Continental Congress, Declaration on the Causes and Necessity of Taking Arms, July 6, 1775.

15. Locke, Second Treatise of Civil Government, chap. 11.

16. James Madison, "Property" (March 29, 1792), in The Founders' Constitution, vol. 1, eds. Philip B. Kurland and Ralph Lerner (Chicago: University of Chicago, 2000), chap. 16, doc. 23, http:// press-pubs.uchicago.edu/founders/documents/v1ch16s23.html.

17. Cicero, On Duties, 161, 162, 164.

18. Locke, Second Treatise of Civil Government, chap. 11.

19. Ibid., chap. 18.

20. Thomas Jefferson, First Inaugural Address, March 4, 1801.

21. The quotations in this paragraph are from Adams, "Thoughts on Government."

22. Alexander Hamilton, Federalist No. 1.

23. John Adams, Inaugural Address, March 4, 1797.

24. In other words, their ability to rule themselves in a moral and educated way; see chapters 5–6.

25. Peter Laslett, ed., *Locke: Two Treatises of Government* (Cambridge: Cambridge University Press, 1988), 415.

26. Michael Grant, trans., *Cicero: On the Good Life* (New York: Penguin Books, 1971), 194.

27. John Adams, "A Dissertation on the Canon and the Feudal Law," no. 3 (September 30, 1765), in *Founding Families: Digital Editions of the Papers of the Winthrops and the Adamses*, ed. C. James Taylor (Boston: Massachusetts Historical Society, 2015), http://www.masshist.org/publications/ apde2/view?&id=PJA01dg2.

28. Thomas Jefferson, letter to Samuel Kercheval, July 12, 1816, Constitution Society, http://www. constitution.org/tj/ltr/1816/ltr_18160712_kercheval.html.

29. James Madison, Speech in the Virginia Constitutional Convention: December 2, 1829, Founders' Quotes, http://foundersquotes.com/quotes/the-essence-of-government-is-power-and-power-lodged- as-it-must-be-in-human-hands-will-ever-be-liable-to-abuse/.

30. Adams, *Defence*, vol. 3, chap. 1.

31. John Adams, letter to Benjamin Rush, January 23, 1809.

32. James Madison, "Parties" (January 23, 1792), in Kurland and Lerner, *The Founders' Constitution*, vol. 1, eds. Philip B. Kurland and Ralph Lerner (Chicago: University of Chicago, 2000), chap. 15, doc. 50, http://press-pubs.uchicago.edu/founders/documents/v1ch15s50.html.

33. Thomas Jefferson to John Adams, June 27, 1813, National Archives, Founders Online, http:// founders.archives.gov/documents/Jefferson/03-06-02-0206.

34. Thomas Jefferson to Henry Lee, August 10, 1824, in Jefferson, *The Works of Thomas Jefferson*, ed. Paul Leicester Ford (New York, London: G. P. Putnam's Sons, 1905).

35. Gerald E. Bevan, trans., *Democracy in America and Two Essays on America* (New York: Penguin Books, 2003), 701-02.

36. John Adams to Thomas Jefferson, November 13, 1815, in H. A. Washington, *The Writings of Thomas Jefferson*, vol. 6 (Washington: Taylor & Maury, 1853–54), 500.

37. John Adams, *Discourses on Davila*, chap. 13, in Adams, *Works*, vol. 6 (Boston: Charles C. Little and James Brown, 1851), Online Library of America, http://oll.libertyfund.org/titles/2104.

38. Adams, Defence, vol. 1.

39. Anne M. Cohler et al., eds., *Montesquieu: The Spirit of the Laws* (Cambridge: Cambridge University Press, 1989), 155.

40. Adams, Defence, vol. 3, chap. 1.

41. Michael Grant, trans., *Cicero: On Government* (New York: Penguin Books, 1993), 187.

42. John Adams to Thomas Jefferson, December 25, 1813, National Archives, Founders Online, http://founders.archives.gov/documents/Jefferson/03-07-02-0040.

43. Adams, Defence, vol. 3, chap. 1.

44. Federalist No. 51.

45. Peter Laslett, ed., *Locke: Two Treatises of Government* (Cambridge: Cambridge University Press, 1988), 363.

46. John Adams to Roger Sherman, July 18, 1789, in Adams, *Works*, vol. 6

47. Adams, *Defence*, vol. 6, chap. 1.

48. John Adams, letter to Thomas Jefferson, June 25, 1813.

49. John Adams, letter to Thomas Jefferson, July 9, 1813.

50. Adams, *Discourses on Davila,* chap. 13.

51. Adams, "Thoughts on Government."

52. Ibid.

CHAPTER 4

1. James Madison, Charters, January 19, 1792.

2. Alexis de Tocqueville, *Democracy in America and Two Essays on America*, trans. Gerald E. Bevan (New York: Penguin, 2003), 52.

3. George Washington to John Jay, August 15, 1786, in *The Founders' Constitution*, vol. 1, eds. Philip B. Kurland and Ralph Lerner (Chicago: University of Chicago, 2000), chap. 5, doc. 11, http://press-pubs.uchicago.edu/founders/documents/v1ch5s11.html.

4. George Washington to John Jay, March 10, 1787, National Archives, Founders Online, http://founders.archives.gov/GEWN-04-05-02-0078.

5. James Madison, speech in the Virginia Constitutional Convention, December 2, 1829.

6. George Washington to Henry Lee, August 26, 1794.

7. James Wilson, speech in Philadelphia, October 6, 1787, at http://www.constitution.org/afp/jwilson0.htm.

8. Thomas Jefferson to John Adams, October 28, 1813.

9. Thomas Jefferson to John Adams, February 28, 1796.

10. John Adams, *A Defence of the Constitutions of Government of the United States of America* [hereinafter, *Defence*], vol. 3, chap. 4, in John Adams, *The Works of John Adams*, 10 vols. [hereinafter, *Works*], vol. 6, ed. Charles Francis Adams (Boston: Charles C. Little and James Brown, 1851), Online Library of America, http://oll.libertyfund.org/titles/2104.

11. George Washington to Edward Newenham, August 29, 1788.

12. Adams, *Defence*, preface, in Adams, *Works*, vol. 4, http://oll.libertyfund.org/titles/2102.

13. James Madison to Thomas Jefferson, October 17, 1788.

14. Alexander Hamilton, Draft of the Second Report on the Further Provision Necessary for Establishing Public Credit (Report on a National Bank), [13 December 1790], National Archives, Founders Online, http://founders.archives.gov/documents/Hamilton/01-07-02-0229-0002.

15. Thomas Jefferson to Joseph C. Cabell, February 2, 1816.

16. John Adams, Draft of an Essay on Power, August 29, 1763.

17. Thomas Jefferson to Nathaniel Macon, August 19, 1821.

18. Adams, *Defence*, chap. 10, in *Works*, vol. 4.

19. Anne M. Cohler et al., eds., *Montesquieu: The Spirit of the Laws* (Cambridge: Cambridge University Press, 1989), 155.

20. Ibid., 63.

21. Thomas Jefferson, letter to Abigail Adams, September 11, 1804.

22. Alexander Hamilton, Federalist No. 23.

23. James Madison, Speech in Congress Opposing the National Bank, February 2, 1791.

24. Federalist No. 45.

25. Tocqueville, Democracy in America and Two Essays on America, 184.

26. Thomas Jefferson, letter to Gideon Granger, August 13, 1800.

27. Thomas Jefferson, "Option against the constitutionality of a National Bank" (1791).

28. James Madison, Government of the United States, February 6, 1792.

29. Merrill D. Peterson, *Jefferson, Writings* (New York: Library of America, 1984), 1245–246.

30. Ibid., 1385.

31. Thomas Jefferson, Autobiography, in Kurland and Lerner, *The Founders' Constitution*, vol. 1, chap. 8, doc. 44, http://press-pubs.uchicago.edu/founders/documents/v1ch8s44.html.

32. Thomas Jefferson, letter to Joseph C. Cabell, February 2, 1816.

33. Thomas Jefferson, letter to John Adams, October 28, 1813.

34. Thomas Jefferson, letter to Joseph C. Cabell, February 2, 1816.

35. James Madison to Edward Livingston, July 10, 1822.

36. George Washington to Bushrod Washington, November 9, 1787.

37. George Washington to Henry Knox, October 15, 1787.

38. Thomas Jefferson to Samuel Kercheval, July 12, 1816, Constitution Society, http://www.constitution.org/tj/ltr/1816/ltr_18160712_kercheval.html.

39. John Rhodehamel, ed., Washington: Writings (New York: Library of America, 1997), 669.

40. Jefferson to Kercheval, July 12, 1816.

CHAPTER 5

1. James Madison, Federalist No. 39.

2. Alexis de Tocqueville, *Democracy in America*, 803.

3. John Adams, letter to Abigail Adams, June 2, 1777.

4. John Adams, Inaugural Address; March 4, 1797.

5. George Washington, Farewell Address, September 19, 1796.

6. Edmund Burke, Letter to a Member of the National Assembly (1791).

7. J. A. Leo Lemay, ed., *Franklin: Writings* (New York: Library of America, 2005), 1384-85.

8. Thomas Jefferson to Peter Carr, August 10, 1787.

9. John Adams, "A Dissertation on the Canon and the Feudal Law," no. 1, August 12, 1765, in *Founding Families: Digital Editions of the Papers of the Winthrops and the Adamses*, ed. C. James Taylor (Boston: Massachusetts Historical Society, 2015), http://www.masshist.org/publications/apde2/view?&id=PJA01dg2.

10. Cicero, Discussions at Tusculum (V), 88, 93.

11. John Adams, *A Defence of the Constitutions of Government of the United States of America*, vol., 3, chap. 4, in John Adams, *The Works of John Adams*, 10 vols. [hereinafter, *Works*], vol. 6, ed. Charles Francis Adams (Boston: Charles C. Little and James Brown, 1851), Online Library of America, http://oll.libertyfund.org/titles/2104.

12. Benjamin Franklin, *Poor Richard's Almanac*, 1746.

13. Gordon Wood, ed., *John Adams: Revolutionary Writings 1755–1775* (New York: The Library of America, 2011), 14.

14. Michael Grant, trans., *Cicero: On the Good Life* (New York: Penguin Books, 1971), 90.

15. Franklin, Poor Richard's Almanac.

16. Benjamin Franklin, letter to Ezra Stiles, March 9, 1790.

17. Tocqueville, *Democracy in America*, 347.

18. Thomas Jefferson, letter to John Adams, April 11, 1823.

19. Thomas Paine, *Miscellaneous Letters and Essays on Various Subjects* (London: W.T. Sherwin, 1817), 62-72.

20. Ibid.

21. Thomas Jefferson, letter to John Adams, April 11, 1823.

22. John Adams, letter to Benjamin Rush, April 18, 1808.

23. Charles Francis Adams, ed., *The Works of John Adams, Second President of the United States*, vol. 9 (Boston: Little, Brown and Company, 1854), 205.

24. Tocqueville, *Democracy in America*, 633.

25. Charles Francis Adams, ed., *The Works of John Adams*, 141.

26. John Adams to Thomas Jefferson, February 2, 1816.

27. James Madison, "Letter to Rev. Frederick Beasley" (November 20, 1825)

28. John Adams, letter to F. A. Vanderkemp, February 16, 1809.

29. Anne M. Cohler et al., eds., *Montesquieu: The Spirit of the Laws* (Cambridge: Cambridge University Press, 1989), 3.

30. John Adams, letter to Thomas Jefferson, September 14, 1813.

31. John Adams, letter to Richard Price: April 19, 1790.

32. Referring to the philosophy of many of the thinkers behind the French Revolution.

33. John Adams, letter to Thomas Jefferson, March 2, 1816.

34. Alexander Hamilton, Memorandum on the French Revolution, 1794.

35. John Adams, letter to Thomas Jefferson, November 13, 1815.

36. From John Adams to Winthrop Sargent, 24 January 1795, Founders Online, National Archives (http://founders.archives.gov/documents/Adams/99-02-02-1630 [last update: 2014-12-01]). (This is an Early Access document.)

37. Thomas Jefferson, letter to John Adams, January 11, 1816.

38. John Adams, letter to Thomas Jefferson, February 2, 1816.

39. Charles Francis Adams, ed., *The Works of John Adams*, 227.

40. Ibid., 206.

41. John Adams, letter to Thomas Jefferson, September 14, 1813.

42. Thomas Jefferson, letter to Peter Carr, August 10, 1787.

43. George Washington, letter to John Jay, August 15, 1786.

44. John Adams: From the Diary, May 29, 1756.

45. Benjamin Franklin, On the Providence of God in the Government of the World, 1730.

46. John Adams, letter to Edmund Jennings, June 11, 1780.

47. Tocqueville, *Democracy in America*, 510–11.

48. Ibid., 511–12.

49. John Adams, letter to Mercy Otis Warren, January 8, 1776.

50. Tocqueville, Democracy in America, 632–33.

51. Thomas Jefferson, letter to Thomas Jefferson Grotjan, January 10, 1824.

52. That is, God (see Luke 14:15–24; John 2:9).

53. Thomas Jefferson, letter to Abigail Adams, January 11, 1817.

54. J. A. Leo Lemay, ed., *Franklin: Writings* (New York: Library of America, 2005), 1308.

55. An observation of Edward Coke, famous English politician and jurist from the seventeenth century.

56. John Adams, letter to Thomas Jefferson, May 6, 1816.

57. John Adams, letter to F. A. Vanderkemp, July 13, 1815.

58. Benjamin Franklin, letter to Joseph Huey, June 6, 1753.

59. Tocqueville, *Democracy in America*, 496–97, 336.

60. John Adams, "Governor Winthrop to Governor Bradford" No. I, January 26, 1767.

61. John Adams, "A Dissertation on the Canon and the Feudal Law" no. 1 (August 12, 1765), in *Founding Families: Digital Editions of the Papers of the Winthrops and the Adamses*, ed. C. James Taylor (Boston: Massachusetts Historical Society, 2015), http://www.masshist.org/publications/apde2/view?&id=PJA01dg2.

62. Anne M. Cohler et al., eds., *Montesquieu: The Spirit of the Laws* (Cambridge: Cambridge University Press, 1989), 478.

63. Adams, "Dissertation" no. 1.

64. Samuel Adams, Speech in Philadelphia, August 1, 1776.

65. A reference to Revelation 17.

66. John Adams, "Dissertation" no. 2 (August 19, 1765), in Taylor, *Founding Families*, emphasis added.

67. John Adams letter to Abigail Adams, August 14, 1776.

68. Adams, "Dissertation" no. 2.

69. John Adams, ibid.

70. Benjamin Franklin, An Imaginary Speech; February 7, 1775.

71. John Adams, "Dissertation" no. 1.

72. Gordon Wood, ed., *John Adams: Revolutionary Writings 1755–1775* (New York: The Library of America, 2011), 153-54.

73. John Adams, Novanglus, no. 3 (February 6, 1775), in Adams, Works, vol. 4, http://oll.libertyfund.org/titles/2102.

74. Adams, "Clarendon" to "William Pym" No. II.

75. Adams, "Dissertation" no. 4 (October 21, 1765), in Taylor, *Founding Families*.

76. Adams, Novanglus no. 4 (February 13, 1775), in Adams, *Works*, vol. 4.

77. Adams, "Dissertation" no. 1.

78. Adams, *Novanglus* no. 4.

79. Ibid.

80. Adams, From the Diary, August 1, 1761.

81. Adams, *Novanglus* No. 4.

82. John Adams, letter to Abigail Adams, August 28, 1774.

83. John Adams, letter to James Warren, April 22, 1776.

84. John Adams, letter to Abigail Adams, October 29, 1775.

85. John Adams, letter to Abigail Adams, October 7, 1775.

86. John Adams, letter to Abigail Adams, September 20, 1774.

87. John Adams, letter to Mercy Otis Warren, January 8, 1776.

88. Abigail Adams, letter to John Adams, June 18, 1775.

89. John Jay, Address of the Convention of the Representatives of the State of New York to Their Constituents, December 23, 1776.

90. John Adams to Abigail Adams, September 16, 1774.

91. John Adams, letter to Abigail Adams, May 17, 1776.

92. John Adams, letter to Abigail Adams, July 7, 1775.

93. Samuel Adams, speech in Philadelphia, August 1, 1776.

94. George Washington, Farewell Address to the Armies of the United States, November 2, 1783.

95. George Washington, Circular to State Governments, June 8, 1783.

96. John Adams, letter to Thomas Jefferson, June 28, 1813.

97. George Washington, Farewell Address, September 19, 1796.

98. Thomas Jefferson, letter to John Adams, February 28, 1796.

99. Anne M. Cohler et al., eds., *Montesquieu: The Spirit of the Laws* (Cambridge: Cambridge University Press, 1989), 22.

100. Samuel Adams, letter to James Warren, November 4, 1775.

101. Tocqueville, *Democracy in America*, 21.

102. Samuel Adams, letter to James Warren, November 4, 1775.

103. Samuel Adams, letter to John Adams, October 4, 1790.

104. Tocqueville, *Democracy in America*, 369.

105. Anne M. Cohler et al., eds., *Montesquieu: The Spirit of the Laws* (Cambridge: Cambridge University Press, 1989), 318.

106. Thomas Jefferson, letter to Madame de Staël, May 24, 1813.

107. Anne M. Cohler et al., eds., *Montesquieu: The Spirit of the Laws* (Cambridge: Cambridge University Press, 1989), 322.

108. Tocqueville, *Democracy in America*, 499.

109. Ibid., 496–97, 340.

110. Ibid., 341.

111. Ibid., 342.

112. Franklin, Poor Richard's Almanac.

113. John Adams, letter to Mercy Otis Warren, April 16, 1776.

114. Abigail Adams, letter to John Quincy, June 10, 1778.

115. John Adams, letter to John Quincy Adams, April 28, 1782.

116. George Washington, letter to Marquis de Lafayette, February 7, 1788.

117. Tocqueville, *Democracy in America*, 21.

118. Ibid., 505–6.

119. Ibid., 342.

120. Quoting Jefferson's letter of May 17, 1818.

121. Gadsden was the main leader of the patriotic movement in South Carolina during the American Revolution.

122. John Adams to Thomas Jefferson, May 29, 1818.

123. Thomas Jefferson, Notes on the State of Virginia, Query XVII (1787).

124. James Madison, Memorial and Remonstrance Against Religious Assessments (1785).

125. Jefferson, Notes on the State of Virginia, Query XVII.

126. Thomas Jefferson, letter to Benjamin Rush, September 23, 1800.

127. Charles Francis Adams, ed., *The Works of John Adams,* Vol 6, 146.

128. Thomas Jefferson, letter to Dr. Thomas Cooper, February 10, 1814.

129. Jefferson, Notes on the State of Virginia, Query XVII.

130. Ibid.

131. James Madison, letter to Edward Livingston, July 10, 1822.

132. James Madison, letter to Edward Everett, March 19, 1823.

133. The First Amendment was at that time applicable only to the federal, not the state governments.

134. James Madison, Detached Memoranda (1819); emphasis added.

135. Tocqueville, *Democracy in America*, 55, 630, 56.

136. Ibid., 343, 340.

137. Ibid., 56.

138. Ibid., 347–48, 352.

139. Benjamin Franklin, "Information to Those Who Would Remove to America," February, 1784.

140. Tocqueville, Democracy in America, 626.

141. Ibid., 630.

142. Ibid., 340.

143. Gordon Wood, ed., *John Adams: Revolutionary Writings 1775-1783* (New York: The Library of America, 2011), 665.

144. Tocqueville, Democracy in America, 340–41.

145. Ibid., 691.

146. Adams, *Defence*, chap. 4, in Adams, *Works*, vol. 4.

147. Tocqueville, *Democracy in America*, 339.

148. George Washington, Thanksgiving Proclamation, October 3, 1789.

149. John Adams, Proclamation, For a National Fast (March 23, 1798).

150. Charles Francis Adams, ed., *The Works of John Adams*, 217.

151. Ibid., 144.

152. James Madison, Proclamation of Day of Fasting and Prayer (July 9, 1812), http://millercenter.org/president/madison/speeches/speech-3616.

153. Benjamin Franklin, Motion for Prayers in the Convention, June 28, 1787.

154. Adams, *Defence*, preface, in Adams, *Works*, vol. 4.

155. John Adams, letter to Benjamin Rush, September 12, 1811.

156. Benjamin Franklin, On the Providence of God in the Government of the World, 1730.

157. George Washington, Speech to the Delaware Chiefs, May 12, 1779.

158. John Adams to Thomas Jefferson, September 14, 1813.

159. "From John Adams to John Quincy Adams, 28 March 1816," Founders Online, National Archives (http://founders.archives.gov/documents/Adams/99-03-02-3058 [last update: 2014-12-01]). [Early access document]

160. John Adams, letter to Benjamin Rush, January 21, 1810.

161. John Adams, letter to Thomas Jefferson, August 9, 1816.

162. John Adams, letter to Thomas Jefferson, September 30, 1816, 490.

163. John Adams to F. A. Vanderkemp: July 13, 1815.

164. John Adams to Thomas Jefferson, September 14, 1813, 374.

165. John Adams, The Works of John Adams, vol. 6 (Defence of the Constitutions Vol. III cont'd, Davila, Essays on the Constitution) (Boston, Charles C. Little and James Brown, 1851).

166. John Adams to Abigail Adams, June 2, 1777.

167. John Adams, Diary, February 11–March 29, 1756 [February 22].

168. John Adam, letter to Benjamin Rush, February 2, 1807.

169. John Adams, letter to Thomas Jefferson, December 25, 1813.

170. John Adams, letter to Thomas Jefferson, February 2, 1816.

171. John Adams, letter to Benjamin Rush, April 18, 1808.

172. John Adams, letter to Thomas Jefferson, April 19, 1817.

173. Thomas Jefferson, letter to Benjamin Rush, April 21, 1803.

174. Paul Ford, ed. *The Works of Thomas Jefferson, Vol. XII* (New York: G.P. Putnam's Sons, 1905), 331-32.

175. Ibid. 332-33.

176. Ibid. 331-32.

177. Jefferson, letter to Benjamin Rush, April 21, 1803.

178. Thomas Jefferson, letter to Dr. Benjamin Waterhouse, June 26, 1822

179. Jefferson, letter to John Davis, January 18, 1824.

180. Thomas Jefferson, letter to John Adams, April 11, 1823.

181. Jefferson, letter to Dr. Benjamin Waterhouse, June 26, 1822.

182. Thomas Jefferson, letter to William Short, October 31, 1819.

183. Thomas Jefferson, letter to Charles Thomson, January 9, 1816.

184. Thomas Jefferson, letter to George Logan, November 12, 1816.

185. Thomas Jefferson, letter to Benjamin Rush, April 21, 1803.

186. Ibid.

187. Thomas Jefferson, letter to John Adams, January 11, 1817.

188. Benjamin Franklin, letter to Catharine Ray, October 16, 1755; a "catechise" was a tool by which Christians were taught basic doctrine and belief.

189. Benjamin Franklin, letter to Jane Mecom, July 28, 1743.

190. J. A. Leo Lemay, ed., *Franklin: Writings*, 179-80.

191. Benjamin Franklin, *Autobiography*, 1382.

192. Franklin, Poor Richard's Almanac.

193. Benjamin Franklin, letter to Joseph Huey, June 6, 1753.

194. Ibid.

195. Benjamin Franklin, Proposed New Version of the Bible; 1779?

196. Benjamin Franklin, letter to Josiah and Abiah Franklin, April 13, 1738.

197. Benjamin Franklin, Compassion and Regard for the Sick, March 25, 1731.

198. Benjamin Franklin, letter to Ezra Stiles, March 9, 1790.

199. Tocqueville, *Democracy in America*, 343–45.

200. Ibid.

201. Ibid.

202. Ibid. 54.

CHAPTER 6

1. Lester J. Cappon, ed., *The Adams–Jefferson Letters* (Univ. of North Carolina Press, 1988), 525.

2. Ibid., 578.

3. John Rhodehamel, ed., *Washington: Writings* (New York: Library of America, 1997), 960.

4. Adams to James Warren, 4 November 1775, in Philip B. Kurland and Ralph Lerner, eds., The Founders' Constitution, vol. 1 (Chicago: University of Chicago, 2000), chap. 18, doc. 6, http://press-pubs.uchicago.edu/founders/documents/v1ch18s6.html.

5.   George A. Peek Jr., ed., *The Political Writings of John Adams* (New York: Liberal Arts Press, 1954), 208.

6.   Ibid., 190.

7.   John Adams to Samuel Adams (18 Oct. 1790), in Kurland and Lerner, *The Founders' Constitution*, vol. 1, chap. 11, doc. 16, http://press-pubs.uchicago.edu/founders/documents/v1ch11s16.html (accessed 9 Nov. 2014).

8.   Peter Laslett, ed., *Locke: Two Treatises of Government* (Cambridge: Cambridge University Press, 1988), 309.

9.   Benjamin Rush, "Of the Mode of Education Proper in a Republic," in ibid., chap. 18, doc. 30, http://press-pubs.uchicago.edu/founders/documents/v1ch18s30.html.

10. Anne M. Cohler et al., eds., *Montesquieu: The Spirit of the Laws* (Cambridge: Cambridge University Press, 1989), 315.

11. Gordon Wood, ed., *John Adams: Revolutionary Writings 1755–1775* (New York: Library of America, 2011), 311.

12. Ibid., 300–1.

13. Gordon Wood, ed., *John Adams: Revolutionary Writings 1775–1783* (New York: Library of America, 2011), 60.

14. Ibid., 490.

15. Ibid., 30–31.

16. Ibid., 300.

17. Wood, John Adams, Revolutionary Writings 1755–1775, 123.

18. Franklin to Samuel Johnson, 23 August 1750, in Benjamin Franklin, *The Works of Benjamin Franklin, vol. 2, Letters and Misc. Writings 1735–1753*, ed. John Bigelow (1904). Available online from the Online Library of Liberty, http://oll.libertyfund.org/titles/2454#Franklin_1438-02_1148.

19. Ibid.

20. J. A. Leo Lemay, ed., *Franklin: Writings* (New York: Library of America, 2005), 324.

21. Ibid., 334–36.

22. Ibid., 336–37.

23. Ibid., 342.

24. Benjamin Rush, "Of the Mode of Education Proper in a Republic."

25. Alexis de Tocqueville, *Democracy in America and Two Essays on America*, trans. Gerald E. Bevan (New York: Penguin, 2003), 53–54.

26. Merrill D. Peterson, *Jefferson: Writings* (New York: Library of America, 1984), 272, 274.

27. Rush, "Of the Mode of Education Proper in a Republic."

28. Noah Webster, "On the Education of Youth in America" (1788), in Kurland and Lerner, The Founders' Constitution, epilogue: http://press-pubs.uchicago.edu/founders/documents/v1ch18s26.html.

29. Peek, The Political Writings of John Adams, 161–62.

30. Wood, John Adams: Revolutionary Writings 1775–1783, 581.

31. Jack N. Rakove, ed., *Madison: Writings* (New York: Library of America, 1999), 809.

32. Ibid., 797.

33. Lemay, *Franklin*, 817.

34. Ibid, 837.

35. Rhodehamel, *Washington, Writings*, 483.

36. Wood, John Adams, Revolutionary Writings 1775–1783, 475.

37. "From John Adams to John Adams, 2 February 1812," Founders Online, National Archives (http://founders.archives.gov/documents/Adams/99-03-02-2099 [last update: 2014-12-01]). [Early access version]

38. The quotations that follow, to Peter Carr, are from Peterson, *Jefferson: Writings*, 814–15, 902–4.

39. Jefferson to Thomas Jefferson Grotjan, 10 January 1824, in Thomas Jefferson, *The Works of Thomas Jefferson*, vol. 12, *Correspondence and Papers 1816–1826*, ed. Paul Leicester Ford (New York and London, G. P. Putnam's Sons, 1905).

40. Tocqueville, Democracy in America and Two Essays on America, 193–94.

41. Ibid., 353.

42. Ibid., 193.

43. Peterson, *Jefferson*, 1110, 935.

44. Webster, "On the Education of Youth in America."

45. Wood, John Adams, Revolutionary Writings 1755–1775, 133–34.

46. Wood, John Adams, Revolutionary Writings 1775–1783, 55.

47. Charles Francis Adams, ed., *The Works of John Adams, Second President of the United States*, Vol. VI (Boston: Little, Brown and Company, 1851), 168.

48. Wood, John Adams, Revolutionary Writings 1755–1775, 123.

49. Cappon, The Adams–Jefferson Letters, 390.

50. Peterson, *Jefferson*, 1149, 1150.

51. Rakove, *Madison*, 791.

52. Peek, The Political Writings of John Adams, 208.

53. Frank Shuffelton, ed., *The Letters of John and Abigail Adams* (New York: Penguin, 2004), 214.

54. Wood, John Adams, Revolutionary Writings 1775–1783, 581.

55. Rush, "Of the Mode of Education Proper in a Republic."

56. Rakove, *Madison,* 503–4, 790.

57. Ibid., 792–93.

58. Rhodehamel, *Washington*, 972.

59. Webster, "On the Education of Youth in America."

60. Rush, "Of the Mode of Education Proper in a Republic."

61. Webster, "On the Education of Youth in America."

62. Peterson, *Jefferson*, 1147, 1149.

63. Ibid., 1387–88.

64. Tocqueville, Democracy in America and Two Essays on America, 786.

65. Ibid., 355–56.

66. Rakove, *Madison*, 500, 502.

67. Peterson, *Jefferson*, 1379.

68. Cohler, *Montesquieu*, 35.

69. Webster, "On the Education of Youth in America."

70. Wood, John Adams: Revolutionary Writings 1755–1775, 298.

71. Lemay, *Franklin*, 283-284.

72. Peterson, *Jefferson*, 999–1000.

73. Ibid., 1147.

74. Jefferson to the Marquis de Lafayette (November 4, 1823) in Ford, ed., *The Works of Thomas Jefferson*, available online from the Online Library of Liberty, http://oll.libertyfund.org/titles/808 #Jefferson_0054-12_344.

75. Jefferson to Col. Charles Yancey (January 6, 1816), in ibid., http://oll.libertyfund.org/titles/807# Jefferson_0054-11_455.

76. Charles Francis Adams, ed., The Works of John Adams, Second President of the United States, Vol. VI, 169.

77. Jefferson to Col. Charles Yancey (January 6, 1816), in ibid., http://oll.libertyfund.org/titles/807# Jefferson_0054-11_455.

CHAPTER 7

1. Jack N. Rakove, ed., *Madison: Writings* (New York: Library of America, 1999), 518.

2. Merrill D. Peterson, *Jefferson: Writings* (New York: Library of America, 1984), 1037.

3. The Constitution of the United States of America and Selected Writings of the Founding Fathers (New York: Barnes & Noble, 2012), 119.

4. Alexis de Tocqueville, *Democracy in America and Two Essays on America*, trans. Gerald E. Bevan (New York: Penguin, 2003), 643.

5. John Rhodehamel, ed., *Washington: Writings* (New York: Library of America, 1997), 973.

6. George A. Peek Jr., ed., *The Political Writings of John Adams* (New York: Liberal Arts Press, 1954), 199.

7. Ibid., 199, 201.

8. Rakove, *Madison,* 167.

9. Tocqueville, Democracy in America and Two Essays on America, 625, 527.

10. Rakove, *Madison*, 515–16.

11. Ibid., 516–17.

12. John Bigelow, ed., *The Works of Benjamin Franklin* (New York: G.P. Putnam's Sons, 1904), 412.

13. Peek, The Political Writings of John Adams, 199.

14. Lester J. Cappon, ed., *The Adams–Jefferson Letters* (Univ. of North Carolina Press, 1988), 388.

15. Peterson, *Jefferson*, 1398.

16. Rakove, *Madison*, 824.

17. Peek, The Political Writings of John Adams, 205.

18. Rakove, *Madison*, 94.

19. Tocqueville, Democracy in America and Two Essays on America, 364.

20. Peterson, *Jefferson*, 522.

21. Rakove, *Madison* 150.

22. Tocqueville, Democracy in America and Two Essays on America, 629.

23. Joanne B. Freeman, ed., *Hamilton: Writings* (New York: Library of America, 2001), 587-88.

24. Tocqueville, Democracy in America and Two Essays on America, 527, 594, 629.

25. Ibid., 332, 191.

26. Peterson, *Jefferson*, 1028.

27. J. A. Leo Lemay, ed., *Franklin: Writings* (New York: Library of America, 2005), 977–79.

28. Ibid., 321.

29. Tocqueville, Democracy in America and Two Essays on America, 65.

30. Lemay, *Franklin*, 979.

31. Ibid., 975, 982.

32. Farmers, largely; though this included any citizens who were self-sufficient.

33. Rakove, *Madison*, 512–13.

34. Tocqueville, Democracy in America and Two Essays on America, 786.

35. Ibid., 594.

36. Rhodehamel, *Washington*, 686.

37. Ibid., 592.
38. Freeman, *Hamilton*, 206.
39. Peterson, *Jefferson*, 300, 1110.
40. Lemay, *Franklin*, 976.
41. Peterson, *Jefferson*, 1028.
42. Ibid., 518–19.
43. Rakove, *Madison*, 513.
44. Lemay, *Franklin*, 981.
45. Tocqueville, Democracy in America and Two Essays on America, 70–71.
46. Peterson, *Jefferson*, 1386.
47. Peek, The Political Writings of John Adams, 157.
48. Peterson, *Jefferson*, 259.
49. Rhodehamel, *Washington*, 191.
50. Lemay, *Franklin*, 1429.
51. Ibid., 587–88.
52. Ibid., 469.
53. Tocqueville, Democracy in America and Two Essays on America, 600.
54. Ibid., 356.
55. Ibid., 594–95.
56. Ibid., 661.
57. Ibid., 599–600.
58. Rhodehamel, *Washington*, 686.
59. Peek, The Political Writings of John Adams, 128–29.
60. Peterson, *Jefferson,* 494-495.
61. Ibid., 808–9.

CHAPTER 8

1. Joanne B. Freeman, ed., *Hamilton: Writings* (New York: Library of America, 2001), 57.
2. J. A. Leo Lemay, ed., *Franklin: Writings* (New York: Library of America, 2005), 800, 678.
3. Ibid., 1154–55.
4. John Jay, letter to R. Lushington, March 15, 1786, available online at http://teachingamericanhistory.org/library/document/letter-to-r-lushington/.
5. George Stade, ed., Thomas Paine: *Common Sense and Other Writings* (New York: Barnes & Noble Classics, 2005), 7.
6. Jack N. Rakove, ed., *Madison: Writings* (New York: Library of America, 1999), 93, 391.
7. "From Thomas Jefferson to William James Macneven, 15 August 1807," Founders Online, National Archives (http://founders.archives.gov/documents/Jefferson/99-01-02-6182 [last update: 2014-12-01]). Source: this is an Early Access document from The Papers of Thomas Jefferson. It is not an authoritative final version.
8. Rakove, *Madison*, 392.
9. Gordon Wood, ed., *John Adams: Revolutionary Writings 1775–1783* (New York: Library of America, 2011), 37.
10. James Madison, letter to Frances Wright (September 1, 1825), on the website of the Online Library of America, http://oll.libertyfund.org/titles/1940#Madison_1356-09_799.
11. George A. Peek Jr., ed., *The Political Writings of John Adams* (New York: Liberal Arts Press, 1954), 172.

12. Ibid., 112.

13. Rakove, *Madison*, 311–12, 310–11.

14. John Rhodehamel, ed., *Washington: Writings* (New York: Library of America, 1997), 701.

15. Ibid., 1023–24; emphasis added.

16. Phillis Wheatley, "His Excellency George Washington," on the website of the Academy of American Poets, http://www.poets.org/poetsorg/poem/his-excellency-general-washington (accessed January 11, 2015).

17. Rhodehamel, *Washington*, 216.

18. John Adams, letter to Robert J. Evans (June 8, 1819), in *John Adams, The Works of John Adams*, vol. 10, ed. Charles Francis Adams (Boston: Little, Brown, 1854), Online Library of America, http://oll.libertyfund.org/titles/2127#Adams_1431-10_1326.

19. Scott J. Hammond, et al, eds., Classics of American Political and Constitutional Thought, vol. 1 (Indianapolis: Hackett, 2007), 152–53.

20. Merrill D. Peterson, *Jefferson: Writings* (New York: Library of America, 1984), 289.

21. Ibid.

22. Ibid., 1344–46.

23. Ibid., 1346.

24. Ted Widmer, ed., American Speeches: Political Oratory from Patrick Henry to Barack Obama (New York: Library of America, 2011), 57–58.

25. Ibid., 61–62.

26. Ibid., 75–76.

27. Alexander H. Stephens, "Cornerstone Address, March 21, 1861," in *The Rebellion Record: A Diary of American Events with Documents, Narratives, Illustrative Incidents, Poetry, etc.*, vol. 1, ed. Frank Moore (New York: O. P. Putnam, 1862), 44–46.

CHAPTER 9

1. Anne M. Cohler et al., eds., *Montesquieu: The Spirit of the Laws* (Cambridge: Cambridge University Press, 1989), 49.

2. Alexis de Tocqueville, *Democracy in America and Two Essays on America*, trans. Gerald E. Bevan (New York: Penguin, 2003), 803–9.

3. Gordon Wood, ed., *John Adams: Revolutionary Writings 1755–1775* (New York: Library of America, 2011), 496, 123, 136.

4. Merrill D. Peterson, *Jefferson: Writings* (New York: Library of America, 1984), 987.

5. Tocqueville, Democracy in America and Two Essays on America, 786–87.

6. Joanne B. Freeman, ed., *Hamilton: Writings* (New York: Library of America, 2001), 44.

7. Wood, John Adams: Revolutionary Writings 1755–1775, 416.

8. Peterson, *Jefferson*, 1177.

9. Lester J. Cappon, ed., *The Adams–Jefferson Letters* (Univ. of North Carolina Press, 1988), 291.

10. Peterson, *Jefferson*, 291.

11. John Rhodehamel, ed., *Washington: Writings* (New York: Library of America, 1997), 679.

12. Charles Francis Adams, ed., *The Works of John Adams, Second President of the United States*, vol. 9 (Boston: Little, Brown, 1854), 458.

13. Peterson, *Jefferson*, 1276–77.

14. Rhodehamel, *Washington*, 527.

15. Gordon Wood, ed., John Adams: Revolutionary Writings 1775–1783, 224.

16. Peterson, *Jefferson,* 287.

17. Adams, letter to Benjamin Rush (September 27, 1808) in Charles Francis Adams, ed., *The Works of John Adams,* http://oll.libertyfund.org/titles/2107#Adams_1431-09_1936.

18. Adams, letter to the Officers of the First Brigade of the Third Division of the Militia of Massachusetts (October 11, 1798), in ibid., http://oll.libertyfund.org/titles/2107#Adams_1431-09_719.

19. Tocqueville, Democracy in America and Two Essays on America, 366.

20. Cohler, *Montesquieu,* 460.

21. Wood, John Adams: Revolutionary Writings 1775–1783, 639.

22. Peterson, *Jefferson,* 1081.

23. Jack N. Rakove, ed., *Madison: Writings* (New York: Library of America, 1999), 497.

24. Wood, John Adams: Revolutionary Writings 1775–1783, 664.

25. Adams to Benjamin Rush, 2 February 1807, in Alexander Biddle, ed., Old Family Letters, Copied from the originals for Alexander Biddle (Philadelphia: J. B. Lippincott, 1892), 128.

26. Cohler, *Montesquieu,* 104.

27. Ibid., 71, 36.

28. Ibid., 23.

29. Ibid., 103, 121-122.

30. Cappon, The Adams–Jefferson Letters, 549–50.

31. J. A. Leo Lemay, ed., *Franklin: Writings* (New York: Library of America, 2005), 1281.

32. Tocqueville, Democracy in America and Two Essays on America, 631-632.

33. Cappon, The Adams–Jefferson Letters, 436.

34. Frank Shuffelton, ed., *The Letters of John and Abigail Adams* (New York: Penguin, 2004), 333–34.

35. Wood, John Adams: Revolutionary Writings 1775–1783, 58.

36. Wood, John Adams: Revolutionary Writings 1755–1775, 406–7.

37. Cappon, The Adams–Jefferson Letters, 203.

38. Wood, John Adams: Revolutionary Writings 1775-1783, 62.

39. Cappon, The Adams–Jefferson Letters, 551.

40. Cohler, *Montesquieu,* 312.

41. The Founders' Constitution, "Balanced Government," *John Adams to Samuel Adams; 18 Oct. 1790,* http://press-pubs.uchicago.edu/founders/documents/v1ch11s16.html (accessed 9 Nov. 2014).

42. Wood, John Adams: Revolutionary Writings 1775–1783, 308–9.

43. Cohler, *Montesquieu,* 109.

44. Rhodehamel, *Washington,* 483, 558.

45. Tocqueville., Democracy in America and Two Essays on America, 236.

46. Ibid., 627–28.

47. Lemay, *Franklin,* 1293–94.

48. Cohler, *Montesquieu,* 503.

49. Ibid., 112, 119, 121.

50. Lemay, *Franklin,* 1140.

51. After all, Ecclesiastes 1:9 does say that there is nothing new under the sun.

52. Rhodehamel, *Washington,* 971.

53. Ibid., 969, 968, 661.

54. Cohler, *Montesquieu,* 803.

55. Rakove, *Madison,* 775, 808.

56. Ibid., 518.

57. Jefferson, letter to William Short (January 8, 1825), on the website of the Online Library of America, http://oll.libertyfund.org/titles/808#Jefferson_0054-12_416.

58. Peterson, *Jefferson*, 1078.

59. Jefferson, letter to the Marquis de Lafayette (November 4, 1823), on the website of the Online Library of America, http://oll.libertyfund.org/titles/808#Jefferson_0054-12_345.

60. Peterson, *Jefferson*, 1448, 75.

61. Rhodehamel, *Washington*, 970–71.

62. Rakove, *Madison*, 764, 502

63. George Stade, ed., *Founding America: Documents from the Revolution to the Bill of Rights* (New York: Barnes & Noble Classics, 2006), 55.

64. Peterson, *Jefferson*, 117.

65. Freeman, *Hamilton*, 470.

66. Peterson, *Jefferson*, 1078–79.

67. Rakove, *Madison*, 498.

68. Ibid., 340.

69. He called this "monuments of deficient wisdom" in the same paper.

70. Rakove, *Madison*, 343.

71. Wood, John Adams: Revolutionary Writings 1775–1783, 74.

72. Peterson, *Jefferson*, 74.

73. Shuffelton, The Letters of John and Abigail Adams, 74.

74. Peterson, *Jefferson*, 987.

75. "James Madison to James Robertson, Jr., 20 April 1831," Founders Online, National Archives (http://founders.archives.gov/documents/Madison/99-02-02-2332 [last update: 2014-12-01]). Source: this is an Early Access document from The Papers of James Madison. It is not an authoritative final version.

76. Rakove, *Madison*, 233–34.

77. Gales, Joseph, 1761-1841. *The Debates and Proceedings in the Congress of the United States, Second Congress, First Session.* Washington DC UNT Digital Library. http://digital.library.unt.edu/ark:/67531/metadc29467/. Accessed February 12, 2015.

78. Ibid., 489.79. ˙ Tocqueville, Democracy in America and Two Essays on America, 368.

80. Lemay, *Franklin*, 1140.

81. Rakove, *Madison*, 503.

82. Ibid., 773.

83. Peterson, *Jefferson*, 1509–11.

84. Ibid., 1079.

85. Lemay, ed., Franklin, 1433.

86. Freeman, *Hamilton*, 591–92.

87. Adams, letter to F. A. Vanderkemp (February 16, 1809), on the website of the Online Library of America, http://oll.libertyfund.org/titles/2107#Adams_1431-09_1955.

88. Adams, letter to Benjamin Rush (February 13, 1811), in Biddle, ed., Old Family Letters, 281.

89. Cappon, The Adams–Jefferson Letters, 539.

90. Wood, John Adams: Revolutionary Writings 1775–1783, 148–49.

91. Ibid., 129.

92. Adams, letter to Benjamin Rush (October 13, 1810), in Biddle, ed., Old Family Letters, 267.

93. Adams, letter to Benjamin Rush (December 27, 1810), in ibid., 272.

94. Peterson, *Jefferson*, 1448.

95. Rakove, *Madison*, 423.

96. Jefferson, letter to George Logan (November 12, 1816), on the website of the Online Library of America, http://oll.libertyfund.org/titles/808#Jefferson_0054-12_40.

97. Adams to Rush, October 13, 1810.

98. Adams, letter to John Taylor (March 12, 1819), at Online Library of America, http://oll.libertyfund. org/titles/2127#Adams_1431-10_1313.

99. Cappon, The Adams–Jefferson Letters, 192.

100. Lemay, *Franklin*, 1001-02.

101. Jefferson to Nathaniel Macon, 19 August 1821, in Thomas Jefferson, *The Works of Thomas Jefferson*, vol. 12, *Correspondence and Papers 1816–1826*, ed. Paul Leicester Ford (New York and London: G. P. Putnam's Sons, 1905).

102. Rakove, *Madison*, 517.

103. Rhodehamel, *Washington*, 972.

104. Eric Foner, ed., *Paine: Collected Writings* (New York: Library of America, 1995), 25.

105. Cohler, *Montesquieu*, 68.

106. Michael Grant, trans., *Cicero: On the Good Life* (New York: Penguin Books, 1971), 149.

107. Cohler, Montesquieu, 14, 113.

108. Peek, The Political Writings of John Adams, 156.

109. Rakove, Madison, 421.

110. Tocqueville, Democracy in America and Two Essays on America, 67, 779.

111. Ibid., 789–90, 736.

112. Peek, The Political Writings of John Adams, 148.

113. John Adams, letter to Samuel Adams, in Philip B. Kurland and Ralph Lerner, eds., *The Founders' Constitution*, vol. 1 (Chicago: University of Chicago, 2000), chap. 11, doc. 16, http://press-pubs. uchicago.edu/founders/documents/v1ch11s16.html.

114. Peterson, *Jefferson*, 1400-1401.

115. Cappon, The Adams–Jefferson Letters, 277.

116. Ibid., 347, 351.

117. Peterson, *Jefferson*, 1220.

118. Peek, The Political Writings of John Adams, 151-152.

119. Rhodehamel, *Washington*, 968, 969–70.

120. Peterson, *Jefferson*, 889–90.

121. Wood, John Adams: Revolutionary Writings 1755–1775, 427–28.

122. Lemay, *Franklin*, 839.

CONCLUSION

1. George A. Peek Jr., ed., *The Political Writings of John Adams* (New York: Liberal Arts Press, 1954), 115.

2. Gordon Wood, ed., *John Adams: Revolutionary Writings 1755–1775* (New York: Library of America, 2011), 169.

3. John Rhodehamel, ed., *Washington: Writings* (New York: Library of America, 1997), 685.

4. Lester J. Cappon, ed., *The Adams–Jefferson Letters* (Univ. of North Carolina Press, 1988), 575.

5. Rhodehamel, *Washington*, 518.

6. Ibid., 733.

INDEX

No publisher in the world has a higher percentage of *New York Times* bestsellers.

 WND Books

A **WND** COMPANY • WASHINGTON DC • WNDBOOKS.COM

"A compelling case that America's public education system must undergo radical change."

—RON PAUL, FORMER CONGRESSMAN AND PRESIDENTIAL CANDIDATE

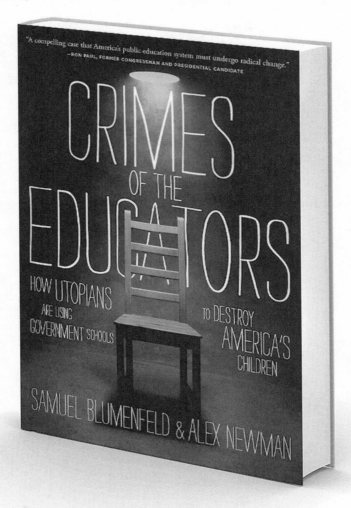

American author and veteran educator Samuel Blumenfeld and journalist Alex Newman have taken on the public education establishment as never before and exposed it for the de facto criminal enterprise it is. CRIMES OF THE EDUCATORS reveals how the architects of America's public school disaster implemented a plan to socialize the United States by knowingly and willingly dumbing down the population, a mission now closer to success than ever as the Obama administration works relentlessly to nationalize K-12 schooling with Common Core.

WND BOOKS • WASHINGTON DC • WNDFILMS.COM